Scuba Diving

SECOND EDITION

Dennis K. Graver, DMT

Human Kinetics

Library of Congress Cataloging-in-Publication Data

Graver, Dennis.
    Scuba diving / Dennis K. Graver. -- 2nd ed.
        p.   cm.
    Includes bibliographical references (p.) and index.
    ISBN 0-7360-0172-7
    1. Scuba diving. I. Title.
GV838.672.G74   1999
797.2'3--dc21   99-12019
                                                                                    CIP

ISBN: 0-7360-0172-7

Developmental Editor: Laura Hambly
Assistant Editor: Leigh LaHood
Copyeditor: Allen Gooch
Proofreader: Bob Replinger
Indexer: Betty Frizzell
Graphic Designer: Robert Reuther
Cover Designer: Jack Davis
Photographer: Dennis Graver
Illustrator: Table 3.2 and Figures 2.5, 2.6, 2.7, 2.12, 3.1, 3.4, 4.3, 4.5, 4.8, 4.21, 4.25, 4.27, 4.28, 4.31, 4.34, 6.9, 7.10, and 7.16 by Argosy; all other illustrations by Thomas • Bradley Illustration and Design

Human Kinetics books are available at special discounts for bulk purchase. Special editions or book excerpts can also be created to specification. For details, contact the Special Sales Manager at Human Kinetics.

Printed in Hong Kong

10   9   8   7   6   5   4   3   2   1

Human Kinetics
Web site: http://www.humankinetics.com/

United States: Human Kinetics, P.O. Box 5076, Champaign, IL 61825-5076
1-800-747-4457, e-mail: humank@hkusa.com

Canada: Human Kinetics, 475 Devonshire Road Unit 100, Windsor, ON N8Y 2L5
1-800-465-7301 (in Canada only), e-mail: humank@hkcanada.com

Europe: Human Kinetics, P.O. Box IW14, Leeds LS16 6TR, United Kingdom
+44 (0)133-278 1708, e-mail: humank@hkeurope.com

Australia: Human Kinetics, 57A Price Avenue, Lower Mitcham, South Australia 5062
(08) 82771555, e-mail: humank@hkaustralia.com

New Zealand: Human Kinetics, P.O. Box 105-231, Auckland Central
09-523-3462, e-mail: humank@hknewz.com

Scuba Diving

SECOND EDITION

Contents

CHAPTER 3: DIVING ADAPTATIONS 33

CHAPTER 4: DIVING EQUIPMENT 55

CHAPTER 5: DIVING SKILLS 93

CHAPTER 6: DIVE PLANNING 133

CHAPTER 7: DIVING ENVIRONMENT 157

CHAPTER 8: DIVING OPPORTUNITIES 181

Preface

My goals in writing this book were to create the most complete, up-to-date text available for entry-level scuba diving and to improve diving safety through education. Toward those ends, I've written *Scuba Diving* for beginners who want to learn to scuba dive and for certified divers who want to refresh their memories and update their knowledge. I've presented the information so that the book will be easy for diving instructors to use with their classes regardless of the training organization that the instructor is affiliated with.

In recent years, the trend has been to simplify diving instruction. Simultaneously, advances in diving medicine, diving equipment, and dive-planning devices have complicated the task of educating the beginning diver. This book provides more information than many scuba texts now available and addresses current issues and topics. Specifically, *Scuba Diving* has several unique features, including

- full-color illustrations and photographs,
- explanations of diving science the average person can understand,
- emphasis on the practical skills of diving,
- modern environmental concerns,
- a detailed explanation of equipment for diving in warm and cold water,
- new, easy-to-understand dive-planning tables, and
- a thorough, yet nonfrightening, explanation of the risks and hazards of diving.

Two other elements that require a bit of explanation are the new terms and "Dive In and Discover." "Dive In and Discover" are lists of specific elements that you will learn about in each chapter. There are also many terms used in scuba diving and by scuba divers. The new terms appear in the text in colored ink, and their definitions are in the glossary at the back of the book. Some of these terms are even highlighted in the book's margins. Be sure you are familiar with the terms in a chapter before you proceed to the next chapter.

The eight chapters of this book introduce you to the scuba diving "community," the diving environment, and diving science, equipment, skills, planning, and opportunities. Everything today's entry-level diver needs to know to enjoy scuba diving in comfort and safety is in *Scuba Diving*. However, you cannot learn everything you need to know in a single course. My focus is on teaching you to dive in average water conditions. You will learn about specialty diving, such as ice diving, night diving, or wreck diving, when you complete intermediate and advanced scuba diving courses. Do not attempt to teach yourself to scuba dive. Do not have a friend who scuba dives teach you. If you want to become a scuba diver, you must complete a sanctioned course of instruction taught by a professional scuba instructor who has been certified by a reputable diver-training organization.

If you are unsure whether scuba is something you would enjoy, many diving businesses offer introductory lessons. You can try scuba diving in shallow water to see if you would like to learn more. Contact a local diving professional and ask about an introductory scuba experience, which requires only a few hours and is often free of charge. By giving yourself the experience, you will introduce yourself to one of the most exciting and enjoyable leisure activities available. Diving evokes feelings of peace and joy that you can experience as soon as you qualify as a scuba diver. Sign up for a course today and start reading!

Dennis K. Graver

Acknowledgments

I am grateful to many individuals and organizations for their assistance with this book. My first thanks go to Rainer Martens, publisher at Human Kinetics, for his persistence in persuading me to write *Scuba Diving*. It also was a pleasure to work with Holly Gilly and Laura Hambly, two of the best developmental editors an author could hope to have, and the rest of the Human Kinetics staff—they are extremely professional.

Many people contributed to the photos in *Scuba Diving*. I wish to thank Bill Oliver of SeaQuest, who provided diving equipment for the models, and Harry Truitt of Lighthouse Diving Center and Dick Long of DUI, who both loaned equipment for photos. I am especially grateful to Skip Commagere, owner of Force E, who provided diving support and photographic models. Cliff Newell of the NOAA in Seattle allowed me to photograph the recompression chambers at the NOAA facility. My longtime friend and diving buddy, Fred Humphrey, provided surf entry and exit shots. While many divers appear throughout the book, I want to thank these in particular: Michelle Anderson, Bill Black, Skip Commagere, Beth Farley, Barbara Graver, Scott Harrison, and Tom McCrudden.

The reviewers have my sincere appreciation, but my deepest gratitude is for the members of the diving community who have taught me for the past 34 years and who continue to teach me now. It is a pleasure to be able to pass on to others some of what I have learned.

Finally, I would like to say a special thank you to my loving wife, Barbara, for all the support she gave me while I completed *Scuba Diving*.

Dennis K. Graver

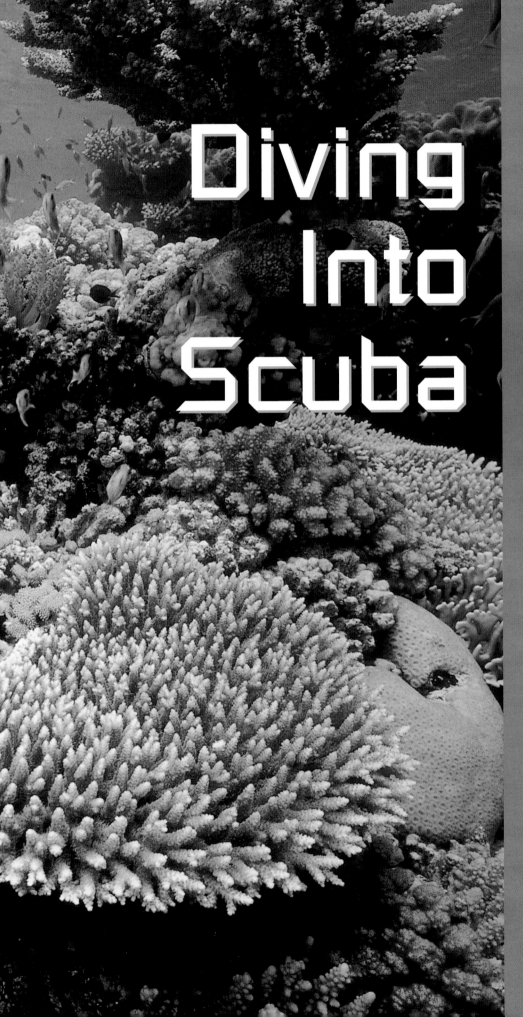

Diving Into Scuba

When you descend beneath the surface of the water, you enter an entirely new and beautiful world. You have opportunities to see incredible life forms that only a few people ever see. Imagine swimming in a giant aquarium, and you can get a glimpse of what you can expect to experience in the underwater world.

By the end of this chapter, you will be able to

- describe the joys of diving,
- define the term C-card,
- explain the scuba diving training requirements for participation in scuba diving activities,
- state the three phases of entry-level training for scuba divers,

- list three medical conditions that would disqualify an individual from scuba diving,
- describe three risks associated with scuba diving,
- list several questions to ask when selecting an entry-level scuba diver training course, and
- explain several responsibilities that you assume when you become a certified scuba diver.

THE JOYS OF DIVING

As a diver, you are weightless and can move in all directions. You approach the freedom of a bird as you move in three dimensions in a fluid environment. Diving weightless in clear water in a forest of underwater plants with sunlight streaming down is only one of many unforgettable experiences awaiting you.

▶ Figure 1.1 Kelp forests are just one of many beautiful sights you'll encounter as a scuba diver.

▶ Figure 1.2 Wrecks teem with underwater life.

Just as there are mountains, plains, and differing environments above the surface of the water, there are differing environments for you to experience underwater. Coral reefs, kelp forests, incredible rock formations, and other natural wonders await divers in various geographical regions (see figure 1.1). Add to this piers, jetties, quarries, mysterious shipwrecks, and other artificial structures, and you can easily see how the variety of underwater sights is limitless (see figure 1.2). There is more to view underwater than anyone could possibly see in a lifetime.

Divers can also enjoy a wide range of activities that enhance their underwater experience. With pursuits like photography, hunting, and collecting, diving is challenging and rewarding. There is an activity to interest everyone. Divers are friendly and easy to get to know. The camaraderie of divers is well known. You will meet fine people and develop lasting friendships. Diving is a sharing activity, and there is much to share. If you enjoy traveling, you will love diving. Dive travel is the number one business of recreational diving. Reasonably priced dive travel vacations to exotic islands abound. Most divers plan one or more diving vacations each year.

The feelings and sensations of diving are fantastic but are difficult to explain. Words are inadequate to describe the peaceful solitude of "inner space." Diving contributes to good health, can help reduce work-related stress, can increase self-esteem, and can make you feel great. You will soon experience the emotions and sensations for yourself. You then will begin to know the joys of diving.

LEARNING ABOUT THE DIVING COMMUNITY

The recreational diving community consists of equipment manufacturers, diving retailers, diving educators, diver-training organizations, dive resorts, diving supervisors, dive guides, dive boats, dive clubs and associations, publishing companies, and certified divers. Commercial, scientific, and highly technical professional diving pursuits are not considered recreational; people who take part in these are in separate "communities."

Few laws pertain to scuba diving. The laws that exist do not govern who may dive. The diving industry is self-regulating. The diving community realizes that it is dangerous when people who have not completed a sanctioned course of instruction attempt scuba diving. Dive businesses require proof of completion of training before they will fill your scuba tanks or allow you to participate in diving activities. Many dive operations also require proof of recent experience documented in a diving logbook (see figure 1.3). If you have not been diving for a year or more, you may be required to do at least one dive under the supervision of a diving professional. The supervised dive requirement helps increase the safety of divers whose skills may need to be refreshed.

When you complete your training requirements as a scuba diver, you receive a certification card called a **C-card**. Most C-cards do not require renewal, but the recreational diving community recommends "refresher" training following periods of inactivity longer than six months.

Certified divers may dive without supervision or may employ the services of a diving guide. Do not assume that a divemaster or diving supervisor aboard a dive boat will be a guide who will dive with you. Guiding services are not necessarily included with dive trips. If you want a guide to lead you about underwater and show you the sights, arrange for guide services in advance.

You will learn more about the community as your diving experience increases. There are many opportunities for adventure and enjoyment. Get actively involved in the community when you complete your training and officially qualify as a scuba diver.

▶ Figure 1.3 You will need to show proof of certification before dive businesses will fill your scuba cylinders.

▶ Figure 1.4 You should make at least four dives in open water during your scuba training.

LEARNING ABOUT DIVER TRAINING

A national diver-training organization must sanction your training. The training organization establishes standards that you must meet before the organization will issue a certification card. The appendix includes a list of national diver-training organizations. Instructors should have credentials that verify their qualifications, and they must have current membership in a training organization. Confirm the qualifications of your instructor.

Your entry-level training course consists of a series of academic sessions, pool or confined water (pool-like conditions in open water) sessions, and open-water (actual diving locations) training. You will learn theory in the classroom, learn skills in controlled conditions, and then apply your skills in the diving environment. This logical progression is common for all approved diver-training courses.

Minimum requirements for your training are four or more academic sessions, four or more pool sessions, and at least four scuba dives in open water. See figure 1.4. You should not make more than two scuba training dives per day.

Your initial training time should total 30 to 40 hours of instruction. Instruction should take place over a period of several weeks instead of a few days. The time between class sessions allows you to reflect upon your training and helps you absorb and retain the knowledge and skills better than a concentrated training schedule would.

DIVING PREREQUISITES

Diving is an exciting activity for anyone over age 12 with normal health and a reasonable degree of physical fitness. You need to be able to swim 200 yards (183 m) nonstop using any combination of strokes. There is no time requirement for the swim. Being comfortable in the water is more important than being able to swim fast.

Normal health means that your heart, lungs, and circulation are normal and that you do not have any serious diseases such as epilepsy, asthma, or diabetes. Any medical conditions—even if controllable under normal conditions—that might incapacitate you in the water could cause you to drown while scuba diving. Air spaces in your body—sinuses, ears, and lungs—must be normal because changes in pressure affect them.

Warning:

Do not attempt to learn scuba diving without instruction from a professional diving instructor.

People with physical disabilities may dive if they have medical approval from a physician.

Women who are pregnant should not scuba dive. Increased pressure can have adverse effects on an unborn child. Pregnant women may, however, participate in snorkeling. A woman's menstrual cycle does not exclude her from diving if her health permits participation in other sports during that time.

You need to be emotionally fit as well as physically fit for diving. If you are terrified of water or of feeling confined, diving probably is not the right activity for you. Normal concerns are to be expected, but stark terror is dangerous underwater.

You should have a physical examination before you begin your training, especially if it has been more than a year since your last exam. Ask your instructor to recommend a diving physician. Sometimes physicians who do not understand the physiology of scuba diving grant approval to individuals who have medical conditions that place them at great risk in and under the water. If your physician grants you medical approval for diving, but your instructor says your medical condition is contrary to diving safely, listen to your instructor. If you have questions about your fitness to dive, call the Divers Alert Network at (919) 684-2948.

THE RISKS OF DIVING

All activities have risk. Risk is involved in walking across the street, driving a car, or skiing behind a boat. To avoid injury while participating in an activity, we take precautions for our safety. There are precautions for scuba diving just as there are for any other pursuit.

Diving is similar to flying. Both are low-risk activities when done with well-maintained equipment according to established rules and in good environmental conditions. Unfortunately, diving and flying are unforgiving if you ignore the rules and recommendations designed to minimize the risks.

The following information and much of this book make you aware of injuries that can occur to scuba divers. The information alerts you to potential hazards and, more important, helps you learn to avoid injury. If you will do what you are taught to do as a diver, your risk will be minimal and all your diving experiences will likely be pleasant ones.

Pressure changes with depth. Changes in pressure can injure body air spaces severely if you are not in good health or if you fail to take steps to keep the pressure in the air spaces equal to the surrounding pressure. To avoid permanent hearing loss or permanent ringing in the ears, you will learn equalizing techniques as part of your training.

Scuba Wise

I nearly drowned when I was 4, so as a child I was terrified of water. When I was 8, I spent a summer with my uncle in Ohio. He would take me to Lake Erie and give me pennies if I would wade into water deep enough to cover my navel! I learned swimming as a Boy Scout at age 11. Although I completed a lifesaving class at age 16, I still was afraid of the water. When I learned skin and scuba diving and *discovered that I could actually relax in water, it became my ally. For the first time in my life, I enjoyed water and was able to rid myself of my childhood fears. Just because a person is afraid of water does not mean that the individual cannot enjoy scuba diving. If you can swim 200 yards, you can learn to dive and to love being in and under the water.*

You normally have gases dissolved in your body. Increased pressure at depth increases the amount of gas dissolved in your body. If you ascend too rapidly from a dive, the gases in your system can form bubbles and produce a serious illness known as **decompression sickness** (DCS). By regulating your depths, the times of your dives, and your rate of ascent, you can avoid decompression sickness. Failure to heed depth and time schedules and ascent rates can result in serious, permanent injuries.

Diving can be strenuous at times. You need sufficient physical fitness and stamina to handle long swims, currents, and other situations. If you become winded from climbing a flight of stairs, you may need to improve your level of fitness before learning to scuba dive. Exhaustion in and under the water is hazardous.

Diving takes place in water, which is an alien environment. You will be using life support equipment to dive, but you must realize that you cannot be entirely dependent on the equipment for your well-being. Aquatic skills are essential in and around water. People with very weak aquatic ability can drown when minor equipment problems occur, problems that could easily be handled by a person with good water competence. You must be comfortable in water to be a scuba diver (figure 1.5).

You should not be overly concerned with the potential risks of diving because injuries are preventable. Learning how to dive with as much personal safety as possible is the purpose of your training. You will learn to minimize the risk of any injury and maximize your enjoyment of the underwater world.

decompression sickness (DCS) —Illness caused by gas bubbles forming in the tissues or blood before the gas can be diffused into the lungs and eliminated; also called venous gas emboli (VGE) and "bends"

▶ Figure 1.5 Being comfortable in the water is important to your enjoyment and safety.

SELECTING A DIVE COURSE

There are many diver training organizations and thousands of professional diving educators. Your phone book lists diving businesses offering sanctioned courses. Many community colleges, YMCAs, and recreational departments also offer scuba courses. Ask about the qualifications, experience, and reputation of several diving instructors in your area to select a course that will provide you with the best possible training. Ask the following questions:

- Which diver-training agency sanctions the training?
- How long has the instructor been teaching scuba diving?
- Which levels of training is the instructor qualified to teach?
- May you speak with the graduates of a recent class?
- Why is the course offered better than others in the area?
- Are assisting and rescue techniques taught in the course?
- How many instructor-supervised open-water dives are included?

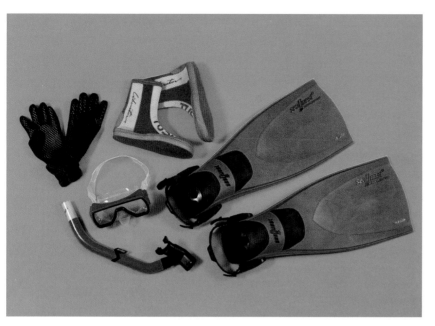

The tuition for diving instruction usually falls between $200 and $300. The lowest-priced course may not necessarily be a bargain. Find out what is included with the course fee and, more important, what the total cost will be for you to become certified as a scuba diver.

You will not have to purchase all the equipment needed to scuba dive, but you will need to have a mask, snorkel, fins, and usually boots and gloves for your training (see figure 1.6). Use of the additional required equipment typically is part of the course tuition.

When you are considering which course to enroll in, find out whether the price includes costs for educational

▶ Figure 1.6   You should purchase a mask, snorkel, fins, boots, and gloves for use during your scuba diving training.

materials and certification There may be additional costs for travel, lodging, parking, boat fees, and equipment rental for open-water training. Determine the complete cost before enrolling in a course.

When you have selected the best program for you and have enrolled in a course, you should receive a reading assignment for your first session. If you are not given an assignment, speak with your instructor; you will learn much better by reading in advance about the topics to be presented in class. Good diving instructors provide a handout with reading assignments.

Select a course and enroll right away. A fantastic new world awaits you underwater. Scuba training is exhilarating, challenging, and enjoyable.

DIVING RESPONSIBILITIES

When you qualify as a scuba diver, you assume many responsibilities. You are responsible for your safety, for the safety of those with whom you dive, for the image of scuba divers, and for the preservation of the diving environment. Responsibilities cannot be given to you; they must be assumed. The diving community encourages divers to accept responsibility for their actions. Because you will be part of the diving community, you need to be a responsible diver. Learn what you should do, then do what you learn.

SUMMARY

Diving can be a source of great joy. There are many exciting experiences awaiting the trained diver. You need dive credentials to participate in diving activities. You must complete diver training to obtain your C-card and logbook. But diving is not for everyone. You must have normal health, good swimming skills, and reasonable physical fitness. Diving poses risks that a well-trained, wise, and fit diver can minimize. Compare training programs and choose the best education, which may not be the quickest or the least expensive. Remember that you accept a great deal of responsibility when you become a diver.

Do not assume that you can transfer the responsibility for a dive accident to someone else. Ultimately you control your actions under water. Become a competent, self-reliant diver who adheres to recommended safety practices and you will discover the joy of diving.

The Responsible Diver Code

I will dive within the limits of my training and ability.

I will evaluate the conditions before every dive and make sure they fit my personal capabilities.

I will be familiar with and check my equipment before and during every dive.

I will respect the buddy system and its advantages.

I will accept responsibility for my own safety on every dive.

I will be environmentally conscious on every dive.

I will be responsible to myself, the people with whom I dive, and the environment.

Diving Science

2

Your body is a marvelous machine. It performs many complex functions automatically. Just as your body is well adapted to a land environment, it can adapt in many ways to the aquatic environment. In this chapter, you will become familiar with some of the structures and functions of your body. You will learn the differences between the land and water environments, and how changes in pressure affect your body.

By the end of this chapter, you will be able to

- list three body air spaces of concern to divers;
- describe the process of hearing in air;
- describe the cardiorespiratory process;
- explain the effect of carbon dioxide on breathing;
- define the terms hyperventilation, hypoventilation, density, pressure, gauge pressure, absolute pressure, squeeze, reverse block, ingassing, outgassing, partial pressure, and defogging;
- explain the principle of buoyancy and the key to controlling buoyancy;

- explain the effects of pressure and temperature on a volume of air in a flexible container;
- explain why it is important to vent your lungs when you ascend in water;
- convert any temperature to absolute temperature;
- explain the process of ingassing and outgassing;
- state the two primary factors that affect the air consumption of a scuba diver;
- list four methods of heat loss;
- describe three potential problems for scuba divers that can be caused by humidity; and
- describe the effects of water on vision and hearing.

ANATOMY FOR THE DIVER

Inside your body are air-filled spaces that are affected by changes in pressure. The three primary body air spaces of concern to you as a diver are the lungs, the ears, and the sinuses. It also helps you as a diver to understand the function of your throat. Figure 2.1 explains the functions of the sinuses, throat, and lungs.

The Sinuses

The sinuses warm and humidify inspired air. They secrete mucus to help protect the body by trapping airborne germs. The small airways that connect the sinuses to the nasal passages normally are open. Congested sinuses pose problems for divers. In the next chapter, you will learn more about sinus problems and their prevention.

Abbreviations

ATA	Atmospheres absolute	**FFW**	Feet of fresh water	**lb**	Pound
ATM	Atmosphere	**FSW**	Feet of seawater	**m**	Meter
CO	Carbon monoxide	**ft**	Feet	**mg**	Milligram
CO$_2$	Carbon dioxide	**ft^3**	Cubic foot	**O$_2$**	Oxygen
°C	Degrees Celsius	**g**	Gram	**PP**	Partial pressure
cm	Centimeter	**hr**	Hour	**psia**	Pounds per square inch absolute
cm^2	Square centimeter	**kg**	Kilogram		
cm^3	Cubic centimeter	**km**	Kilometer	**psig**	Pounds per square inch gauge
°F	Degrees Fahrenheit	**L**	Liter		

Function of the sinuses, throat, and lungs

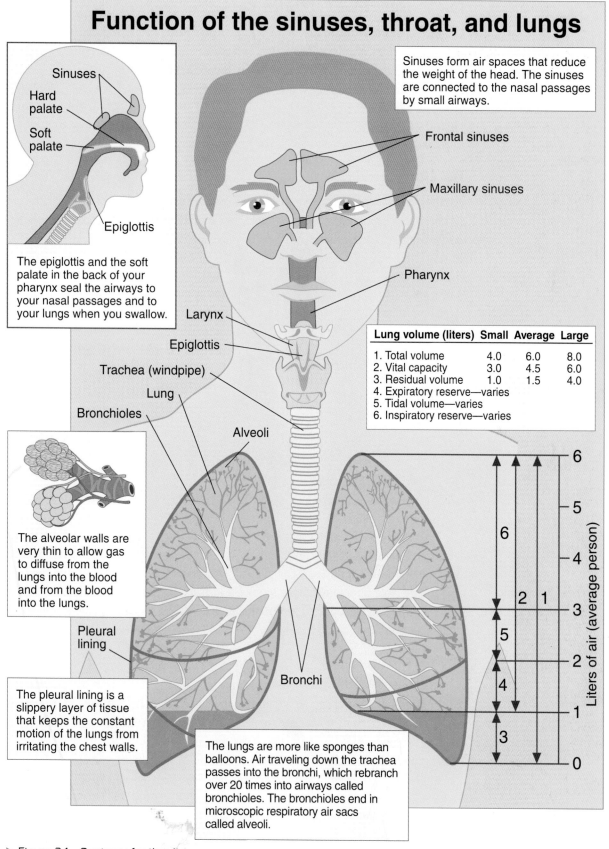

Sinuses

Hard palate

Soft palate

Epiglottis

The epiglottis and the soft palate in the back of your pharynx seal the airways to your nasal passages and to your lungs when you swallow.

Sinuses form air spaces that reduce the weight of the head. The sinuses are connected to the nasal passages by small airways.

Frontal sinuses

Maxillary sinuses

Pharynx

Larynx

Epiglottis

Trachea (windpipe)

Lung

Bronchioles

Alveoli

The alveolar walls are very thin to allow gas to diffuse from the lungs into the blood and from the blood into the lungs.

Pleural lining

The pleural lining is a slippery layer of tissue that keeps the constant motion of the lungs from irritating the chest walls.

Bronchi

The lungs are more like sponges than balloons. Air traveling down the trachea passes into the bronchi, which rebranch over 20 times into airways called bronchioles. The bronchioles end in microscopic respiratory air sacs called alveoli.

Lung volume (liters)	Small	Average	Large
1. Total volume	4.0	6.0	8.0
2. Vital capacity	3.0	4.5	6.0
3. Residual volume	1.0	1.5	4.0
4. Expiratory reserve—varies			
5. Tidal volume—varies			
6. Inspiratory reserve—varies			

Liters of air (average person)

▶ Figure 2.1   Anatomy for the diver.

13

The Throat

In addition to being the organ of voice, the larynx helps prevent foreign matter from entering the lungs. If something foreign, such as food or water, comes into contact with the larynx, a reflex action causes a spasm of the voice box. Coughing expels the foreign substance. You have experienced this sensation when something has gone "down the wrong pipe." Review the throat section of figure 2.1. During your scuba diving training, you will learn how to keep water out of your larynx to avoid coughing and choking in and under the water.

The Lungs

Healthy lungs are essential for scuba diving. The lungs are large air sacs contained within the chest cavity. Your lungs have a maximum capacity and a minimum capacity. When you exhale completely, your lungs are not empty. They contain about 2 pints (1 L) of air. The air remaining in your lungs after you have exhaled completely is your residual volume. The amount of air you move in and out of your lungs is your tidal volume. When you are at rest, your tidal volume is small. When you exert, your tidal volume increases until you reach both your maximum lung volume and your residual volume with each breath. Your vital capacity is the difference between the volume of air for a maximum inhalation and the volume of air for a maximum exhalation—typically about 6 to 8 pints (2.8 to 3.8 L). In the next chapter, you will learn several reasons why your lungs are the most critical air spaces in diving.

The Teeth

You may be surprised to learn that there are dental concerns for divers. Pressure may affect air pockets in improperly filled teeth and may cause tooth pain. If a tooth hurts only under pressure or only following a dive, see your dentist and tell him or her what you suspect. The roots of some upper molars extend into the sinus cavities. Postpone diving for several weeks after you have had a tooth extracted.

Your mouth and jaw are designed for an even bite. If you bite hard on a mouthpiece with your front teeth only for prolonged periods, your jaws will become sore. Special mouthpieces designed for a proper bite can help reduce the problem. You should not have to bite hard on a mouthpiece to hold it in place. If you find biting necessary, get lighter equipment. Prolonged improper biting that irritates your jaw can lead to serious inflammation of your jaw and ears.

The Ears

Behind your eardrum is an air space called the middle ear (see figure 2.2). The pressure in the middle ear must equal the pressure in the outer ear or the eardrum will not move freely. The next chapter explains how to keep pressure inside your ears equal to external pressure. Your eustachian tube allows the equalization of pressure in the middle ear. The liquid-filled cochlea contains hairlike projections called cilia, which convert mechanical movement to electrical signals for the brain. The movement of the oval window—moved by the bones of hearing—causes the liquid and the cilia to move back and forth. The oval window movement could not take place except for a second window in the hearing organ—the round window. When the oval window moves inward, the round window moves outward, and vice versa.

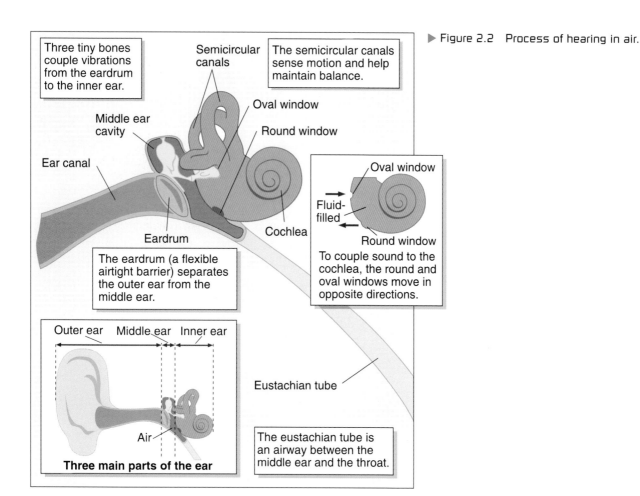

If the motion sensed by your semicircular canals and the visual clues received by your eyes are not in harmony, motion sickness can result. Sudden changes in temperature or pressure in the middle ear can affect your semicircular canals and cause temporary disorientation. (See chapter 3 for a discussion of potential ear problems for divers, how to avoid them, and how to handle them should they happen.)

RESPIRATION AND CIRCULATION

One of the fascinating processes within the human body is your ability to breathe in air and circulate oxygen to tissues with no conscious effort. As your level of exertion increases, your heart and lungs automatically adjust to meet the increased demands for oxygen and nourishment. An understanding of the gases involved in respiration and the basics of respiration and circulation will help you understand the effects and the demands of diving on your lungs and heart.

Gases We Breathe

Several gases affect recreational divers, and you need to know about their effects on your body.

About 80 percent of air is nitrogen (N_2). At sea level pressures, nitrogen has no effect on your body. At a depth of about 100 feet, the increased pressure of the gas does have a

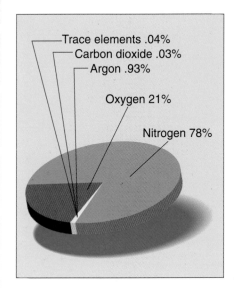

Trace elements .04%
Carbon dioxide .03%
Argon .93%

Oxygen 21%

Nitrogen 78%

▶ Figure 2.3   Composition of air.

detrimental effect, which is called nitrogen narcosis Excessive nitrogen in your body at the end of a dive can produce a serious illness known as decompression sickness. You will learn more about nitrogen narcosis and decompression sickness in the next chapter.

Oxygen (O_2) is the gas that supports life. Any other gas mixed with oxygen serves only as a vehicle for oxygen to be inspired. Approximately 20 percent of air is oxygen (see figure 2.3). You need to breathe at least 10 percent oxygen to remain conscious, but oxygen breathed under high pressure is poisonous and causes convulsions. You must have compressed air—not pure oxygen—in your scuba tanks. A specialty form of diving uses a nitrogen-oxygen mixture with a higher percentage of oxygen than is found in air. The mixture, which reduces the effects of nitrogen at depth, is called Nitrox. The use of mixed gases, including Nitrox, requires special training, equipment, and procedures.

As your body tissues use oxygen, they produce carbon dioxide (CO_2). CO_2 is the primary stimulus for respiration. The greater the level of carbon dioxide in your body, the greater the urge to breathe. If the level of carbon dioxide in your body becomes too great, unconsciousness results.

Carbon monoxide (CO) is a poisonous gas produced by the incomplete combustion of gas or oil. The exhaust from an internal combustion engine contains carbon monoxide. An oil-lubricated air compressor that overheats can produce CO. Even a minute amount of carbon monoxide in your scuba tank can poison you, which can lead to unconsciousness or death. Air filling stations must take care to avoid contamination of air with carbon monoxide.

Breathing and Circulation Mechanics

When you need to breathe, sensors at the base of your brain send a signal that stimulates your diaphragm to contract. This draws air into your lungs in the same way an old-fashioned bellows draws in air when you expand it. Your diaphragm and the muscles of your chest expand your chest cavity to inspire air. Figure 2.4 illustrates how the heart, lungs, and circulatory system work together in the process of respiration.

Scuba Wise

There is an old joke about a young woman who returned home from her first session of scuba diver training and was unenthusiastic when her father asked if she enjoyed the class. Her reply was, "First the instructor told us all the ways that we could die, then he worked us in the water until I thought that I was going to die." Thankfully, instructors do not teach classes that way today. The reason for learning about potential injuries is to understand how to prevent them. Armed with knowledge that we con-

vert to wisdom through proper application, we can avoid all the potential problems identified in this chapter. The use of scuba diving instruction for fitness training also is outdated. Reasonable physical fitness is a prerequisite for scuba diving. Any healthy person who can swim 200 yards continuously is fit enough to dive. The objective of modern scuba training is to help you learn to relax in and under the water, not to "whip you into shape."

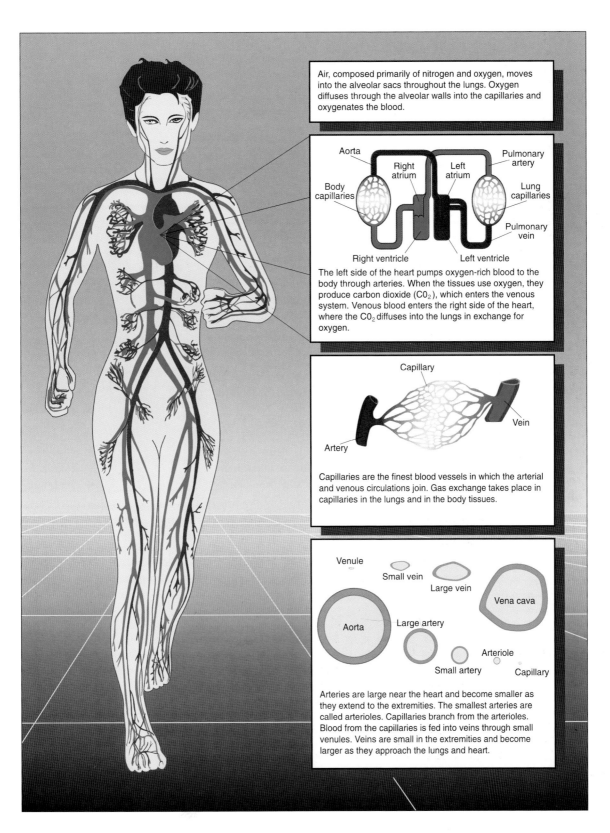

Air, composed primarily of nitrogen and oxygen, moves into the alveolar sacs throughout the lungs. Oxygen diffuses through the alveolar walls into the capillaries and oxygenates the blood.

The left side of the heart pumps oxygen-rich blood to the body through arteries. When the tissues use oxygen, they produce carbon dioxide (CO_2), which enters the venous system. Venous blood enters the right side of the heart, where the CO_2 diffuses into the lungs in exchange for oxygen.

Capillaries are the finest blood vessels in which the arterial and venous circulations join. Gas exchange takes place in capillaries in the lungs and in the body tissues.

Arteries are large near the heart and become smaller as they extend to the extremities. The smallest arteries are called arterioles. Capillaries branch from the arterioles. Blood from the capillaries is fed into veins through small venules. Veins are small in the extremities and become larger as they approach the lungs and heart.

▶ Figure 2.4 The cardiorespiratory system.

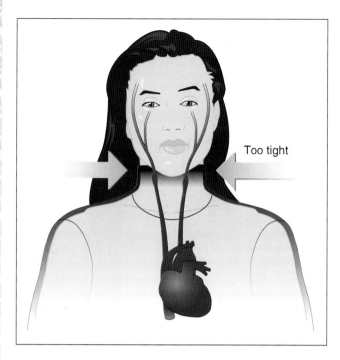

Too tight

▶ Figure 2.5 Cartoid sinus reflex. Pressure on your neck can slow your heart rate and lead to unconsciousness.

Blood consists of plasma, a colorless liquid, and a variety of cells. Hemoglobin, a blood component, is the primary oxygen-carrying mechanism in the blood. Approximately 45 percent of the blood is hemoglobin. Hemoglobin releases oxygen when it reaches tissues that need oxygen.

When the tissues use oxygen, they produce carbon dioxide. The carbon dioxide enters the venous system. Carbon dioxide diffuses into the lungs in exchange for oxygen. This completes a circulatory cycle, which takes about 30 seconds.

Carotid sinuses on each side of the neck sense blood pressure within the circulatory system. Excessive pressure on the carotid sinuses during exercise causes the heart to slow when it should be working hard to meet the oxygen demands of the body. Decreased output from the heart can lead to insufficient oxygen for the brain, which can cause unconsciousness. A blackout caused by pressure on the carotid sinuses is a carotid sinus reflex, which figure 2.5 illustrates. Therefore, beware of diving equipment that is tight around your neck.

Exhalation usually is a passive process. To exhale carbon dioxide-laden air from the lungs, the diaphragm relaxes and the elasticity of the chest cavity forces air from the lungs. You ventilate your lungs approximately 12 to 14 times per minute when at rest. Respiration functions automatically. The key to respiration is the level of carbon dioxide in your circulatory system. When the carbon dioxide in your body reaches a certain level, your brain stimulates respiration. When you voluntarily hold your breath, the buildup of carbon dioxide within your body urges you to breathe. Many people believe the amount of oxygen in the body controls respiration, but it is the level of carbon dioxide that regulates breathing.

Hyperventilation is rapid, deep breathing in excess of the body's needs. Limited hyperventilation—three to four breaths—enhances breath holding, but if you hold your breath after excessive hyperventilation you may lose consciousness before being stimulated to breathe. There are no warnings. A breath-holding diver who loses consciousness from lack of oxygen usually blacks out near the surface during ascent. The sudden loss of consciousness near the surface is shallow water blackout. Loss of consciousness can cause drowning. Figure 2.6 illustrates shallow water blackout.

If you breathe rapidly and shallowly, carbon dioxide continues to build in your system, but you do not expel it from your lungs. Inadequate breathing is hypoventilation. Shallow breathing is dangerous, especially when you exert yourself, because you can lose consciousness from lack of oxygen. It is essential to breathe sufficiently to exchange the air in your lungs.

CONTRASTING AIR AND WATER ENVIRONMENTS

We live immersed in air, which is a fluid. A fluid is either a gas or a liquid. Air has weight and takes up space. We don't pay much attention to our immersion in air because we are adapted to the environment, we have lived in it all our lives, and we cannot see the air.

The weight of the atmosphere does affect us, however.

Air weighs about 0.08 lb/ft³ (1.28 mg/cm³) at sea level. As altitude increases, air becomes thinner, so its weight per cubic foot (or mg/cm³) is less in the mountains than it is at the seashore (see figure 2.7). The change in the weight of air affects the air spaces in our ears when we fly or when we drive in the mountains.

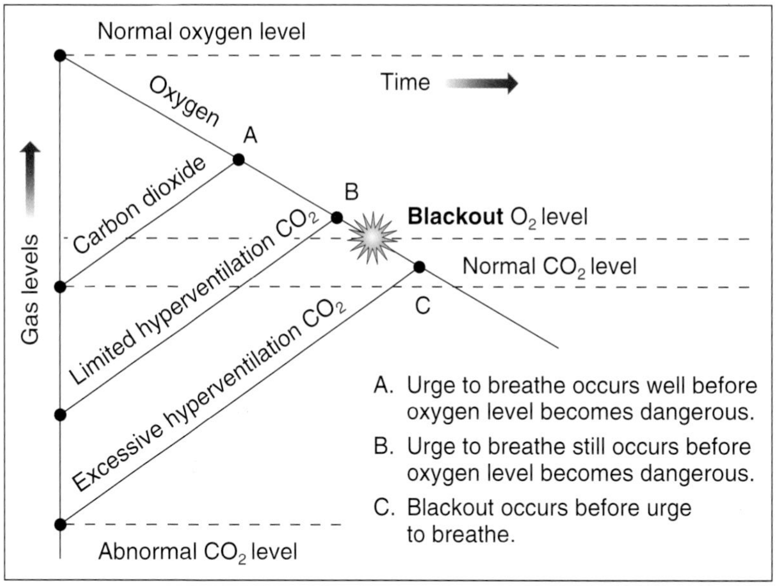

Density

Density is mass per unit volume (for example, pounds per cubic foot). Water is a fluid, but it is much heavier than air. Seawater weighs about 64 lb/ft³ (1.025 g/cm³), which makes it about 800 times denser than air. Fresh water, because it does not contain salt, weighs a little less than seawater: 62.4 lb/ft³ (1.0 g/cm³). Temperature affects the density of water; cold water is slightly denser than warm water.

Air compresses, but water essentially is incompressible. While air becomes thinner as altitude increases, water density remains constant throughout the water column.

Drag is a force that retards movement. Resistance to movement is much greater in water than in air. Factors affecting drag include the viscosity of the fluid, the speed of motion, and the size and shape of an object. The denser the fluid, the faster the motion, the larger the object, and the more irregular the surface of the object, the greater the drag.

A. Urge to breathe occurs well before oxygen level becomes dangerous.

B. Urge to breathe still occurs before oxygen level becomes dangerous.

C. Blackout occurs before urge to breathe.

▶ Figure 2.6   Shallow water blackout.

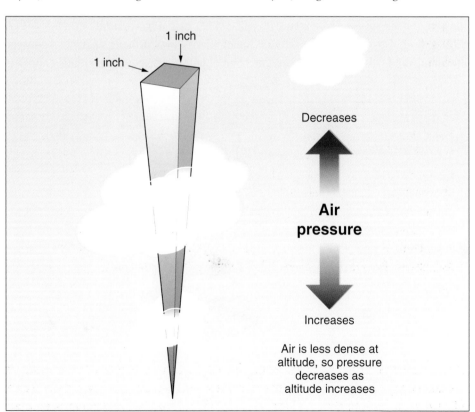

▶ Figure 2.7   Density and pressure according to altitude.

Because of higher density, the molecules of water are much closer together than those of air. The tightly packed molecules affect the transmission of light, sound, and heat (see table 2.1). Light travels about 27 percent slower in water than in air. Sound travels about four times faster in water than in air. Water conducts heat nearly 25 times faster than air. Water has an enormous capacity for absorbing heat with little change in its temperature. The higher density of water affects you in many ways when you dive. The next chapter explains how to deal with the effects of water density.

Buoyancy

An object's ability to float in a liquid depends on the density of the object compared with the density of the fluid. Water pressure at any point exerts equally in all directions, even upward. You can feel the upward force (buoyancy) of water when you try to push something under the water. Buoyancy results from the difference in pressures on the upper and lower surfaces of an object. The weight of an object plus the weight of the fluid (air, water, or both) above the object exert a downward force. Fluid pressure pushes upward from below. The difference between these two forces is the buoyancy of the object.

Calculations prove that the force of buoyancy acting on a submerged object equals the weight of the water displaced. A hot air balloon floats in air because hot air inside the balloon weighs less than the volume of cooler air the balloon occupies. The weight of the water that a diver displaces buoys the diver upward with a force equal to the weight of the water displaced (see figure 2.8). If you and your equipment weigh less than the weight of the amount of water being displaced, you will float (be buoyed up) and have positive buoyancy. If you and your equipment weigh more than the weight of the water being displaced, you will sink. An object that sinks has negative buoyancy. An object that weighs exactly the same as the amount of water being displaced neither floats nor sinks. Instead, the item remains at the depth where it is placed because it has neutral buoyancy.

As a diver, you can float at the surface, sink to the bottom, or hang suspended between the bottom and the surface. If the volume of an object increases with very little change in

Table 2.1 Water Compared With Air

Property	Air	Water	Comparison
Density	.08 lb/ft³	62.4 to 64 lb/ft³	Water 800 times denser than air
Compressibility	Yes	No	Air density varies; water density constant (at dive pressures)
Speed of light	186,000 mi/sec	140,000 mi/sec	Light travels 25% slower in water
Light absorption	Low	High	Water absorbs color quickly
Speed of sound	1,125 ft/sec	4,900 ft/sec	Sound travels 4 times faster in water
Conductivity	.17	3.86 to 4.12	Heat loss is 22 to 24 times faster in water than in air
Heat capacity	.24	.94 to 1.0	The heat capacity of water is 4 times greater than air

▶ Figure 2.8   Principles of buoyancy.

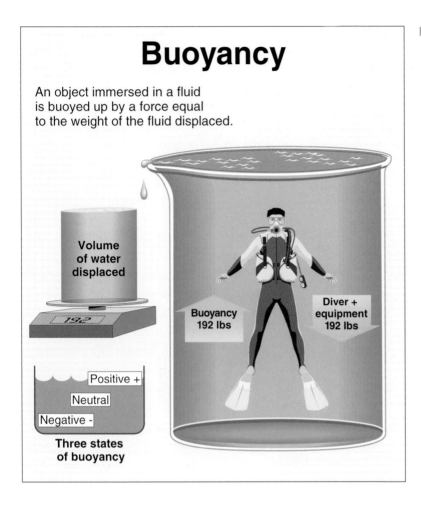

its weight, buoyancy increases. This happens when you add air to an inflatable jacket or vest. The next chapter addresses the factors affecting buoyancy and the principles of buoyancy control.

Pressure Measurement

The force (often weight) of something per unit area, such as pounds per square inch or grams per square centimeter, is pressure. The envelope of air surrounding the earth is the atmosphere. The weight of one square inch of the atmosphere at sea level is 14.7 lb (1.03 g/cm²), or 1 "atmosphere" (ATM) of pressure. As you descend in water, the weight of the fluid—the pressure—exerted upon each square inch of your body increases. One square inch of salt water that is 33 ft (10.06 m) in height weighs 14.7 lb (1.03 kg/cm²), 1 ATM or 1.01 Bar. One square inch of fresh water 34 ft (10.36 m) in height also exerts a pressure equivalent to 1 ATM. Because 1 Bar is almost identical to 1 ATM, we will assume them to be identical. Remembering that water does not compress (for the pressures involved with recreational diving), you should be able to grasp that water pressure increases by 1 ATM or Bar for every 33 ft (10 m) of salt water (FSW) and for every 34 ft (10.36 m) of fresh water (FFW). Figure 2.9 shows how atmospheric pressure and water pressure are measured.

The reference for pressure is either atmospheric pressure at sea level or zero pressure (outer space). A pressure gauge that reads zero at sea level displays only the pressure in

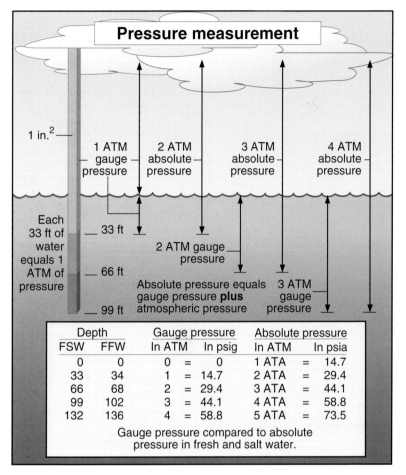

Pressure measurement

1 in.²

1 ATM gauge pressure

2 ATM absolute pressure

3 ATM absolute pressure

4 ATM absolute pressure

Each 33 ft of water equals 1 ATM of pressure

33 ft

66 ft

99 ft

2 ATM gauge pressure

Absolute pressure equals gauge pressure **plus** atmospheric pressure

3 ATM gauge pressure

Depth		Gauge pressure				Absolute pressure		
FSW	FFW	In ATM		In psig		In ATM		In psia
0	0	0	=	0		1 ATA	=	14.7
33	34	1	=	14.7		2 ATA	=	29.4
66	68	2	=	29.4		3 ATA	=	44.1
99	102	3	=	44.1		4 ATA	=	58.8
132	136	4	=	58.8		5 ATA	=	73.5

Gauge pressure compared to absolute pressure in fresh and salt water.

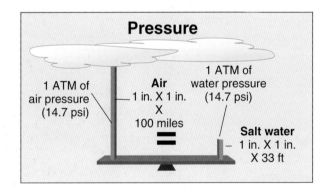

Pressure

1 ATM of air pressure (14.7 psi)

Air
1 in. X 1 in. X 100 miles

=

1 ATM of water pressure (14.7 psi)

Salt water
1 in. X 1 in. X 33 ft

▶ Figure 2.9   Principles of pressure.

Boyle's law—The pressure of a given quantity of gas whose temperature remains unchanged varies inversely with its volume, while the density varies directly with the absolute pressure.

excess of 1 ATM. Tire gauges and depth gauges are good examples of instruments that indicate gauge pressure, which is abbreviated "psig" (pounds per square inch gauge).

The total pressure exerted is what matters to divers. Both the pressures of the atmosphere and the water apply to diving. The reference for the total pressure is zero. The total pressure is absolute pressure, which is abbreviated "psia" (pounds per square inch absolute). When we express absolute pressure increments of atmospheres, we measure the pressure in atmospheres absolute (ATA).

You obtain absolute pressure by adding atmospheric pressure to gauge pressure. Be sure you understand the concept because we use absolute pressure when we deal with the effects of pressure in this and later chapters.

GAS LAWS

When you compress a quantity of gas, you reduce its volume and increase its density. Boyle's law states, "For any gas at a constant temperature, the volume varies inversely with the absolute pressure while the density varies directly with the absolute pressure."

Effects of Boyle's Law

If you compress a closed, flexible air space, such as a balloon, you reduce its volume in proportion to the increase in pressure. When you double the pressure, a closed, flexible air space occupies only half the volume that it did at the surface. No air is lost. The molecules compress into a smaller area. The density of the air is twice as great as it was at the surface.

When you return the compressed air space to the surface, the air inside expands until the object reaches its original volume. You compress your lungs during a breath-hold descent, and they return to normal volume when you return to the surface, provided you do not expel air underwater.

Scuba equipment provides air to you at the exact pressure of the surrounding water. This allows you to expand your lungs to their normal volume regardless of the depth. The density of the air inside the lungs increases so the air pressure equals the water pressure. Figure 2.10 shows the relationships between pressure, volume, and density.

When compressed air equalizes an air space at a pressure greater than sea level, Boyle's law also takes effect when you reduce the surrounding pressure. As outside pressure decreases, compressed air in a closed, flexible container expands in proportion to the reduction in pressure; that is, if the pressure halves, the volume doubles. If a container filled with compressed air at depth vents correctly during ascent, expanding air escapes through the vent, and the container remains full throughout the ascent. If the container is not vented, pressure inside increases when the container reaches its maximum volume. If the container is weak, the increase in pressure will rupture the container. This concept is important to scuba divers, who have many air spaces equalized with compressed air. Vented air spaces do not pose a hazard. If your lungs are not vented during ascent, life-threatening injuries will result. If you do not vent air from a flotation jacket during ascent, control of buoyancy will be lost as air expands and the jacket volume increases.

Figure 2.10 shows an interesting point about the rate of change of pressure (and volume) in water. The pressure doubles from 1 ATM to 2 ATM in 33 ft (10 m) of seawater. To double the pressure again requires a depth of 99 FSW (30 m). Note that you must ascend from 99 ft (30 m) to a depth of 33 ft (10 m)—a distance of 66 feet (20 m)—to experience the same rate of change of pressure that you experience when you ascend from 33 feet (10 m) to the surface. In other words, the closer you get to the surface, the greater the rate of change of pressure (and of the volume of an air space). You must be more attentive to compressed air in air spaces the nearer you are to the surface.

Perhaps the most significant challenge of diving is the change in pressure you experience during descents and ascents in water. Changes in pressure have direct, mechanical effects on your body. Pressure imbalance in your body air spaces can cause discomfort. You feel pressure changes in air as a result of changes in altitude, although pressure changes in water occur at a much greater rate than in air. You can sustain serious injury unless you keep the pressure in air spaces inside and attached to you equalized with the surrounding water pressure. Boyle's law causes squeezes and reverse blocks, which figure 2.11 illustrates. Knowledgeable and experienced divers routinely manage the task of equalization to avoid squeezes and blocks. Keeping air spaces

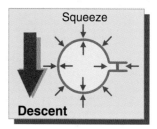

Depth	Pressure	Volume	Density
0 ft	1 ATM	1.0	X 1
33 ft	2 ATM	1/2	X 2
66 ft	3 ATM	1/3	X 3
99 ft	4 ATM	1/4	X 4

▶ Figure 2.10 Pressure, volume, and density relationships.

▶ Figure 2.11 Equalizing pressure.

Squeezes and blocks

If the pressure inside an air space is less than the surrounding water pressure, the outside pressure attempts to compress the air space. This condition is a "squeeze."

During descent, squeezes may occur in ears, sinuses, the mask, and other air spaces in or attached to the body.

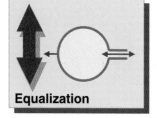

Squeeze

Descent

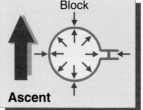

Block

Ascent

During ascent, the pressure surrounding an air space decreases. If the air inside the space, which was equalized to a higher pressure during descent, cannot escape, a situation that is the reverse of a squeeze occurs. When the pressure inside an air space is greater than the surrounding pressure, the condition is a "reverse block."

A "block" describes a situation where some form of blockage prevents compressed air from escaping along the route by which it entered an air space.

Prevention of both squeezes and blocks involves keeping the pressure within an air space equalized with the surrounding pressure.

Equalization

Guy-Lussac's law—For any gas at a constant volume, the pressure of the gas will vary directly with the absolute temperature.

equalized with the surrounding pressure is a challenge you will learn to meet and is one of the main subjects of the next chapter.

Guy-Lussac's Law

Boyle's law begins, "For any gas at a constant temperature . . ." because there are relationships between the temperature, pressure, and volume of a gas. Guy-Lussac's law explains these relationships: "For any gas at a constant volume, the pressure of the gas will vary directly with the absolute temperature." Just as absolute pressure must be used for pressure calculations, absolute temperature must be used for temperature computations. The absolute temperature scale for Fahrenheit temperatures is Rankine. To convert a Fahrenheit temperature to Rankine, add 460 degrees. The absolute temperature scale for a Celsius temperature is Kelvin. To convert a Celsius temperature to Kelvin, add 273 degrees.

You can observe the effect of Guy-Lussac's law with a scuba tank, which has a constant volume. When you decrease the temperature of the air in a tank, the pressure decreases. When you increase the temperature of the air in the tank, the pressure increases. A scuba tank taken from the trunk of a hot car and cooled in water experiences a drop in pressure although you do not release air from the cylinder. Pressure increases or decreases in a standard 80 ft³ (2,266 L) aluminum scuba cylinder at a rate of about 6 psig per degree Fahrenheit temperature change. Pressure increases or decreases in a standard 71.2 ft³ (2,016 L) steel scuba cylinder at a rate of about 5 psig per degree Fahrenheit temperature change.

Dalton's and Henry's Laws

Dalton's law—The partial pressure of a given quantity of gas is the pressure it would exert if it alone occupied the same volume. Also, the total pressure of a mixture of gases is the sum of the partial pressures of the components of the mixture.

A gas diffuses into or out of a substance. When a gas comes into contact with a liquid, the gas dissolves into the liquid. The amount of gas that diffuses into the liquid depends on the density and temperature of the liquid, the pressure of the gas in contact with the liquid, and the length of time the gas is in contact with the liquid. Another term for the process of gas diffusion into a liquid is ingassing. Because the human body is primarily liquid, the gases you breathe diffuse into your body tissues.

In a mixture of gases, such as air, the percentage of the total pressure exerted by each gas is the partial pressure (PP). Dalton's law states, "The total pressure exerted by a mixture of gases is the sum of the pressures that would be exerted by each gas if it alone were present and occupied the total volume." It is the partial pressure of a gas that determines the amount of that gas that dissolves into a liquid. Henry's law expresses gas absorption and says, "The amount of a gas that will dissolve in a liquid at a given temperature is directly proportional to the partial pressure of that gas." Table 2.2 shows the partial pressures of gases in the air at 1 ATM.

The partial pressure of a gas is the percentage of the gas in the mixture times the absolute pressure of the mixture. The partial pressure of a gas at depth has the same effect as a higher percentage of that gas at the surface. If a mixture of gas contains 2 percent carbon dioxide (CO_2) at sea level (14.7 psia or 1.03 kg/cm²), the partial pressure of the CO_2 is 0.294 psia (21 g/cm²). If the absolute pressure of the same mixture of gases increases to the pressure found at a depth of 99 feet (58.8 psia or 4.12 kg/cm²) in the ocean, the partial pressure of the CO_2 is 1.176 psia (0.082 mg/cm²). The amount of carbon dioxide sensed by the body at 99 ft (30 m) is four times greater than the amount that is sensed at the surface. Breathing 2 percent CO_2 at a depth of 99 ft (30 m) is the same

Henry's law—At a constant temperature, the amount of a gas that dissolves in a liquid with which it is in contact is proportional to the partial pressure of that gas.

Air composition	Percentage of gas	Partial pressure at 1 ATA	Partial pressure at 1 ATA (metric)
Nitrogen	78%	11.466 psia	.803 kg/cm²
Oxygen	21%	3.087 psia	.2163 kg/cm²
Argon	0.93%	0.137 psia	.0095 kg/cm²
Trace gases	0.04%	0.006 psia	.0004 kg/cm²
Carbon dioxide	0.03%	0.004 psia	.0003 kg/cm²
TOTALS	100%	14.7 psia	1.03 kg/cm²

Table 2.2 Partial Pressures of Gases in Air at 1 ATM

as breathing 8 percent CO_2 at the surface! A high level of CO_2 has a profound effect on respiration. The surface equivalent effect of partial pressures makes minute amounts of contaminants in breathing gases unsafe at depth. Table 2.3 shows the surface equivalent effect of partial pressures at various depths.

When a liquid has absorbed all of a gas that it can hold, the liquid is saturated. When you reduce the partial pressure of the gas in contact with the liquid, gas diffuses out of the liquid. This process is outgassing. Ingassing and outgassing provide a foundation for the dive tables used to prevent decompression sickness; these tables are presented in chapter 6.

AIR CONSUMPTION

The volume of air you breathe per minute during exertion is much more than the volume you breathe at rest—up to 17 times more on land and about 14 times more in the water. Pressure on the torso in the water allows only 85 percent of normal inhalation.

Table 2.3 Surface Equivalent Effect of Partial Pressures

Depth	Pressure	O_2[a]	CO[b]	CO_2[c]
0 ft (0 m)	1 ATA	20%	1%	2%
33 ft (10 m)	2 ATA	40%	2%	4%
66 ft (20 m)	3 ATA	60%	3%	6%
99 ft (30 m)	4 ATA	80%	4%	8%
132 ft (40 m)	5 ATA	100%	5%	10%

[a] Breathing air (20% oxygen) at 132 ft (40m) has the same effect as breathing 100% oxygen at the surface.

[b] Breathing a (toxic) mixture containing 1% CO at 66 ft (20 m) is the same as breathing 3% CO at the surface.

[c] Breathing a mixture containing 2% CO_2 at 99 ft (30 m) is the same as breathing 8% CO_2 at the surface and causes labored breathing.

Additional Information About Gas Laws

The following gas law formulas may be used to make precise mathematical calculations of pressure, volume, and temperature.

Boyle's law: $P_1V_1 = P_2V_2$

P_1 = Initial pressure (psia or ATA)
P_2 = Final pressure (psia or ATA)
V_1 = Initial volume
V_2 = Final volume

Example: A balloon with 2 pints of air floats from 2 ATA to the surface (1 ATA). What is the volume of the balloon at the surface?

P_1 = 2 ATA
P_2 = 1 ATA
V_1 = 2 pints
V_2 = Unknown

Rearranging the formula to solve for V_2, we find that
$V_2 = P_1V_1/P_2 = (2 \times 2)/1 = 4$ pints

Partial Pressure (PP) = psia × percent of gas

Example: What is the partial pressure of oxygen if the gas comprises 20 percent of a gas mixture that has an absolute pressure of 58.8 psi?

PP = 58.8 × 0.2 = 11.76 psia

Guy-Lussac's law: $P_1/T_1 = P_2/T_2$

P_1 = Initial pressure (psia or ATA)
P_2 = Final pressure (psia or ATA)
T_1 = Initial temperature (°R or °K)
T_2 = Final temperature (°R or °K)

Example: A scuba tank with a pressure of 2,250 psig and a temperature of 70 °F is heated to a temperature of 150 °F. What is the pressure of the scuba tank at the higher temperature? First, convert readings for pressure and temperature to absolute measures.

P_1 = 2,250 psig + 14.7 psia = 2,265 psia
P_2 = unknown
T_1 = 70 °F + 460 = 530 °R
T_2 = 150 °F + 460 + 610 °R

Rearranging the formula to solve for P_2, we find that

$P_2 = (P_1T_2)/T_1 = (2,265 \times 610)/530 = 2,607$ psia
2,607 psia – 14.7 psia = 2,592 psig

Because the density of the air breathed increases with depth, depth is a significant factor affecting the rate at which you consume air. For a given level of exertion, a supply of air lasts only half as long at a pressure of 2 ATA as it does at a pressure of 1 ATA. With heavy exertion at a pressure of 4 ATA (99 ft [30 m]), you exhaust an air supply over 40 times faster than you would the same volume of air when at rest at the surface! The rapid depletion of your air supply is one reason why you must avoid heavy exertion while diving.

The rate of air consumption is expressed in cubic feet per minute (liters per minute) or psig (ATMs or Bars) per minute. By knowing your consumption rate for various levels of activity, you can plan your dives. When you know your consumption rate and the amount of air available, you can calculate air supply duration for future dives.

HEAT, HUMIDITY, LIGHT, AND SOUND

You experience many changes when you enter water. You lose body heat faster, you lose body moisture when you use scuba equipment, what you see is deceiving, and what you hear may cause confusion. When you understand what happens to you and why, you can manage the differences between the water and air environments.

The Transfer of Heat

The net effect of the various forms of heat transfer is that you can chill quickly while diving. Radiation, convection, and conduction transfer heat from one medium to another (see figure 2.12). Heat waves radiate from exposed surfaces, heat travels upward through fluids by convection, and heat is transferred directly via conduction through substances in contact with each other. Metals are good conductors. Water is a poor conductor compared with metal, but conducts heat 25 times faster than air. Conduction and convection are the primary means by which heat transfers from a diver to the surrounding water. Heat rises from the skin and water carries the heat away. You lose body heat through the process of evaporation. Moisture evaporates from your lungs when breathing underwater and from the surface of your skin when you perspire above water. Scuba equipment expands high-pressure air and cools it. Your body heat warms the air you breathe, and you lose the heat energy with each exhalation.

You can slow the transfer of heat by insulating yourself with a material that is a poor conductor of heat. Exposure suits help insulate you from the environment, but insulation does not help reduce heat lost through respiration. The next two chapters present ways to manage the problems of heat loss.

Humidity

Scuba divers must guard against the effects of humidity, or the amount of water vapor present in a gas. The temperature of the gas determines the amount of water vapor a gas can absorb and retain. The warmer the gas, the more humidity the gas can contain.

You humidify inspired air. The process of compressing the air that is put into scuba tanks dehumidifies the air in the cylinder. You draw moisture from body tissues when you humidify dry scuba air during respiration. The resulting fluid loss can cause partial dehydration, an undesirable condition, especially for a scuba diver. In the next chapter, you will learn how to avoid the problems of dehydration.

Diving poses other humidity problems that you must manage. Moisture in the air inside your mask condenses on the faceplate of your mask as the air cools. Unless you thoroughly clean your mask lens in advance so the condensation runs off in a thin sheet, foggy beads of condensation form and blur your vision. Chapter 6 presents the process for cleaning, or defogging, your mask.

In freezing temperatures, moisture from your exhaled breath may cause a scuba regulator to freeze. Water in other items of diving equipment also may freeze. If you intend to

▶ Figure 2.12 Heat transfer and loss.

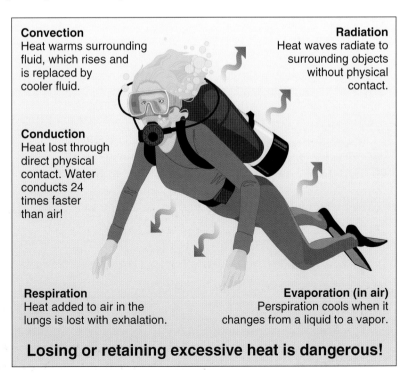

Convection
Heat warms surrounding fluid, which rises and is replaced by cooler fluid.

Conduction
Heat lost through direct physical contact. Water conducts 24 times faster than air!

Radiation
Heat waves radiate to surrounding objects without physical contact.

Respiration
Heat added to air in the lungs is lost with exhalation.

Evaporation (in air)
Perspiration cools when it changes from a liquid to a vapor.

Losing or retaining excessive heat is dangerous!

Additional Information About Air Consumption

The following air consumption formulas are used to calculate consumption rates and air supply duration. To calculate air consumption, you need three items of information: the depth at which you have remained for a period of time, the length of time you have remained at that depth, and the amount of air you have used during that time. To determine your air consumption rate:

1. Determine your depth air consumption rate (DACR). This is simply the amount of air used divided by the time at depth. For example, the DACR for a diver who uses 1,000 psig (68 ATMs or Bars) in 10 minutes is 100 psig (6.8 ATMs or Bars) per minute.

$$DACR = \frac{\text{Air used}}{\text{Time at depth}}$$

2. Convert the DACR to the surface air consumption rate (SACR). You need to express the rate in terms of volume rather than pressure. After you do this, you can apply the air consumption rate to any depth and to a cylinder of a different size than the one used initially to calculate the air consumption rate. Obtain the surface consumption rate by multiplying the DACR times the ratio of the pressure at the surface to the pressure at depth. Because you can express pressure in terms of depth, you can use the following formula:

$$SACR = DACR \times \frac{\text{33 ft (or 10 m)}}{\text{Diving depth in ft + 33 ft (or 10 m)}}$$

If, for example, your depth consumption rate for a depth of 33 ft (10 m) is 30 psig/min (2 ATMs or Bars/min), your SACR is 30 (33/66) = 15 psig/min (1.0 ATM or Bar/min).

3. Convert the rate to volume, establish a ratio of the tank volume and pressure (when the tank is full) to the breathing rate volume and pressure, then solve for the breathing rate volume (BRV). You solve for BRV as follows:

If

$$\frac{V_1}{P_1} = \frac{V_2}{P_2}$$

where

V_1 = Full tank volume
V_2 = Breathing rate volume

P_1 = Full tank pressure
P_2 = Breathing rate pressure

then

$$BRV = \frac{V_1 \times P_2}{P_1}$$

For example, the breathing rate volume (BRV) for a diver with an 80 ft³ (2,286 L), 3,000 psig (204 ATMs/Bars) tank and an SACR of 30 psig/min (2.04 ATMs/Bars) is

$$BRV = \frac{\text{80 ft}^3 \times \text{30 psig/min}}{\text{3,000 psig}} = 0.8 \text{ ft}^3/\text{min}$$

$$\text{Metric BRV} = \frac{\text{2,266 L} \times \text{2.04 ATM/min}}{\text{204 ATM}} = 22.7 \text{ L/min}$$

4. For the same level of activity, you can calculate the approximate duration (in minutes) of any amount of air from a tank of any size used at any depth. Here is an example: how long will 1,750 psig (119 ATMs or Bars) of air from a 71.2 ft³ (2,016 L), 2,475 psig (168 ATM) tank last at a depth of 70 ft (21.3 m) for a diver with a breathing rate volume (BRV) of 0.8 ft³ (22.9 L) per minute?

First, determine the volume of air in the tank at a pressure of 1,750 psig (119 ATMs or Bars). The formula for determining the volume of air in the tank is

$$V_2 = \frac{V_1 \times P_2}{P_1}$$

where

V_1 = Full tank volume
V_2 = Partially filled tank volume
P_1 = Full tank pressure
P_2 = Partially filled tank pressure

The air supply volume for the partially filled tank is, therefore,

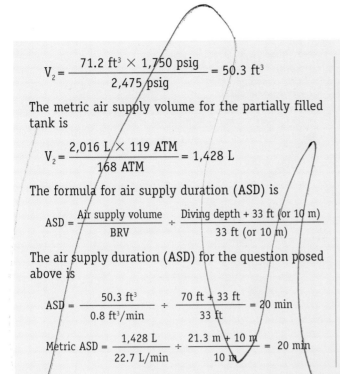

$$V_2 = \frac{71.2 \text{ ft}^3 \times 1,750 \text{ psig}}{2,475 \text{ psig}} = 50.3 \text{ ft}^3$$

The metric air supply volume for the partially filled tank is

$$V_2 = \frac{2,016 \text{ L} \times 119 \text{ ATM}}{168 \text{ ATM}} = 1,428 \text{ L}$$

The formula for air supply duration (ASD) is

$$\text{ASD} = \frac{\text{Air supply volume}}{\text{BRV}} \div \frac{\text{Diving depth} + 33 \text{ ft (or 10 m)}}{33 \text{ ft (or 10 m)}}$$

The air supply duration (ASD) for the question posed above is

$$\text{ASD} = \frac{50.3 \text{ ft}^3}{0.8 \text{ ft}^3/\text{min}} \div \frac{70 \text{ ft} + 33 \text{ ft}}{33 \text{ ft}} = 20 \text{ min}$$

$$\text{Metric ASD} = \frac{1,428 \text{ L}}{22.7 \text{ L/min}} \div \frac{21.3 \text{ m} + 10 \text{ m}}{10 \text{ m}} = 20 \text{ min}$$

These calculations may seem complicated at first, but the ideas are simple. The calculations become easy with practice. Let's review the four steps of air consumption calculations: (1) determine your depth air consumption rate (DACR); (2) determine your surface air consumption rate (SACR); (3) determine your breathing rate volume (BRV); and (4) determine the air supply duration (ASD) for a quantity of air. The abbreviated formulas for the calculations are:

$$\text{DACR} = \frac{\text{Air used}}{\text{Time at depth}}$$

$$\text{SACR} = \text{DACR} \times \frac{33 \text{ ft (or 10 m)}}{\text{Diving depth} + 33 \text{ ft (or 10 m)}}$$

$$\text{BRV} = \frac{V_1 \times P_2}{P_1}$$

$$\text{ASD} = \frac{\text{Air supply volume}}{\text{BRV}} \div \frac{\text{Diving depth} + 33 \text{ ft (or 10 m)}}{33 \text{ ft (or 10 m)}}$$

dive in a cold environment, you should complete special training and know how to prepare and use your equipment in those conditions.

Light and Vision

The density of water makes it challenging to interpret what we see and hear. Light travels slower in air than in water. When rays of light traveling in water pass through the lens of your mask, they accelerate and bend (refract). The effect is that what you see underwater is magnified. Objects appear three-fourths of their actual distance (25 percent closer) and one-third larger (four-thirds of their actual size). The visual distortion requires adjustments, and you will learn to make these with experience. An object 12 ft (3.7 m) away appears to be only 9 ft (2.7 m) away. A fish that appears about 2 ft (0.6 m) long actually is only 1½ ft (0.5 m) in length. Many new divers discover that items they remove from the water while diving are much smaller than they perceived them to be when the objects were underwater. Figure 2.13 illustrates how light is perceived differently in water.

One difficulty caused by the refraction of light is that distant objects appear closer than they are. This can create a hazard in clear water when you look downward on a drop-off. You may be tempted to go to a point that appears close, but if you go there you will exceed your planned maximum depth. You must realize that distance perception is inaccurate, and you must rely on your depth gauge instead of your vision.

You have two types of vision: day vision and night vision. You use different parts of your eyes for each type. When you move from a brightly lighted area into a dimly lighted area, your visions needs 15 to 30 minutes to adapt to the lower level of light. Even after the adaptation, your ability to see fine details is much less than your ability with day vision. In addition, particles in water diffuse, scatter, and attenuate light. The deeper you go, the less light there is. The amount of light decreases very quickly with depth in turbid water. A dive in turbid water involves a change from day vision to night vision.

▶ Figure 2.13   Vision underwater.

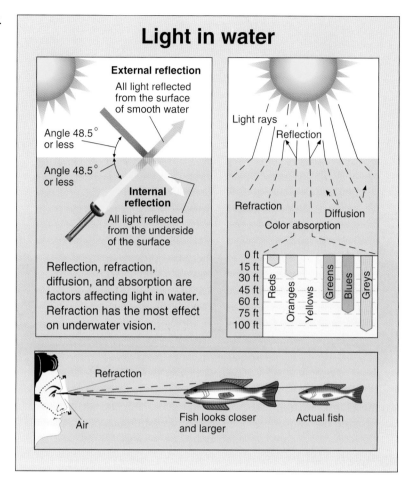

Water affects light in many ways. The surface of water reflects light. When light strikes the surface of calm water at an angle of less than 48 degrees, the water reflects all the light. Early morning and late afternoon sunlight do not penetrate calm water. Light rays going toward the surface from underwater also reflect from the interface, making the underside of the surface appear as a mirror when the viewer is at the proper angle.

Objects you view underwater often lack their natural colors. White light, such as sunlight, comprises all the colors of the spectrum. Increasing depth absorbs various colors. The water absorbs warm colors, such as red and orange, with only 30 ft (10 m) of depth. Cooler colors, such as blue, penetrate deepest. This is why deep, clear water is blue. The underwater scene appears drab at depths below 100 ft (30 m). Fortunately, you can restore all the colors of the spectrum underwater by using an artificial light at close range.

Sound and Hearing

Sound travels well in water. You will hear many sounds while diving. On land you can determine the direction of a sound by the time difference between a sound reaching one ear and then the other. This delay interval is brief, but it is sufficient for your brain to discern. Underwater, you hear when sound conducts through water and the bones of your head to your inner ears. Sound travels about four times faster in water than in air. The time delay for sound to reach the hearing organ in one ear and then in the other one is so small that directional discernment is difficult underwater.

Sound also does not transfer well from air to water. Only 0.01 percent of sound can travel directly between air and water. You must use special devices to make voice communications effective underwater.

SUMMARY

The aquatic environment affects your body in several ways. Pressure affects your air spaces—your ears, sinuses, and lungs. The rate of change of pressure in water is many times greater than in air and increases as you approach the surface during ascent. Changing pressures also affect the diffusion of gas into and out of liquids. The level of carbon dioxide in your body controls your respiration. The difference in density between air and water affects your buoyancy, mobility, heat loss, vision, and hearing. Temperature affects the pressure of a constant volume of gas. Depth and activity have the greatest effect on air consumption. Water absorbs heat from the body, so divers need insulation to help prevent excessive heat loss. Finally, humidity can cause several problems for scuba divers. Now that you are aware of the effects of the aquatic environment on your body, you are prepared to learn to adapt to the underwater environment.

Diving Adaptations

3

In chapter 2, you learned about the effects of water on your body. In this chapter, you learn how to deal with those effects. Most people with average intelligence and normal health can make aquatic environment adaptations, such as buoyancy and the equalization of pressure. Many adaptations you will make automatically, but some you must make consciously. Learning to make the transition from an air environment to the underwater environment requires professional instruction and guidance. You need to learn what to do, then do what you have learned.

By the end of this chapter, you will be able to

- *define hypothermia, hyperthermia, vasoconstriction, heat exhaustion, heatstroke, buoyancy compensator, Toynbee maneuver, Valsalva's maneuver, trapdoor effect, skip breathing, barotrauma, pulmonary barotrauma, arterial gas embolism, mediastinal emphysema, subcutaneous emphysema, pneumothorax, vertigo, perfusion, half-time, compartment, decompression illness, and nitrogen narcosis;*

- *state the cause, effect, signs and symptoms, first aid, treatment, and prevention of hyperthermia,*

hypothermia, squeezes, reverse blocks, respiratory distress, pulmonary barotrauma, vertigo, seasickness, decompression illness, and nitrogen narcosis;

- *explain three ways to control buoyancy while scuba diving;*

- *explain when to equalize pressure in your ears during descent and what to do if the pressure does not equalize; and*

- *explain how to minimize resistance to movement for underwater swimming.*

To function effectively underwater, you need specific attitudes, equipment, and knowledge. This chapter provides the fundamental knowledge and begins shaping the attitudes required to minimize the risk of injury. You will apply the basics of anatomy, physiology, and physics you have learned to a typical person descending into the depths and ascending back to the surface.

THERMAL ADAPTATIONS

Maintaining body core temperature within a few degrees of normal is challenging in water. When you are immersed in water, you lose body heat. A water temperature of 50° F (10° C) can incapacitate an unprotected diver within 15 minutes. Even water at a temperature of 80° F (27° C), which feels relatively warm, can chill a diver within an hour. Wearing only a swimsuit in 80° F water is the same as being without any clothing in air that is 42° F (6° C).

Your brain regulates your body functions to maintain your body temperature. If your core temperature is less than 95° F (35° C), you will suffer from hypothermia. You need to guard against two types of hypothermia—mild and severe—both of which can be dangerous. If your core temperature is higher than normal, you experience the effects of hyperthermia. You need to understand the effects of two types of hyperthermia—heat exhaustion and heatstroke—and prevent the conditions. They both can be dangerous.

Hypothermia—Excessive loss of heat from the core of the human body

Heat Loss

Your body has a variety of physiological responses to the loss of heat. Respiration increases automatically when you get chilled, which is undesirable because as you heat and moisturize inspired air, you lose the heat and moisture with each exhalation. The more you breathe, the more heat and moisture you lose to the surrounding environment. Water depth compounds the problem because the greater the surrounding pressure, the greater the density of the air that you breathe. Denser air requires more heat than air that is less dense. The deeper you dive, the quicker you get cold.

Anything that affects the function of your body—excitement, fear, seasickness, and other forms of illness—may increase heat loss. Therefore, good health and a confident state of mind are safety recommendations.

Hyperthermia—Higher than normal body core temperature

One way your body responds to cold is to shunt blood from the extremities through vasoconstriction. The circulatory shunting reduces heat loss because it keeps warm blood from losing heat when it passes through areas of your body that have little insulation.

Your head, underarms and sides, groin, and hands and feet are most prone to heat loss underwater (see figure 3.1). Fortunately, you can insulate these areas easily. You can lose considerable heat from your head in cold water because the head receives a large supply of warm blood and because it lacks natural insulation. Your body does not shunt blood from your head the way it does from other body extremities. In water at a temperature of 70° F (21° C) or less, it is important to insulate your head.

Hands have large surface areas compared with their volume. To prevent losing excessive heat through your hands when you get cold, your body shunts blood from them until they reach a temperature of 50° F (10° C). At this temperature, your body restores circulation to your hands to rewarm them partially. Hands quickly lose their warmth to the water. If you dive without hand protection in cold water, you lose body heat through your hands. Although your hands may become numb when they get cold, you should insulate them to conserve body heat.

Small people chill more quickly in water than large people. Small people have less muscle mass to generate and store heat. Insulation is important for all divers, but protection against heat loss is more critical for those of smaller stature.

Failure to wear adequate insulation leads to hypothermia. So does repeated or prolonged exposure. Slow chilling of your body is undesirable. You lose muscle strength and feeling, and your muscles may cramp. Severe heat loss also affects your ability to reason.

Another body response to heat loss is shivering, which restores heat through muscular activity. Shivering generates about five times as much heat as your body produces at rest. Shivering is helpful on land, but it is not beneficial in water. Water conducts away the heat you produce by shivering, and you get colder. Uncontrollable shivering indicates that you have lost too much heat from the core of your body and that you cannot rewarm yourself without getting out of the water. When you are shivering, terminate the dive. Rewarm yourself thoroughly before making any additional dives. Warm, dry clothes, warm surroundings, and warm nonalcoholic drinks help to return your body temperature to normal.

There is a difference between warming the surface of your body and warming the core of your body. You may feel rewarmed, but your deep core temperature may remain below normal. If you return to the water in this condition, you quickly will become chilled. The only way to be sure that you are thoroughly rewarmed is to keep warming yourself until you begin to perspire. Perspiration occurs when the core temperature begins to rise above normal body temperature.

Overheating

You can prevent excessive loss of body heat by insulating your body with an exposure suit, but insulation can cause another problem.

Vasoconstriction—Narrowing of the blood vessels

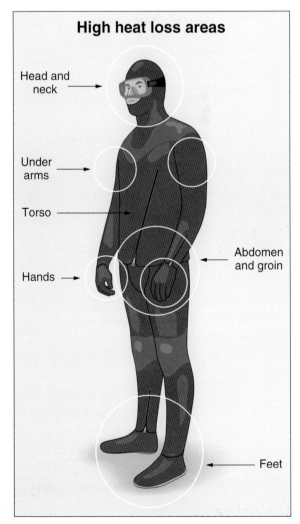
▶ Figure 3.1 Hands and feet are low heat loss areas in air, but they can be high heat loss areas in cold water if unprotected.

High heat loss areas

Head and neck

Under arms

Torso

Hands

Abdomen and groin

Feet

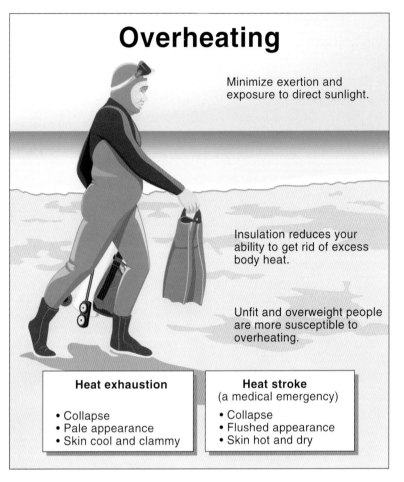

Overheating

Minimize exertion and exposure to direct sunlight.

Insulation reduces your ability to get rid of excess body heat.

Unfit and overweight people are more susceptible to overheating.

Heat exhaustion	Heat stroke (a medical emergency)
• Collapse • Pale appearance • Skin cool and clammy	• Collapse • Flushed appearance • Skin hot and dry

▶ Figure 3.2 Don't allow yourself to become overheated when preparing to dive.

When you insulate your body to reduce heat loss in water, you reduce your body's ability to rid itself of excess heat above water. The evaporation of the perspiration helps cool your body, but if you cover your body, perspiration cannot evaporate. You may become overheated in warm climates when you are preparing to dive. It is a challenge to maintain your body temperature within acceptable limits before, during, and after dives. Figure 3.2 shows the effects of overheating.

When a person is unable to stop the rise of core temperature, heat exhaustion occurs. This condition is serious. A person affected by heat exhaustion becomes weak and may collapse. The victim looks pale and feels sweaty. Move the person with this condition to a cool place and take steps to lower his or her body temperature.

A more serious form of hyperthermia is a heatstroke, which occurs when the body temperature becomes so high that the body's temperature-regulating ability shuts down. A victim of heatstroke looks flushed and has hot, dry skin. This condition is extremely serious. Cool the patient's body immediately and summon medical assistance.

Preventing hyperthermia is much better than treating it. Avoid prolonged exposure to higher temperatures when wearing insulation. If the air temperature is high, douse yourself with water after donning your exposure suit and before donning the remainder of your diving equipment. Stay out of direct sunlight if possible. All thermal considerations for diving are especially important for divers whose physical fitness is marginal.

BUOYANCY ADAPTATIONS

Exposure suits and other equipment affect your buoyancy. You must adapt your weight to blend weightlessly into the aquatic environment. When you are buoyant, you must fight to remain submerged; when you are overweighted, you must work hard to keep from sinking or to stay off the bottom. You need to maintain the weightless state of neutral buoyancy underwater and a state of positive buoyancy at the surface. In chapter 2, you learned the principle of buoyancy and the three states of buoyancy. Here, you will learn some practical applications of buoyancy.

Your body, composed of solids, liquids, and air spaces, has an average density nearly the same as water. A typical human body immersed and relaxed in water has a positive buoyancy of a few pounds when the lungs are filled with air and negative buoyancy of a couple of pounds when the lungs contain the minimum amount of air.

Factors Affecting Buoyancy

Usually you wear some type of exposure suit to dive. Most exposure suits increase buoyancy, so you wear weights to offset the buoyancy of the suit and achieve neutral buoyancy. The weights you use are made of lead, which is about 12 times denser than water.

Your initial state of buoyancy in water depends on the weight of the volume of water you and your equipment displace. You can vary your volume—with a negligible increase or decrease in your weight—by adding air to or venting air from an inflatable device, called a **buoyancy compensator** (BC). A BC is standard equipment for divers. Increasing BC volume increases buoyancy, while decreasing BC volume decreases buoyancy.

Your buoyancy is affected by your physical size, your lung capacity, the equipment you wear, and the items you carry (see table 3.1). Exposure suits use air or small bubbles of gas for insulation. When you wear an exposure suit and descend, pressure compresses your suit and reduces its volume, so you become less buoyant. You must add air to your BC to compensate for buoyancy lost from suit compression. On the other hand, buoyancy increases as you consume air from your scuba cylinder. Remember that air weighs 0.08 lb/ft^3 (1.28 mg/cm^3). A typical scuba tank contains 80 ft^3 (2,266 L) of air. A full tank weighs 6 lb (2.9 kg) more than an empty tank. As you consume air from your scuba tank, you can vent some of the air that you added to your BC to compensate for suit compression. The trade-off helps you keep buoyancy constant during a dive.

Inflating your lungs increases your buoyancy, while deflating them reduces buoyancy. A high average lung volume makes you float; a low average volume makes you sink. When you become excited or begin moving quickly, your respiration increases and affects your buoyancy. For optimum control of buoyancy, maintain a calm, relaxed state.

The density of water also affects buoyancy. Salt water is denser than fresh water, so you are more buoyant in the ocean than in a lake. This means if you are weighted for neutral buoyancy in the ocean, you must remove some weight to achieve neutral buoyancy for freshwater diving. The amount of weight you remove is about 3 percent of the combined

Table 3.1	Factors Affecting Buoyancy
Factor	**Effect**
Size and weight of diver	Larger divers are more buoyant
Type and amount of equipment	Bulky equipment is more buoyant
Amount of weight worn	Weights offset positive buoyancy
Amount of air in BC	Increasing volume increases buoyancy
Amount of air in tank	Buoyancy increases as air decreases
Amount of air in lungs	Exertion or excitement increases volume and buoyancy
Suit compression	Pressure decreases volume and buoyancy
Item carried	Added weight decreases buoyancy
Type of water	Denser water increases buoyancy

dry weight of you and your equipment. For example, if a neutrally weighted 160 lb (73 kg) diver with 60 lb (27 kg) of equipment, including 16 lb (7.2 kg) of weights, wants to dive in fresh water instead of seawater, the diver must remove about 7 lb (3 kg) of weight to be weighted correctly.

Ways to Control Buoyancy

You control buoyancy three ways: (1) by the amount of weight you wear; (2) by the amount of air in your BC; and (3) by the amount of air in your lungs. These means of control are coarse, medium, and fine adjustments respectively. The skills you need to learn to adapt to the aquatic environment include determining the correct amount of weight to be worn, regulating the amount of air in your BC, and varying your breathing for minor buoyancy adjustments. Chapter 5 addresses these skills.

EQUALIZING PRESSURES

One of the most important adaptations you must learn is how to handle the effects of pressure changes in water. Pressure changes rapidly as you descend and ascend. You must keep air spaces inside and on your body equalized to avoid discomfort and injury. In this section, you will learn the procedures for pressure **equalization**

Equalizing the Sinuses

Your sinuses equalize pressure automatically as long as they are healthy. But when you have a cold or respiratory illness, the membranes lining your sinuses become swollen. The swelling can close the narrow air passages leading to the sinuses. If you descend with swollen sinus membranes, a sinus squeeze will result. Because the sinuses are formed with bone, they do not compress as a flexible container does. When the pressure inside the sinuses is less than the surrounding pressure, the reduced pressure draws fluids into the cavities to reduce their volume and equalize the pressure by compressing the air that is there. Do not attempt this painful method of equalization because your problems are not over after you descend. When you ascend in the condition just described, the compressed air in the sinuses expands to its original volume. The expansion can force the fluid in your sinuses out through the openings, which are swollen shut. Avoid this painful process; don't dive unless your head is clear and normal. Figure 3.3 shows what happens to both healthy and congested sinuses under pressure.

▶ Figure 3.3 How pressure is equalized in the sinuses.

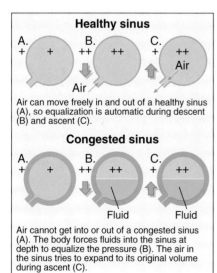

Healthy sinus

A. + + B. ++ ++ C. + ++ Air

Air

Air can move freely in and out of a healthy sinus (A), so equalization is automatic during descent (B) and ascent (C).

Congested sinus

A. + + B. ++ ++ C. + ++

Fluid Fluid

Air cannot get into or out of a congested sinus (A). The body forces fluids into the sinus at depth to equalize the pressure (B). The air in the sinus tries to expand to its original volume during ascent (C).

Do not use medications to relieve stuffiness and congestion caused by an illness and then dive. Increased pressure may reduce the medication's effects and the duration of its effectiveness. Decongestants do not cure an illness; they simply mask its symptoms. When medication taken to open swollen airways wears off, a "rebound" effect occurs. The airways become more swollen than they were before you took the medication. If the rebound occurs while diving, you can trap high-pressure air in your sinuses. If you are not well enough to dive without medications, do not dive.

Equalizing the Ears

You will be more involved with the equalization of pressure in your ears than with any other air space. Whereas the air passages to your sinuses normally are open, the eustachian tubes leading to your ears normally are closed. You need to learn how to open the tubes at will to allow air to pass through them and equalize pressure in the air spaces of your middle ears.

There are several movements you can make that will open the ends where the eustachian tubes connect with the throat. Swallowing, yawning, lifting the base of your tongue, and jutting the jaw forward (either individually or in combination) should produce a "cracking" sound in your ears. The opening of the tubes causes the sound. Some divers are fortunate because they can use simple movements to equalize pressure in their ears during descent. Most people require a more forceful means of equalization. Many divers use a technique known as the Toynbee maneuver, which you do by blocking your nostrils, closing your mouth, and swallowing. The Valsalva's maneuver is a more forceful maneuver you do by blocking your nostrils, closing your mouth, and gently attempting to exhale.

You must avoid excessive force when you use the Valsalva's method or you can permanently damage your ears by rupturing the round window. When pressure in the outer ear increases, the eardrum bulges inward. The bones of hearing in the middle ear transmit the movement to the oval window in the inner ear. When you attempt to exhale against closed airways, you create an internal pressure that your body transmits to your inner ears. The attempted exhalation pressure, in conjunction with the water pressure exerted on the oval window, can cause the round window to rupture, a serious injury that can result in a permanent high frequency hearing loss and constant ringing in the ear. Because you control how hard you attempt to exhale in a Valsalva's maneuver, you can prevent this injury. Be careful!

You must equalize your middle ear air spaces frequently. If you delay equalization during descent, increasing pressure holds your eustachian tubes closed, and attempting to force air through them only closes them tighter. This is the trapdoor effect, a difficulty you can avoid by keeping the pressure in your middle ears and your throat equal. You can then open your eustachian tubes and allow air to pass through them. Figure 3.4 shows the trapdoor effect.

Equalize pressure in your ears before descending and about every 2 ft (0.6 m) for the first 15 ft (4.6 m) of descent, about every 3 ft (0.9 m) from 15 to 30 ft (4.6 to 9.2 m), and as needed thereafter. You will feel and hear air enter your ears when you "clear" them of any difference in pressure. If you attempt to equalize and cannot get air into your ears, ascend several feet to reduce the pressure on your eustachian tubes and try again. If that works, continue your descent. If that does not work, ascend a little farther and try again. Your initial descents may appear somewhat jerky until you become accustomed to equalization techniques.

Failure to equalize pressure in your middle ears is as bad as trying to equalize forcefully. Pressure bows the eardrum inward in an unequalized middle ear. If

Toynbee maneuver—A method of opening the eustachian tubes by blocking the nostrils, closing the mouth, and swallowing

Valsalva's maneuver—A method of opening the eustachian tubes by blocking the nostrils, closing the mouth, and gently trying to exhale

▶ Figure 3.4   Ear equalization technique.

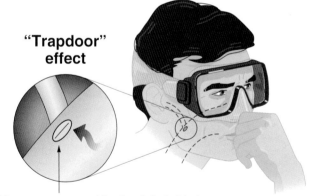

Methods:
- Blowing gently with mouth closed and nostrils blocked.
- Swallowing with mouth closed and nostrils blocked.
- Jutting the jaw forward while yawning with mouth closed.

"Trapdoor" effect

When pressure equalization falls behind water pressure during descent, the pressure difference holds the opening of the Eustachian tube closed and prevents any further equalization until the diver ascends enough to relieve the pressure on the end of the Eustachian tube.

the squeeze continues, pressure forces blood and fluid into the middle ear to reduce the volume. The process takes time and usually, but not always, is painful. It does, however, damage the ear. If you feel discomfort or pressure in your ears during descent, reascend until the pain is gone, then ascend another couple of feet before trying to equalize.

If you ignore an ear squeeze and continue your descent, the pressure differential can rupture your eardrum. The rupture instantly equalizes the pressure in your middle ear but damages your ear in the process. A rupture of your eardrum causes a temporary loss of hearing and a feeling of "fullness" in your ear. Cold water rushing into the middle ear may also cause temporary disorientation. See the section on vertigo later in this chapter. If you suspect an ear injury, see a physician; prompt treatment can minimize the risk of permanent injury.

You can cause an outward rupture of an eardrum if you block the ear canal with a plug or cover your ears with a watertight covering. When you obstruct an ear canal, the air in your outer ear remains at surface pressure while the pressure in your middle ear increases with equalization during descent. The difference in pressure between the middle and outer ear pushes the eardrum outward until it breaks. You can and must prevent such an injury. Do not wear earplugs while diving, and avoid waterproof seals over your ears.

It is easier to equalize when you descend in an upright position than in a head-down position. Membranes line the airways in your head, and gravity affects blood in the vessels within the membranes. When you are upside down in water, the membranes of your air passages swell and narrow.

Ear equalization difficulties during ascent are uncommon. Air expanding inside the middle ear escapes through the eustachian tube. Air passes out through the tube much more easily than it goes in; you do not have to do maneuvers to open your tubes so the air can escape. But if a plug of mucus happens to block a tube, pressure will build up in the middle ear and cause a reverse block. This can cause discomfort. If you feel pain or pressure in an ear during ascent, stop the ascent. Pressure inside the ear usually will work its way out, if given time. If you are forced to surface, the pain will increase and an injury may result. Have the ear examined by a physician, especially if you have reoccurring reverse blocks.

Equalizing the Mask

Inside the dive mask is an air space affected by changes in pressure. If you descend without increasing the amount of air inside your mask, pressure pulls your face and eyes into the mask slightly. The pulling sensation, if ignored, ruptures capillaries in your eyes and on your face and causes a mask squeeze. After a dive, the whites of your eyes will be red, and your face will be red and puffy. There is no excuse for a mask squeeze. You can prevent the problem by exhaling through your nose as needed during descent to keep the pressure inside your mask equal to the surrounding pressure.

BREATHING ADAPTATIONS

Breathing in water differs from breathing on land in several ways. You cannot breathe as freely in water. Pressure on the lungs from immersion in water prevents you from breathing as fully as you can in air. Also, it is not as easy to get large quantities of air from a scuba system as it is to breathe deeply above water.

When you ascend, compressed air in your lungs expands, which can cause your lungs to rupture unless you allow the excess air to escape. A normal breathing pattern allows expanding air to escape; breath holding does not. A primary rule of scuba diving is to always breathe continuously. There is a chance that you will inhale some water, which

▶ Figure 3.5   A breath-holding ascent after breathing compressed air can cause lung rupture. Breathe continuously while ascending.

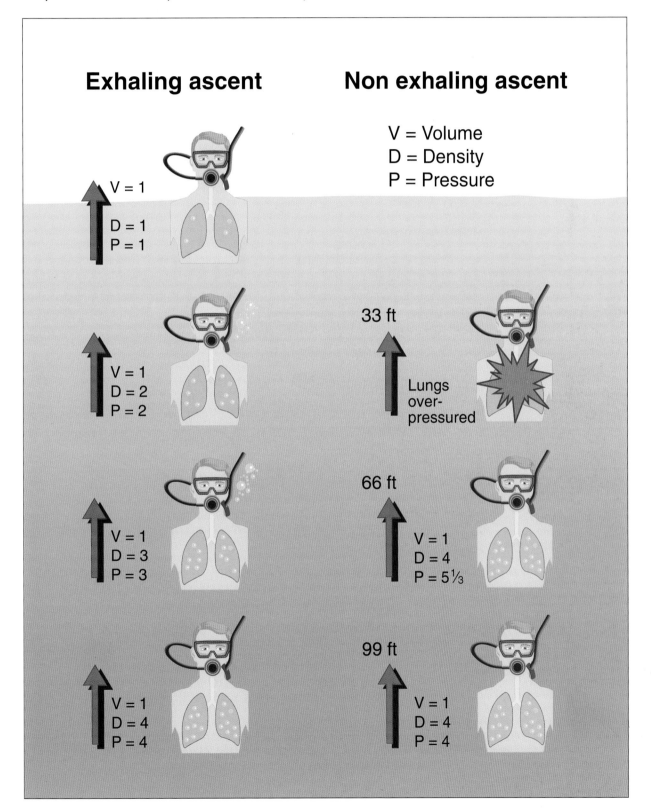

Exhaling ascent

V = 1
D = 1
P = 1

V = 1
D = 2
P = 2

V = 1
D = 3
P = 3

V = 1
D = 4
P = 4

Non exhaling ascent

V = Volume
D = Density
P = Pressure

33 ft
Lungs over-pressured

66 ft
V = 1
D = 4
P = 5⅓

99 ft
V = 1
D = 4
P = 4

The most important rule of scuba diving: Always keep breathing. Do not hold your breath.

will cause you to choke and gasp when the water strikes your vocal chords. You need to learn the correct methods of breathing while in and under the water.

Lung Overexpansion

The most important aquatic breathing adaptation you will make is overcoming the instinct to hold your breath underwater. When you breathe compressed air at depth, the density of the air in your lungs is greater than it is at the surface. When you ascend, the air in your lungs expands as the surrounding pressure decreases. If you hold your breath, your lungs expand until they reach their maximum volume, then rupture with an ascent of as little as 4 ft (1.2 m). It is imperative that you avoid breath holding when breathing compressed air underwater. You may breathe continuously or may exhale a small amount of air continuously but never hold your breath during ascent after breathing compressed air. Figure 3.5 (on page 41) illustrates why you must breathe continuously. Table 3.2 describes the possible consequences of breath holding while ascending with compressed air in your lungs.

Skip Breathing

Some divers attempt to extend their air supplies by holding each breath for several seconds. This dangerous practice is called skip breathing. When you hold your breath, you increase the amount of carbon dioxide in your circulatory system. A high carbon dioxide level in your body reduces your ability to cope should a difficulty arise. And if you skip breathe, you may forget to exhale while ascending. It is important to breathe continuously when breathing compressed air.

Breathing Problems

Divers may encounter respiratory difficulties if they overexert themselves, breathe contaminated air, inhale water, or run out of air. Fortunately, you can (and should) prevent all these problems.

Overexertion   Scuba equipment allows you to breathe comfortably while underwater. A regulator delivers air with little respiratory effort, but breathing underwater requires more effort than breathing above water. If you do not maintain your scuba equipment properly, the effort required to inhale and exhale can be excessive and may cause respiratory distress.

Scuba regulators have a limited capacity to supply air and are not for activities involving heavy exertion. Commercial divers use helmets with air hoses to supply large amounts of air to meet their needs. You must avoid strenuous activities underwater because you can overbreathe your equipment and experience air starvation, a suffocating feeling of not being able to get enough air.

While diving, make your breaths longer and slower than your breaths on land. Pace your activity to keep respiration at a slow, controlled rate. If breathing becomes rapid or labored, cease all activity immediately and exhale deeply until your respiration returns to a controlled rate.

Contaminated Air   If the compressed air in your tank comes from an air compressor that is not operated or maintained properly, your tank will contain contaminated air. The contamination is likely to be CO (carbon monoxide), a gas produced by incomplete

Table 3.2 Potential Lung Injuries

Pulmonary Barotrauma

Barotrauma is trauma or injury caused by pressure. *Pulmonary barotrauma* is any lung injury caused by pressure. Failure to allow expanding air to escape from the lungs during ascent can cause several forms of pulmonary barotrauma, either singularly or in combination.

Arterial Gas Embolism

An *embolism* is a blockage of circulation. An embolism resulting from an air bubble blocking the arterial circulation is an *arterial gas embolism* (AGE). This occurs when air expanding in the lungs forces bubbles of air into the circulation. Air bubbles enter the capillary beds of the lungs and pass through the heart, which pumps the bubbles into arteries supplying blood to the body. The diameter of an artery decreases as the distance from the heart increases. At some point a bubble lodges in an artery and becomes an embolus (plug). It is common for an arterial gas embolism to occur in an artery leading to the brain. The embolus has the effect of a stroke, causes unconsciousness, and is an extremely serious injury. Anytime a diver loses consciousness after a dive, you should suspect AGE. The temporary obstruction of an airway, such as that caused by a cold, increases the risk of AGE. Healthy lungs are a prerequisite for diving.

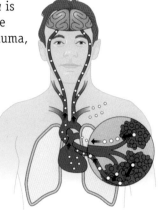
Air embolism

Mediastinal Emphysema

If a rupture of the lung does not force air into the circulation, the air may travel along the bronchi and enter the middle area of the chest, called the *mediastinum*. This results in a *mediastinal emphysema,* which means air in the tissues in the middle of the chest. The injury causes a dull ache or tightness that worsens with coughing, swallowing, or taking a deep breath. Expanding air may interfere with the circulation of the heart and can cause loss of consciousness.

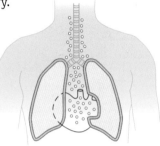
Mediastinal emphysema

Subcutaneous Emphysema

Expanding air in the mediastinum may migrate upward along the breastbone. The air will then swell the tissues around the neck, producing an injury known as *subcutaneous emphysema*, which is air in the tissues under the skin. The injury can cause changes in the voice, crackling of the skin, and a feeling of fullness in the neck.

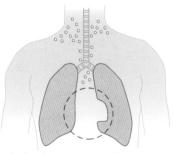
Subcutaneous emphysema

Pneumothorax

If a lung rupture forces air into the space between the lungs and the lining of the chest wall, a condition known as *pneumothorax* occurs. The term means air trapped in the chest cavity. As air trapped in the pleural space expands during ascent, it collapses the lung and may affect the action of the heart. Symptoms are severe pain and breathing difficulty.

Lung injuries are serious and can be life threatening. Life support may be required. This is one reason why you should complete a course in cardiopulmonary (heart and lung) resuscitation (CPR). You may have to administer first aid until professional medical treatment (which all lung injuries require) is available.

Failing to allow excess air to escape causes nearly all lung overexpansion injuries. You can prevent injuries by breathing continuously. If you remove the scuba regulator from your mouth for any reason, exhale lightly and continuously to avoid breath holding.

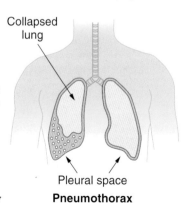
Collapsed lung
Pleural space
Pneumothorax

combustion. CO in the body impedes the blood's ability to transport oxygen. Blood hemoglobin's affinity for CO is 210 times greater than its affinity for oxygen. Hemoglobin normally exchanges oxygen for CO_2 about every half-minute, but when CO attaches to hemoglobin, the contaminant remains bonded to the hemoglobin for hours. Breathing contaminated air under pressure can make you ill and render you unconscious. Avoid contaminated air by having your tank filled only with pure air. CO is an odorless, tasteless gas, but usually other gases that have a foul taste and odor accompany it. If the air from a scuba tank smells or tastes foul, do not use it. Report the situation immediately to the facility that filled the cylinder. Good air stations have their air tested regularly to ensure purity.

Water Inspiration　If you inhale water, your larynx goes into a spasm as a reflex action to keep the liquid out of your lungs. Avoid coughing and choking in water; not only are these reflexes unpleasant, but they may cause you to inspire more water and lose buoyancy. You need to breathe differently underwater than you do on land. Avoid quick inhalations. Begin a breath with a light, slow inhalation to ensure you are inhaling air and not water. Once air begins flowing, the remainder of your inhalation can be normal.

You also can prevent droplets of water from going down your throat by placing the tip of your tongue on the roof of your mouth behind your upper teeth to form a splashboard. If you do inhale some water and start coughing, try swallowing hard three times in rapid succession. The swallowing helps you overcome your reflex.

If water does enter your lungs, it interferes with respiration. If an extensive area of the lungs is irritated by water, you can drown. This is a risk you face in any aquatic pastime. The purpose of your training is to allow you to enjoy the aquatic environment with the minimum risk of injury—especially drowning. When you follow the rules and practices you learn, the risk of injury while diving will be negligible.

An automatic response to the inhalation of water is to swallow it in an effort to keep your airways dry. When you swallow salt water, you may experience illness, nausea, or diarrhea. If you swallow several mouthfuls of salt water while diving, terminate the dive.

Running Out of Air　Some divers do not monitor their air supplies and run out of air at depth. There is no more excuse for running out of air underwater than there is for running out of gas on the freeway when you have a working fuel gauge. There are ways to manage an out-of-air situation, but it is much better to avoid the problem.

HEART AND LUNGS

Immersion changes your cardiac workload. When you are upright in water, there is a greater pressure on your lower limbs than on the upper part of your body. The pressure differential shifts more blood than normal into the upper part of your body. Your heart pumps a greater volume with each beat and works from one and one-third to over one and one-half times harder in this situation than it does on land.

Water temperature alters the rate and rhythm of your heart, and physical and emotional stress compound the issue. The combined effects of water pressure, exercise, cold, and stress can cause serious problems if your heart is not healthy. If you have heart problems and wish to dive, you should obtain approval from a diving physician. Even minor heart problems can cause you to suddenly lose consciousness in the water, and you could drown. Fitness for diving is an important safety issue.

ONLY FOOLS STRETCH THE RULES

Your ability to exert in water is not as good as it is on land. Your heart and lungs do not function as well as normal when under pressure. Trying to work hard underwater will lead to overexertion and a frightening sensation of suffocation. To adapt to your cardiopulmonary limitations, you must learn to limit your activities and pace yourself.

EQUILIBRIUM ADAPTATIONS

If you rupture an eardrum, water colder than body temperature may come into contact with the semicircular canals of your inner ear. The canals—your center of equilibrium—are sensitive to temperature and pressure changes. Cold water cooling the semicircular canals can cause *vertigo*—a feeling of dizziness and disorientation; a feeling that passes when the water in the middle ear warms to body temperature. Obviously it is better to prevent vertigo than to deal with it.

A sudden change in pressure in the middle ear air space of one ear that affects the semicircular canals also can produce dizziness called alternobaric vertigo. The disorientation from alternobaric vertigo passes quickly when the inner ear recovers.

There are many causes of vertigo. Fortunately, instances of severe disorientation are rare in diving. If you experience disorientation while underwater, try to grasp a solid object for a point of reference until the feeling passes. If suspended in the water, close your eyes and hug yourself to reduce the effects of the vertigo. Avoid panic by telling yourself that the sensation will not last long.

Motions detected in your inner ears, visual references, and joint pressures on your limbs all affect your equilibrium. When your brain receives mixed signals from your inner ears, eyes, and body, you may experience motion sickness. You must avoid seasickness because vomiting in and under the water is hazardous.

Medications can help reduce the tendency to be seasick. The medicine dulls the senses of the organs of balance in your ears. Unfortunately, the medications can have other undesirable effects. If you are prone to seasickness, consult a diving physician about the medication you should try. Take some of the medicine several days before you plan to dive, and note the effects, if any. If the medication produces drowsiness or blurred vision, do not use it while diving. Seek an alternative that does not produce side effects. Medications that cause dizziness, drowsiness, changes in heart rhythm, or blurred vision may cause you to lose consciousness under pressure. Many divers do successfully use medications to prevent seasickness; you need to find a type that works for you. Take motion sickness medication at least 30 minutes before you are exposed to motion.

If you do not want to use medication, there are other techniques you can use to reduce the tendency toward seasickness. Eat a good, nonspicy meal in advance. An empty, acid-filled stomach becomes upset more easily than does a full one. People whose breakfast before diving consists of coffee and orange juice are good candidates for motion sickness. When aboard a vessel, position yourself as near the center of the boat as possible. Avoid sitting in the front end of the boat, breathing engine fumes, and reading. You can hasten your adaptation to motion, described as getting your "sea legs," by lying down for a while with your eyes closed. Being still allows your inner ears to adapt to the motion without visual signals confusing your brain.

You may become disoriented when you are weightless in a dimly lighted environment. Under some conditions, you may have difficulty telling which way is up if you rely on your sense of balance. To prevent disorientation, learn to recognize clues about your orientation in the water. Water in your mask settles to the lowest point, bubbles ascend, and heavy objects you hold (such as your weight belt) orient themselves up and down.

VISUAL ADAPTATIONS

Experience will help you adapt to magnified vision underwater. You can adapt so quickly to distance corrections in water that you will have to readapt when you surface from a dive. At the end of a dive, the distance to a boat or to the shore may look much greater than it is. You may be surprised to find that you require less time than you think to swim to a destination.

You also will compensate for color differences. When you know the color something is supposed to appear, it looks more like that color. Artificial light at close range will help you view the rich and magnificent colors in the underwater world.

Your vision adapts to low light levels, but the process takes time. Short, deep dives in turbid water will not allow you to complete your adaptation, and details will not be clear. You will not be able to see well without artificial light. You can improve your ability to see while diving by avoiding bright light and glare before a dive. Wear good, dark sunglasses above water during the day. When you complete training for night diving, you will learn other techniques to help adapt your eyes for diving at night.

Humidity can cause condensation to form on the lens of your mask and obscure your vision. A clean glass surface will not fog, so make sure you clean the lens or lenses of your mask thoroughly.

INGASSING AND OUTGASSING ADAPTATIONS

You absorb nitrogen underwater, and there are limits to the amount of nitrogen that you can safely eliminate at the end of a dive. If you exceed these limits, you may be injured.

Decompression Theory

Gases diffuse by moving from areas of greater concentration to areas of lesser concentration. When pressure increases, gases diffuse from your lungs into your blood and then

Scuba Wise

At some point, many divers discover a special feeling of becoming part of the underwater world. I remember vividly an overwhelming feeling—a strange combination of peace and exhilaration—that I experienced during a dive in the Red Sea. The goal of training is to help you adapt to a new environment. When we are able to make the adaptations, we can relax; when we can relax, we focus more on our exciting new surroundings than we do on ourselves. It is challenging to meet the demands of diving, but when you succeed, the exuberance is worth every adaptation you have to make. We can adapt well to new situations. Training helps us adapt faster, easier, and safer than we can by trial and error. Study the remaining chapters carefully so you can learn how to adapt to the subaquatic environment. I want you to feel what I felt in the Red Sea and have felt many times while diving. The feeling of being one with the sea is powerful, moving, and unforgettable.

from your blood into your tissues. When the **ambient pressure** (surrounding pressure) decreases, diffusion occurs in the reverse sequence.

Two factors affecting diffusion are time and **perfusion** (the circulation in a tissue). The greater the circulation in a tissue, the sooner the pressures of the gases in that tissue come into balance with the pressures of the gases you breathe. Reaching this state of equilibrium takes time. The amount of time that a tissue uses to accumulate half the gas it can hold for a given pressure is a **half-time**. A tissue is saturated (holds all a gas it can for a given pressure) after 6 half-times. If perfusion permits 50 percent of a gas to diffuse into a tissue in 5 minutes, the tissue saturates in 30 minutes. Outgassing also occurs in 6 half-times.

Air is primarily nitrogen and oxygen. The oxygen in the air you breathe is of no consequence to you within the limits of recreational diving (130 ft or 39.6 m maximum) because you use the oxygen. Nitrogen, the primary component of air, is inert. Your body cannot use the nitrogen, so when you ascend you must eliminate the excess nitrogen you absorb at depth. Because nitrogen diffuses from your body, there is no problem unless the reduction in pressure is so great that you cannot eliminate the nitrogen fast enough. When you reduce the pressure on a liquid rapidly, and there is sufficient gas dissolved in the liquid, the gas forms bubbles. An excellent example of this is CO_2 dissolved in carbonated beverages (see figure 3.6). The gas remains dissolved in a sealed, pressurized container. When you reduce the pressure suddenly by opening the container, the gas forms bubbles because it cannot diffuse out of solution slowly. If a beverage container has a tiny leak, however, the carbon dioxide comes out of solution slowly without bubbling. There is no bubbling when you open a container that has a slow leak because the gas has diffused out of solution.

You must be concerned about the amount of nitrogen in solution in your body and the rate at which you eliminate it. If you absorb too much nitrogen while diving and do not ascend in a manner that allows the excess nitrogen to be eliminated without forming bubbles, the bubbles are likely to cause decompression sickness or the bends, a serious diving illness.

Mathematical models provide estimates of the amount of nitrogen in different parts of your body. Because perfusion varies, tissues absorb nitrogen at differing rates. Decompression experts use mathematical models, called **compartments**, to estimate gas absorption and elimination by various areas of the body. A compartment is identified by its half-time. One with a half-time of 5 minutes is a 5-minute compartment. Experts use compartments ranging from 5 minutes to as long as 960 minutes when calculating gas absorption and elimination.

A compartment that has absorbed gas will withstand some lowering of pressure before bubbling occurs. Originally, scientists believed that a reduction in pressure by a ratio greater than two to one would cause bubbling to occur in divers who were saturated for a particular depth. This was the surfacing ratio that could not be exceeded. Then scientists discovered that because of differences in perfusion, the surfacing ratios are different for various compartments. Those that eliminate gas quickly have a higher surfacing ratio than do compartments that eliminate gas slowly. The difference in ratios posed an interesting and complex problem for divers because one tissue controlled how long a diver could remain at one depth, while another tissue controlled how long the diver could remain at another depth. The **controlling compartment** was used to

▶ Figure 3.6 When you reduce the pressure on a liquid rapidly and there is sufficient gas dissolved in the liquid, the gas forms bubbles.

controlling compartment—The area of the body that determines how long a diver can remain at a given depth. The determination is made by how quickly a gas diffuses from that compartment.

establish our modern time limits for diving. Do not remain at any depth longer than the time it takes the controlling compartment to exceed its surfacing ratio. If you do, you must prevent bubble formation by stopping during the ascent and eliminating the excess gas. The time limits for various depths have been conveniently arranged into tables and included in dive computer software to help you keep the amount of nitrogen in solution in the various tissues of your body within the surfacing ratio of each and every compartment.

It takes time to eliminate excess gas from tissues. The rate at which you reduce pressure (ascend) is important. The dive tables in chapter 6 use a pressure reduction rate no greater than 30 feet per minute. Some dive computer mathematical models use rates two and three times slower than the dive tables. It is important to ascend slowly to prevent the formation of bubbles in your body tissues.

Decompression Sickness

Commonly known as the bends, decompression sickness (DCS) is the result of a reduction in pressure (decompression) that is too rapid for the amount of gas in solution in body tissues. The gas forms bubbles in the tissues or in the blood before it can be diffused into the lungs and eliminated.

Scientists do not fully understand what occurs when DCS strikes. The symptoms may appear immediately after surfacing from a dive or days after diving. About half of all DCS cases occur within one hour after diving. The symptoms vary depending on the amount and location of the bubbles. Severe cases of decompression sickness can have severe neurological effects and produce permanent paralysis.

Common Symptoms of DCS

- A mottled skin rash
- Joint pain
- Numbness
- Tingling
- Weakness
- Paralysis

Factors That Increase the Chances of DCS

- Lack of sleep
- Alcohol and its aftereffects
- Dehydration
- Illness
- Age
- Cold water
- Exercise during and after diving
- Altitude after diving

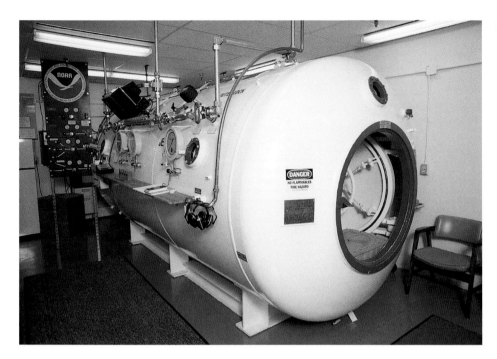

Some experts believe that you should avoid postdive activities that stimulate circulation because increased perfusion may contribute to DCS. Specific activities to avoid include engaging in physical exercise, drinking alcoholic beverages, and taking hot showers or baths. Reduced pressure at altitude is an additional factor because flying in a plane or driving into the mountains too soon after diving can cause the bends. Shun all activities that increase the likelihood of decompression sickness.

A person suffering from DCS requires prompt first aid and medical treatment. The illness worsens with time. The best first aid measure is to administer oxygen in the highest concentration possible. Breathing oxygen eliminates nitrogen in inspired air and enhances the diffusion of nitrogen from the body. The patient should remain still and sip water. Make arrangements to have the patient transported to the nearest medical facility. After initial medical treatment, the medical staff will arrange to transfer the patient to a facility that has a hyperbaric (high pressure) chamber. The patient will be placed inside a large vessel called a recompression chamber. Hyperbaric treatment consists of increasing the pressure in the chamber to reduce or eliminate the symptoms, administering medications, and then slowly decompressing the patient. Recompression must be done in a chamber. (Figure 3.7 shows an example of a recompression chamber.) Never attempt the in-water decompression of a victim of the bends.

Decompression sickness is extremely serious because it can cause permanent injury. To reduce the likelihood of DCS, remain well within the established time/depth limits for diving. Surface at a rate no greater than that specified for the dive planning device you use (see figure 3.8). Stop during every ascent for 2 to 3 minutes at a depth between 10 and 30 ft (3 and 9 m) to eliminate excess nitrogen before surfacing. The processes of ascending and stopping are forms of decompression that reduce the likelihood of decompression sickness. The final way to avoid DCS is to delay excursions to altitude after diving. The details of the time delays are contained in chapter 6.

▶ Figure 3.8 Be sure to complete all necessary precautionary decompression stops when ascending after a dive.

decompression illness (DCI)—Condition with symptoms of both AGE and DCS, where a diver has minor symptoms of AGE upon surfacing, recovers, and then develops a severe case of DCS

Decompression Illness

When a patient has symptoms of both arterial gas embolism (AGE) and DCS, the medical diagnosis is decompression illness (DCI). This is a relatively new term used to describe a unique condition. A diver surfaces from a dive, has some minor symptoms of AGE, recovers somewhat, then develops a severe case of DCS. Seek medical attention immediately for any diver who has neurological symptoms after a dive.

Nitrogen Narcosis

The increased partial pressure of nitrogen can cause a condition known as nitrogen narcosis, or "rapture of the deep," at depths of about 100 ft (30 m) and deeper. Scientists do not know the exact mechanism of narcosis, but its effects are similar to those of anesthetic gases. The feelings associated with narcosis range from euphoria to overconfidence to terror. Narcosis impairs thinking and affects judgment, reasoning, memory, and the ability to do physical tasks. Narcosis is hazardous; it reduces your awareness and ability to respond to an emergency. Susceptibility to narcosis varies from person to person and within an individual from day to day.

Narcosis begins suddenly at depth. You can relieve its symptoms rapidly by ascending to a shallower depth to reduce the narcotic effect.

The following factors predispose a person to narcosis:

- A high level of system CO_2 caused by exertion
- Alcohol or its aftereffects
- Anxiety
- Cold
- Medications
- Social drugs

Experience, frequent diving, and concentration reduce susceptibility to narcosis, but preventing narcosis is better than attempting to cope with it.

DEHYDRATION PREVENTION

You need to preserve body fluids to prevent dehydration. When your body becomes cold, you produce more urine than normal. You receive air underwater by creating an inhalation pressure that opens valves in an air delivery system. The inhalation pressure is slight, but it is greater than normal. Inhaling harder than normal is negative-pressure breathing, which also has the physiological effect of increasing urine production. Breathing underwater compounds the problem of dehydration.

Some types of diuretic beverages (such as coffee and alcohol) and medications cause increased urine production. Avoid ingesting anything that makes you urinate more than normal. You must prevent excessive dehydration because the condition predisposes you to diving injuries. Do the following to prevent dehydration:

- Insulate yourself to stay as warm as possible.
- Keep your regulator well maintained so it breathes as easily as possible.
- Avoid diuretic drinks and medications.
- Replenish body fluids frequently; drink fluids before and between dives.

MOBILITY ADAPTATIONS

The equipment that you wear for diving limits your mobility. It reduces your range of motion and makes walking difficult. The colder the water, the thicker your exposure suit and the less your range of movement.

Diving equipment is fairly heavy, and it is challenging to lift and move. Improper lifting techniques can cause back injuries. Squat down and lift with your legs to pick up a tank or weight belt instead of bending over.

The weight of the equipment changes your center of gravity and affects your balance. Keeping your balance can be challenging on a rocking boat or an uneven bottom during entries and exits. Move carefully and hold on to something or someone for support when you move around out of the water.

You wear fins so that you can use the large muscles of your legs for propulsion. To adapt to diving, you need to learn to use your legs for swimming and your body angle to control direction. These actions free your hands for other uses underwater. Do not use your hands for propulsion. Fins make it difficult for you to walk. Shuffle your feet while moving backward or sideways, keep your knees bent, and be careful not to fall.

Drag retards your ability to move in the water. One factor affecting drag is the speed of motion. The greater the speed, the greater the resistance to movement. The average diver can sustain a speed of a little more than 1 mph (1.6 km/hr). Doubling the speed increases the energy requirement fourfold. Trying to move in water as if it were air causes exhaustion quickly. Use a slow, steady pace and slow, deliberate motions to reduce the effects of drag.

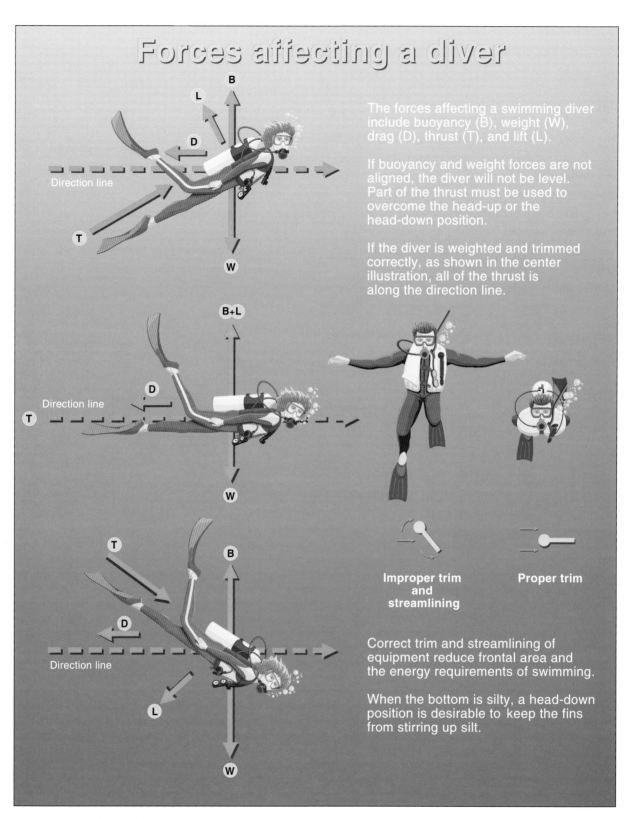

Forces affecting a diver

The forces affecting a swimming diver include buoyancy (B), weight (W), drag (D), thrust (T), and lift (L).

If buoyancy and weight forces are not aligned, the diver will not be level. Part of the thrust must be used to overcome the head-up or the head-down position.

If the diver is weighted and trimmed correctly, as shown in the center illustration, all of the thrust is along the direction line.

Improper trim and streamlining

Proper trim

Correct trim and streamlining of equipment reduce frontal area and the energy requirements of swimming.

When the bottom is silty, a head-down position is desirable to keep the fins from stirring up silt.

▶ Figure 3.9 Weight, lift, thrust, and drag affect divers as they move through the water.

Another factor affecting drag is the size of the object in motion. The larger the surface area exposed, the greater the resistance. A swimming diver is under the influence of four forces. Weight pulls the diver downward, lift (positive buoyancy) pulls the diver upward, thrust moves the diver forward, and drag retards forward progress (see figure 3.9). Divers usually wear weight around the waist, which pulls the lower half of the body downward. Because air in a BC rises to the top, buoyancy from the BC lifts the upper half of the body. The effect of these forces increases the surface area of the diver and, therefore, drag. Adjust the amount of weight you wear so your body is as horizontal as possible in the water. Correct weighting minimizes drag and the effort required to swim.

Water flows smoothly across a smooth and rounded surface but flows turbulently across an irregular surface. When the surface is irregular, the turbulent flow increases drag. Just as vehicles designed to travel through fluids are streamlined to reduce drag caused by turbulent air flow, you can choose and configure your equipment so it presents the smoothest surface possible to the flow of water.

SUMMARY

You have to make many changes in your normal behavior to adapt to the underwater environment. The way you breathe is the most important adaptation. You must breathe continuously and avoid breath holding when you use scuba equipment. You must also limit your activity and pace yourself to avoid overexertion. Managing the mechanical and physiological effects of pressure requires major adaptations. You must keep pressure equalized in your air spaces and limit depth and time at depth to avoid nitrogen narcosis and decompression sickness. Being in the underwater environment seems strange at first, but you can adapt to weightlessness and other strange feelings. The sensations of diving become exhilarating as you gain experience in the new world beneath the surface.

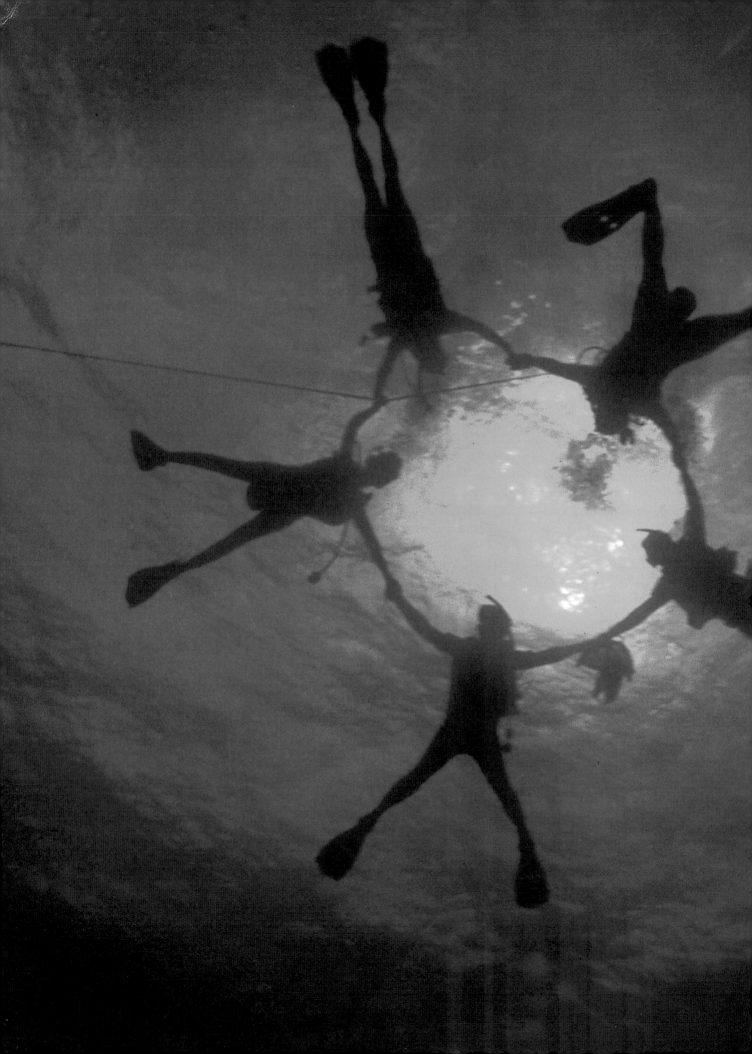

Diving Equipment

4

Equipment helps people adapt to the underwater environment. It allows them to see, breathe, move, and rest. Diving is an equipment-intensive activity. In this chapter, you will learn what equipment you need, how to select the best equipment for your needs, and how to care for your equipment. You will become familiar with the following equipment:

- Masks
- Snorkels
- Fins
- Skin diving vests
- Exposure suits
- Weighting systems
- Buoyancy compensators
- Scuba cylinders
- Cylinder valves
- Scuba regulators
- Alternate air sources
- Instrumentation
- Dive knives, accessories, and specialized equipment

By the end of this chapter, you will be able to

- *describe the purpose, types, features, selection criteria, and care and maintenance procedures for skin and scuba diving equipment;*
- *contrast steel and aluminum scuba cylinders, wet and dry suits, integrated and nonintegrated weighting systems, and reserve and nonreserve valves;*

- *define the terms jumpsuit, Farmer Johns, K-valve, J-valve, DIN-valve, burst disk, O-ring, port, stage, octopus, capillary gauge, Bourdon tube, submersible pressure gauge (SPG), blowout plug, alternate air source (AAS), pony tank, Spare Air unit, lubber line, console, and ceiling; and*
- *state the training requirements for the use of specialized scuba equipment that uses gases other than compressed air.*

You need to be equipped properly to dive in open water. A snorkeler (a diver who remains at the surface) should wear a mask, a snorkel, fins, and a skin diving vest. A skin diver (a breath-hold diver who dives beneath the surface) uses snorkeling equipment and may wear an exposure suit and a weight belt (if the suit requires weights). Complete scuba equipment includes, at a minimum, mask, snorkel, fins, an exposure suit, a weighting system (if needed), a buoyancy compensator, a scuba unit (cylinder, valve, regulator, alternate air source), instrumentation, and a dive knife. For cold water, a diver also needs a hood, boots, and gloves. Figure 4.1 shows fully equipped divers.

BASIC EQUIPMENT FOR ALL DIVERS

The mask, snorkel, fins, and some type of flotation device are basic equipment for all types of recreational diving: snorkeling, skin diving, and scuba diving.

Masks

The eyes require an air space in front of them to focus sharply. Your mask provides an air space and a window to another world. There are many styles of masks, but only two basic recreational types: purge and nonpurge. A purge is a one-way valve through which you can expel water that enters the mask. As you will learn in the next chapter, you can remove water from a mask without a valve, so many masks do not feature a purge valve. A third type of mask, a full-face mask, is for commercial and specialty applications only. Figure 4.2 shows the most common types of masks.

The type of mask you choose is not nearly as important as the fit of the mask on your face. The mask must fit your facial contours perfectly so that it will feel comfortable and remain watertight throughout a dive. Fit and comfort are the most important features to consider when you select a mask. To test the fit, remove the strap or position it on the front of the mask. Tilt your head back and lay the mask (do not push it) on your face. Make sure your hair is not under the sealing edge of the mask; then inhale gently. If the mask pulls onto your face snugly from

▶ Figure 4.1 Fully equipped cold-water (left) and warm-water (right) divers.

the partial vacuum created by your inhalation, the mask fits. If you have to push the mask to get it to seal on your face, the mask probably will leak when you use it underwater.

Some features of a mask affect its fit and comfort. Consider the style, type of material, and type of sealing edge. The best masks are made from silicone, which is soft, pliable, and nonallergenic and resists deterioration better than rubber compounds (see figure 4.3).

The buoyancy of smaller masks poses no problems, but the tug of buoyancy of masks with larger volumes may affect the seal. Low volume masks are easier to clear of water and provide excellent visibility. A wide, double-edged seal does a better job of excluding water than a single-edge seal.

A film of oil from production is on the surfaces of the glass lenses of new masks. You must remove the film completely or the mask will fog continuously underwater. Clean your mask thoroughly with scouring powder. The glass is too hard to be scratched by the abrasive, so do not be timid when cleaning your mask. Commercial defogging solutions help keep your mask clear while you dive. If a clean mask fogs slightly during use, you can allow a small amount of water into the mask and wash it across the fogged area to resolve the problem.

Several visual correction options are available for diving. If you wear soft contact lenses, you can use them for diving after you complete your training, but you should not use them during training because you may lose them when you are learning how to clear water from your mask. Some contact lens wearers prefer a mask with a small purge valve because they can expel water from the mask with little risk of losing a contact lens. Several companies prepare and bond corrective lenses into any diving mask. If you require only a simple correction, you may be able to use interchangeable corrective lenses that are available for some masks. You may be able to obtain corrective lenses for your mask when you purchase it.

Store your mask in a mask box when you are not using it. The box helps keep the mask from getting damaged and helps prevent discoloration of silicone.

Snorkels

A human head weighs about as much as a bowling ball. If you had to swim while holding

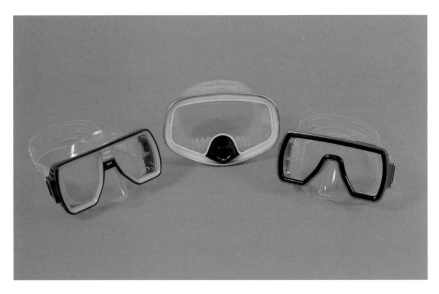

▶ Figure 4.2   Many different masks are available for divers including purge (center) and nonpurge types.

▶ Figure 4.3   Fit and comfort are the most important considerations when selecting equipment.

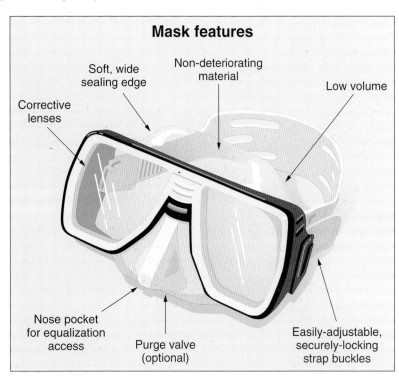

Mask features

Soft, wide sealing edge

Non-deteriorating material

Low volume

Corrective lenses

Nose pocket for equalization access

Purge valve (optional)

Easily-adjustable, securely-locking strap buckles

a bowling ball out of water, you would become exhausted quickly. If you try to swim while holding your head above water, you will tire rapidly. But if you allow buoyancy to support your head in the water, you can relax and swim for hours. A snorkel allows you to breathe while water supports your head—allowing you to conserve energy and enjoy continuous underwater viewing.

In its simplest form, a snorkel is nothing more than a breathing tube that extends from a diver's mouth to a point above the waterline. A basic diving snorkel is a J-shaped tube with a mouthpiece on one end. Just as with masks, there are two basic recreational types of snorkels: purge and nonpurge (see figure 4.4). A purge snorkel has a one-way valve through which you may expel water that enters the tube. As you will learn in chapter 5, you can clear water from a snorkel that lacks a purge valve, so some snorkels do not have a valve. Some types of purge snorkels are self-draining: gravity drains water from the tube automatically when you are at the surface of the water.

There are additional snorkel features, such as a swivel mouthpiece. Another is a flexible hose for the lower half of the tube so the lower part that usually is curved hangs straight down when you are not using your snorkel (see figure 4.5). The flex-hose snorkel also reduces interference between the snorkel and your scuba regulator. Also, there are special mouthpieces to maximize comfort and devices to prevent water from entering the top end of the snorkel, although water exclusion devices are not essential.

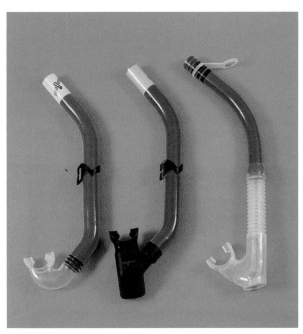

▶ Figure 4.4 The two common types of snorkels are nonpurge (left) and purge (center and right).

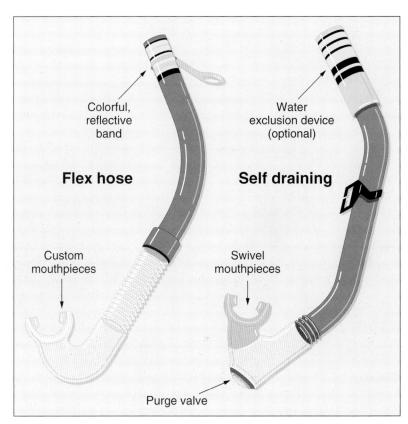

▶ Figure 4.5 Snorkel features.

The fit of your snorkel is the most important consideration, much more important than the type. The mouthpiece must not irritate your mouth, gums, or jaw when in place for extended periods. The angle of the mouthpiece in the mouth must not require you to bite hard to hold the mouthpiece in place. A snorkel that fits poorly may cause sore gums or jaws. A snorkel tube should have an inside diameter of approximately ¾ in. (1.9 cm) so that resistance to airflow through the tube will not make breathing difficult.

Attach the snorkel to your mask strap on the left side using a snorkel keeper. There are several types of keepers. Popular keepers are the simple ones depicted in figure 4.6. The adjustment is correct if the snorkel mouthpiece remains in your mouth when you open your mouth widely.

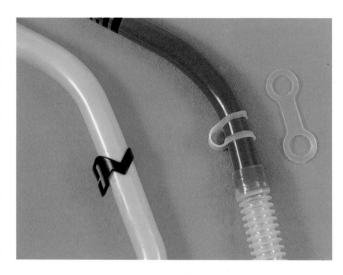

▶ Figure 4.6 Two types of snorkel keepers.

Fins

Diving would be much less enjoyable without fins. They increase your ability to move in the water and free your hands for many activities. You move in water by pushing against the water. Fins increase your ability to move by increasing the size of the area you move against the water; fins present a larger surface area than your hands. The muscles of your legs are much larger and stronger than your arm muscles. Your arms would tire quickly if fins were attached to your hands, but your legs are strong enough to handle the load. Fins help stabilize you in water by providing a surface of resistance to movement. The resistance provides leverage for countermovement and directional control.

The two basic types of fins are shoe fins and open-heel fins. Shoe fins slip onto bare feet, so they are good snorkeling fins for tropical climates. You wear open-heel fins with foot coverings called boots. Open-heel fins, generally used for scuba diving, usually are larger and stiffer than shoe fins. Small, flexible snorkeling fins may be inadequate for the harder work of scuba diving. Figure 4.7 shows examples of different types of fins.

Special materials and designs abound. The fundamental features of a fin are the size and stiffness of the blade (see figure 4.8). The larger and stiffer the blade, the greater the

▶ Figure 4.7 Open-heel fins (left) and shoe fins (right) provide alternatives for different diving needs.

physical demand when you move the fin through the water. A blade that is too stiff can cause you to cramp and become fatigued. It is best to begin with fins of a moderate size and stiffness. When you can use those fins for extended periods without difficulty, you may then consider fins that can provide greater propulsion.

The most important criteria for the selection of any item of diving equipment are fit and comfort, and this is especially true of fins. To help ensure proper fit, sit down and try on a fin. Wear a boot if trying an open-heel fin. Hold your foot in the air and wiggle it up and down and from side to side. The fin and your foot move as a single unit. If

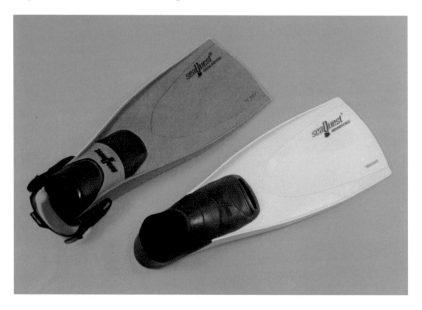

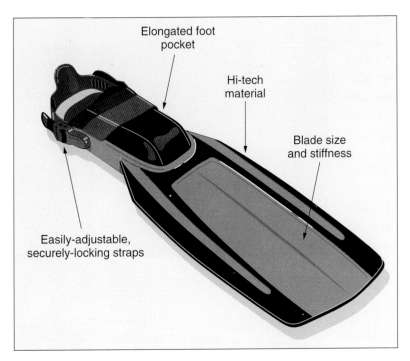

Elongated foot pocket

Hi-tech material

Blade size and stiffness

Easily-adjustable, securely-locking straps

▶ Figure 4.8   Features of dive fins.

▶ Figure 4.9   Skin diving vests.

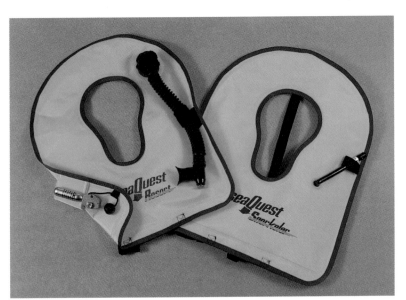

your foot moves inside the foot pocket, the fin is too large. Diving equipment should fit snugly, but not tightly. A fin that is too tight can cause your foot to cramp. The foot pocket of the fin should fit but should not exert pressure on your foot. Select your fins using fit, comfort, and blade size and stiffness as your primary selection criteria. Features, fashion, and cost should be secondary considerations.

Skin Diving Vests

Positive buoyancy is invaluable when you want to rest at the surface or carry items you have collected while diving. Wear a buoyancy vest whenever you dive.

Divers use one basic type of skin diving vest, and it fits around the neck and secures at the waist (see figure 4.9). A standard feature of a skin diving vest is an oral inflation tube, which comes in various sizes. It is easier to use larger tubes with mouthpieces than smaller tubes without mouthpieces. Some vests feature a CO_2 detonator. You must care for the mechanism at the end of every day of diving, or it will not function reliably.

Care and Maintenance

Your skin diving equipment will provide years of service if you take care of it properly. Rinse the equipment with clean, fresh water after use; dry it in the shade, and store it in a cool, dark, smog-free location. Prolonged sunlight, smog, salt crystals, and swimming pool chlorine harm your equipment. Fill a skin diving vest partially with fresh water after use, and swish the water inside. Drain the vest completely, then inflate it for drying and for storage. If the vest has a CO_2 detonator, remove the CO_2 cartridge, rinse the cartridge and assembly thoroughly, and lubricate the cartridge threads. Screw the cartridge back into the assembly only after the vest has dried thoroughly. Periodically inspect the straps on your mask and fins for drying and cracking and replace straps when they begin to deteriorate. After your mask has dried, rub a drop of defogging solution on the lens to help keep the lens clean during storage.

EXPOSURE SUITS

Wear some type of exposure protection for diving regardless of the water temperature. An exposure suit protects you from scrapes and stings and provides insulation.

The two basic types of exposure suits are wet suits and dry suits. Generally speaking, the colder the water, the thicker your suit and the more of your body you cover with the suit. There are many suit configurations, but most are one piece or a combination of a jacket and pants. Vests are accessories that help conserve heat in vital organs. Hoods, boots, and gloves help reduce heat loss from the head, feet, and hands, respectively.

Wet Suits

A wet suit is a good exposure suit for water temperatures ranging from 60° to 85° F (15.6° to 29.4° C). A wet suit allows water inside, but any water that enters also can exit and carry heat with it. The better the fit of the suit, the less water inside and the warmer the suit. Table 4.1 provides a comparison of wet suit types. The descriptions in the text that follows provide some additional information.

Spandex suits are thin, stretchy, attractive, full-body garments that are popular for diving in tropical waters. The garments, made from a special nylon material called spandex, provide 45 percent more insulation than bare skin and provide protection against stings, scrapes, and sunshine. Spandex suits are light and compact for travel. They also are useful as undergarments for thicker neoprene wet suits. They add an extra layer of insulation beneath a neoprene suit and allow the wearer to slip into a heavier suit more easily. If you live in a temperate climate, you can use a spandex body suit beneath a neoprene wet suit for local diving and use the spandex suit by itself for vacation diving in the tropics (see figure 4.10).

▶ Figure 4.10 Common styles of warm-water wet suits: foam neoprene (left and center) and nylon (right). The style of the suit on the left is a jumpsuit. The suit in the center is a "shorty."

Table 4.1 Wet Suits			
Type	**Warmth**	**Features**	**Temperature range**
Spandex	45% more than bare skin	Light, compact; useful as undergarments for thicker suits	78° F (25.6° C) +
Thermoplastic	30% warmer than spandex	Neutrally buoyant; no weights required; wicks perspiration; windproof	76° F (24.4° C) +
Plush-lined thermoplastic	10% warmer than unlined	Same as thermoplastic	72° F (22.2° C) +
Foam neoprene • ⅛ in. (2-3 mm) • 3/16 in. (4 mm) • ¼ in. (5-6.5 mm) • Titanium (4-6 mm)	20-100% warmer than plush-lined thermoplastic	Buoyant; weights required; long drying time; evaporation chills wearer; minor repairs easy to do	Down to 60° F (15.6° C)
Hoods, vests, boots, and gloves or mitts	16-66% more warmth	Reduces water circulation; layering allows flexibility for various temperature	Down to 60° F (15.6° C)

Thermoplastic—sandwiched between two layers of spandex—is another type of wet suit material. A suit made from this three-ply material is about 30 percent warmer than a spandex suit. Thermoplastic suits are thin (1.2 to 1.4 mm) and designed for use in tropical waters (75° to 85° F [24° to 29° C]). Some suits feature soft, plush lining for extra warmth. The plush lining increases the warmth of the suit by about 10 percent. You can wear a thermoplastic suit beneath a neoprene wet suit for extra warmth in colder water (see figure 4.10).

Thermoplastic material offers several advantages: the balance between weight and volume of the unique material make it neutrally buoyant, so you may not need a weight belt. The stretchy fabric allows you to move freely. The material draws perspiration away from your body but is windproof.

A third type of wet suit material is foam neoprene, as shown in figure 4.11. The foam consists of tiny bubbles of inert gas, which provide insulation. The thicker the wet suit material, the greater the insulation quality of the suit. A ⅛ in. (2 to 3 mm) neoprene wet suit is about 20 percent warmer than a plush thermoplastic suit.

Wet suit material ranges from ⅛ in. (2 to 3 mm) for warm water diving to ⅜ in. (9 mm) for extreme cold water diving. The most common wet suit thicknesses are ⅛ in. (2 to 3 mm), ³⁄₁₆ in. (4 mm), and ¼ in. (5 to 6.5 mm). You can layer wet suit material on critical areas of your body to reduce heat loss, but the thicker the insulation you wear, the more difficult it is for you to control buoyancy. Select the thickness of wet suit material used by experienced divers in the area where you plan to dive.

Nylon usually covers both sides of the neoprene used for wet suits. The nylon increases the strength and durability of the suit, which is glued and sewn together. You can make minor repairs with wet suit cement, but you should have a wet suit manufacturer do the extensive repairs.

Neoprene wet suits require weights to achieve neutral buoyancy. The suit provides immediate buoyancy when you release the weights, but the buoyancy of the suit can be either a benefit or a hazard. Neoprene is not windproof, and the evaporation of water from the suit between dives may cause you to chill. You can get wet suit overgarments to retain warmth between dives. Wear an overgarment between dives in colder climates. Neoprene suits require longer to dry than other types of exposure suits. Mobility of movement is good with thin neoprene wet suits but decreases as the thickness of the material increases.

There are numerous wet suit designs, including the **shorty**, the one-piece **jumpsuit**, and **Farmer Johns** (see figures 4.10 and 4.11).

Consider several features when selecting a wet suit design. The more zippers a suit has, the more water that circulates inside the suit, and the greater the loss of heat. You can get zipperless suits for cold-water diving. Good wet suits feature a spine pad to minimize water

▶ Figure 4.11 Common styles of cold-water wet suits.

circulation along the channel formed by your spine, and some suits for cold-water diving have attached hoods to minimize water circulation at the neck. You may spend time kneeling around and in the water, so kneepads are a desirable feature.

Heat packs are available for wet suits. These packs contain a nontoxic reusable chemical that heats to about 130° F (54° C) for half an hour or more, depending on conditions. The packs fit into heat pack pockets, an optional suit feature.

You can buy wet suits in standard sizes, or you can have a suit tailored for a custom fit. The fit of a wet suit is its most important feature. The suit must fit snugly all over but must not fit so tightly that it hampers your breathing and circulation. A suit that fits well may feel slightly restrictive out of the water. The true test of the fit of a suit is to dive with it. You may be able to rent a wet suit identical to one you would like to purchase.

▶ Figure 4.12 Various types of footwear.

Wet Suit Accessories

Scuba divers usually wear foot protection. There are several types of footwear for various needs (see figure 4.12). Foot coverings, usually made from neoprene, may cover only the foot or both the foot and the ankle. Diving footwear, called boots or booties, ranges from inexpensive neoprene socks to sturdy footwear with durable, molded soles. Boots may or may not have zippers. Zippered boots are easier to don and remove, but boots without zippers are warmer.

You should wear hand coverings when the water temperature is less than 70° F (21.1° C). Some divers wear gloves for protection, such as when catching lobsters. Hand coverings include gloves, mitts, and gauntlets (see figure 4.13). Wear mitts in cold water because they are thicker and have less surface area for heat dissipation than gloves have. Wear gauntlets (neoprene mitts with long cuffs) when the water is extremely cold. Thin neoprene gloves provide sufficient insulation in temperate water. Do not wear gloves in tropical areas. You are more likely to touch things when wearing gloves, and grabbing delicate coral reefs and marine animals while wearing gloves harms the animals.

A hood is an important warmth accessory that can reduce your heat loss from 20 to 50 percent, depending on the temperature of the water. Two basic types of hoods, attached hoods and separate hoods, are available for wet suits (see figure 4.14). Cold-water divers like attached hoods because they restrict water circulation in a suit more than separate hoods do. Some separate hoods have skirts that end at the base of the neck, and other, cold-water hoods have large bibs that cover the neck and shoulder area.

▶ Figure 4.13 Gloves and mitts provide protection for divers' hands.

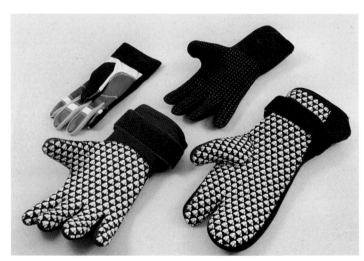

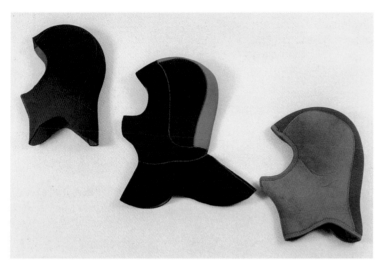

▶ Figure 4.14 Hoods conserve warmth.

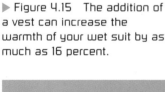

▶ Figure 4.15 The addition of a vest can increase the warmth of your wet suit by as much as 16 percent.

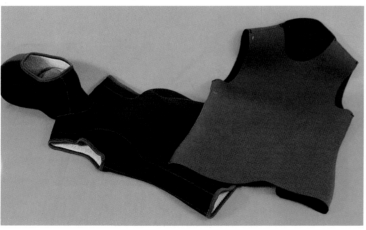

There are thin hoods for protection in warm water and thicker hoods for insulation and protection in cold water.

You can increase the warmth of your wet suit by as much as 16 percent by wearing a vest. Wet suit vests come in all types of material to add warmth with layers of insulation (see figure 4.15). Layering is an effective technique that reduces water circulation while increasing insulation. Some vests have attached hoods.

Wet Suit Care and Maintenance

With proper care, wet suits can provide years of service. Soak your wet suit in clean, fresh, warm water. If you cannot soak your suit, rinse it. Hang your suit on a specially designed, wide wet suit hanger; dry the suit in the shade, and store it on the hanger in a cool, dark, smog-free location. A garage is a poor environment for storing equipment. Do not fold your wet suit for storage because folds can form permanent creases, which insulate poorly. Inspect your suit regularly for seam integrity and tears. Make repairs or have them made as needed.

Dry Suits

When the water temperature is less than 60° F (15.6° C), consider using a dry suit, an exposure suit that excludes water. Dry suits are much warmer than wet suits for three reasons:

1. Air, not water, is in contact with your skin. Because air conducts less heat than water does, you lose less heat via conduction.
2. You wear undergarments beneath a dry suit. The undergarments provide a layer of air, which is a good insulator.
3. Suit compression affects two of the three types of dry suits only slightly, so the insulating ability of those types of dry suits remains nearly constant with depth.

The type of material from which the dry suit is made denotes the type of suit. Table 4.2 compares the three most common types of dry suits. The foam neoprene dry suit is made of the same material as a wet suit, but the dry suit has seals at the wrists and neck, attached dry boots, and a waterproof zipper. See figure 4.16.

A dry suit can cost two to five times as much as a wet suit, but with proper care and maintenance, a good dry suit will last many times longer than a wet suit. If you dive primarily in cold water, a dry suit is a good investment.

Table 4.2 Dry Suits		
Type	**Advantages**	**Disadvantages**
Foam neoprene	Form fitting and streamlined	Long drying time; hard to locate and repair leaks; buoyancy control difficult
Crushed neoprene	Durable; easy to repair; long lasting; less buoyant than foam neoprene	Less insulation than foam neoprene; expensive; somewhat bulky
Shell (two kinds) • Coated nylon • Rubberized fabric	Fast drying; easy to repair; nylon suits inexpensive; rubberized suits long lasting	Easily punctured; bulky; nylon suits do not last long; rubberized suits expensive

A dry suit is a closed air space subject to squeezes. A low-pressure inflator valve, a standard feature, allows you to add air to the suit during descent to prevent suit squeeze. Because air expands during ascent, an exhaust valve is another standard feature. Get a dry suit that has a constant volume exhaust valve that automatically maintains a constant state of buoyancy during ascent.

Diving is a diuretic activity—it increases the amount of urine you produce. Urination in a wet suit is a regular practice by divers in open water, but the problem is more complex when you wear a dry suit. An optional feature for a dry suit is a relief zipper, which is useful only when you are out of the water. Dry suit divers have to exit the water to urinate, and those without a relief zipper must disrobe.

There are several types of undergarments for dry suits. Some are inexpensive, but compress with depth and lose insulating ability when wet. More expensive undergarments are highly resistant to compression and retain most of their insulating quality even if wet. Many dry suit divers prefer to wear two layers of undergarments: a thin garment against the skin to carry perspiration away from the body and a thicker overgarment for the bulk of the insulation. Moisture conducts heat, so you are warmer when you wick perspiration away from your body.

Dry suits have several drawbacks. Controlling buoyancy is more difficult with a dry suit than with a wet suit. Rapid, uncontrolled ascents can occur unless you control the suit. Training is essential before attempting to dive in a dry suit.

Dry suits are bulkier than wet suits. It is easier to don and remove a dry suit than a wet suit, but the bulkiness of a dry suit makes surface swimming difficult, and a dry suit restricts your mobility more than a wet suit does. The inconveniences of a dry suit are of little consequence, however, when warmth is your primary concern.

▶ Figure 4.16 Dry suits can be made from foam neoprene (left), crushed neoprene (center), or nylon (right).

▶ Figure 4.17 Dry suit boots and gloves help keep divers warm.

Dry Suit Accessories

Most dry suits have attached boots, a common and desirable feature. The boots may be thin latex booties on less expensive suits or hard-soled boots on more expensive suits. With latex booties, you wear heavy socks for insulation, and you must wear wet suit boots over the latex booties to protect them. The end result is that dry suit divers usually need fins with large foot pockets.

You can wear neoprene gloves or mitts with a dry suit. If the water is extremely cold, you can get dry gloves with insulating liners that attach to some dry suits. An attached latex dry hood is an option for some models, but most dry suit divers use a separate neoprene dry suit hood. Figure 4.17 shows examples of dry suit accessories.

Dry Suit Care and Maintenance

Dry suits require more care than wet suits. The zipper is expensive to replace, as are the control valves, so do not allow salt crystals to form in the zipper or in the valves. Soak and rinse the zipper and valves in clean, fresh water as soon as possible following a saltwater dive. Wash the neck and wrist seals with soapy water, and then rinse them. Coat latex seals with pure talc after they dry. The talc helps protect the rubber against the elements. Fold dry suits in half over a wide hanger for drying. Lubricate the suit zipper according to the manufacturer's instructions; then store the suit with the zipper open. If the suit needs to be repaired, have an authorized dealer make the repairs.

Exposure Suit Selection

There are many factors to consider when you select an exposure suit and accessories: your physical characteristics, where you intend to dive, how you intend to dive, how much diving you intend to do, and what you intend do while diving. The amount of money you invest also is a factor, but keep in mind that buying an inexpensive suit may be false economy. If the suit does not meet your needs, you will have to spend more money for another suit.

The amount of diving you intend to do is an important factor. If you plan to make only one dive per day, your insulation requirements are not as great as if you plan to dive several times per day. The more time you plan to spend in the water, the warmer the suit you should have.

If you are a thin person who gets chilled easily, you need more insulation than the average-size person for a given water temperature. People with above-average body fat may not need as much insulation as those with average body fat; natural fat is a good insulator. Thermal comfort is essential for diving safety and enjoyment.

If you intend to do most of your diving in the local area, the most popular type of suit in the area probably is the best type for you. If the local waters are cold, you will have to choose between a wet suit and a dry suit. If you choose to get a wet suit as your first exposure suit for cold-water diving, a layered design with Farmer John pants, a vest, and a step-in jacket with an attached hood retains more warmth than high-waisted pants, a regular jacket, and a separate hood. A custom fit retains more warmth than a suit of a standard size.

Dry suits are not desirable for long surface swims because you can overheat, and the drag caused by the bulkiness of some dry suits may cause you to tire or cramp. On the other hand, dry suits retain much more warmth at depth than wet suits. If you believe most of your diving will be deeper than 40 ft (12 m), if the water will be 60° F (15.6° C) or colder, and if you can avoid long surface swims, a dry suit is a good choice as long as you obtain training before using the suit.

If you plan to dive in a variety of climates, a spandex or thermoplastic suit combined with a neoprene wet suit may be a good option. You can wear different parts of the suits to meet different warmth requirements. Your diving activity affects your needs. An underwater hunter looking for game generates more body heat than does an underwater photographer whose movements are minimal. The less active you are while diving, the more insulation you need. Your desires, needs, and budget determine the features you select for your exposure suit. Features that are popular with local experienced divers and diving leaders can help you identify desirable features for your suit.

The accessories you select for your suit depend upon the type of suit you choose, the temperature of the water, the activity you intend to pursue, and your budget. A hood may be thin and short for warmer water, thick with a long skirt for colder water, or a dry suit type. Foot coverings may be low cut, ankle-high, or attached to the suit. The soles may be soft or rugged. Hand coverings may range from nothing to thick mitts, gauntlets, or dry gloves.

Local diving professionals can help you select an exposure suit and accessories. No matter what type of exposure suit you choose, keep in mind that it is an investment in your enjoyment of diving. Diving is not fun if you get cold.

▶ Figure 4.18　Weight belts or integrated weighting systems are two options for divers.

WEIGHTING SYSTEMS

Exposure suits increase your buoyancy. You need weights for ballast so you can achieve neutral buoyancy. One type of weighting system is a weight belt; another type integrates the weights into the scuba unit. Figure 4.18 shows examples of weighting systems.

Weight Belts

You can attach weights to, or insert them into, a belt that you wear around your waist. The belt is heavy nylon webbing 2 in. (5 cm) wide. You can thread the belt through lead weights, wrap pouches of lead shot around the belt, or put weights or pouches of lead shot into pockets on pocket-type belts. A hollow fabric belt that you can fill with lead shot is more comfortable on your hips than hard weights. Lead shot, which comes in different sizes, causes less damage than hard lead weights if you drop a belt accidentally. Smaller diameter shot allows more weight per volume than larger shot, so the more weight you need, the smaller the shot you should use.

Because exposure suits compress with pressure, a weight belt around your waist loosens unless it has a means of compensating for the suit compression. A compensator is a desirable feature for a weight belt; you can select from a variety of designs.

Secure the weights on your weight belt so that they will not shift position. Pocket-type belts are good in this respect. When you thread separate weights onto a belt, secure the first and last weights with retainers (which are an accessory item).

The most important feature of any weighting system is the quick release. In the event of an emergency, you must discard weights quickly to establish positive buoyancy. No matter what type of system you choose, a positive, easily located, and easily operated quick release is essential.

Types of Weights

Several types of weights are available. Large, curved hip weights help offset the buoyancy of cold-water exposure suits. Smaller, rectangular weights are popular because they are economical. Coated weights are attractive and practical. Manufacturers mold weights into various shapes and offer a heavy vinyl coating as an option. The coating reduces pollution from lead, improves appearance, makes the weights easier to see in the water, and reduces exposure suit abrasion. Fabric mesh packets filled with lead shot are popular. You can get bulk lead shot for hollow fabric belts. Coated lead shot, although slightly more expensive, is better than uncoated shot. There are shot-filled tubular ankle weights, although some diving experts believe ankle weights are unnecessary.

Another useful type of weight is a tank weight. These weights allow you to remove some weight from your waist and move it to a place higher on your body. This action allows you to trim your buoyancy so that you are horizontal while hovering. And tank weights can be a rescue aid for an unconscious diver at the surface; if properly adjusted, they will roll an unconscious, buoyant diver into a face-up position.

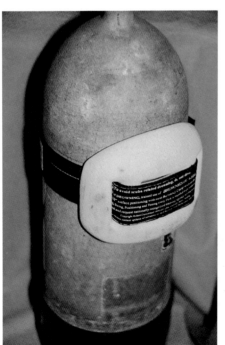

▶ Figure 4.19 Tank weights help distribute weight for better trim.

Integrated Weighting Systems

An integrated weighting system eliminates the need for a weight belt by holding lead weight in the **backpack** that holds the scuba cylinder or in the BC. An integrated weighting system makes the scuba unit heavier, but it also allows better distribution of weight than a separate system can provide. Some divers prefer an integrated weighting system because weights are less likely to shift, a suit compression compensator is not needed, and weights placed above your waist will improve your trim in the water and reduce strain on your lower back. However, when you raise your center of gravity, you are more likely to lose your balance and fall when you are out of the water. You need strength, good balance, and caution to use an integrated weighting system. The type of weight used in integrated systems usually is lead shot, either in bulk or in pouches.

Tank Weights

You can obtain some of the advantages of an integrated weighting system by removing some of the weight from your weight belt and adding the weight to your tank. Several designs are available and are depicted in figure 4.19.

Care and Maintenance

Weighting systems do not require as much care and maintenance as other items of diving equipment. Do not soak or rinse raw lead after use because lead in the runoff will pollute the environment. If "gray water" seeps from your weight system, replace the lead with new, coated lead. (You can recycle old lead, so do not throw it away.) Pocket-type weighting systems allow you to remove the weights and rinse the remainder of the system.

Inspect the functional aspects, such as the quick release and the compensator, regularly. If you use a belt, inspect the weight retainers to make sure they are not broken, and make sure the end of the belt is clean and neat for easy insertion into the buckle. If the end of your belt is frayed, trim and singe it. Be careful when you fix a frayed end that you do not cut or burn yourself.

Weighting System Selection

When selecting a weighting system, consider your physical characteristics, the amount of weight you need, and how frequently you will need to change the amount of weight you use.

If your waist is larger than your hips, a weight belt may not work well—especially if you need more than 30 lb (13.6 kg) of weight. Consult with divers whose physical characteristics are similar to yours for advice on weighting systems.

If you require more than 30 lb (13.6 kg) of weight, you may need weights on a weight belt plus an integrated system. If you require only a small amount of weight, nearly any type of weight system is acceptable.

If the type of diving you do varies, the amount of weight you need also varies. If you dive in fresh water and in salt water, you need to adjust your weights. When you vary your exposure suit configuration, you also need to vary the amount of weight you wear. The more you need to change weights, the more you need a weighting system that allows changes to be made easily.

BUOYANCY COMPENSATORS

A buoyancy compensator (BC) helps you control buoyancy. You can inflate your BC at the surface to increase buoyancy, deflate it to reduce buoyancy for descent, and add air to it to achieve neutral buoyancy underwater. Most BCs also contain a backpack to hold your scuba cylinder.

▶ Figure 4.20 Buoyancy compensators come front-mounted (left), jacket-style (center), or back-mounted (right).

Types of Buoyancy Compensators

The three types of BCs are jacket-style, back-mounted, and front-mounted. Figure 4.20 shows examples of the types, and table 4.3 compares them. Most BCs used in diving today are a wraparound jacket design, which provides front and rear buoyancy. There are two basic jacket designs. One style has inflation tubes over the shoulders. A newer style has straps over the shoulders. The straps have convenient, adjustable releases.

Back-mounted BCs place buoyancy chambers behind you. These systems are useful for

Type	Location of buoyancy chamber	Advantages	Disadvantages
Jacket-style	Front and rear	Even lift; diver can remain upright	Not suitable for skin diving
Back-mounted	Rear	Does not interfere with dry suit valve operation	Pushes diver forward; difficult for diver to remain upright
Front-mounted	Front	Suitable for skin diving; allows diver to remain upright	Need separate backpack for cylinders; requires disconnection of inflator hose before removal; does not provide as much lift as jacket

Table 4.3 Buoyancy Compensators

underwater modeling and for specialty diving activities. Models look better without bulky BCs covering them, and back-mounted units do not interfere with dry suit valve operation as much as other types of BCs.

Front-mounted BCs fit around your neck and cover your chest area. This was the first type of BC, but few divers use front-mounted buoyancy compensators today. You can use a front-mounted BC for both skin diving and scuba diving. BC jackets and back-mounted BCs are not suitable for skin diving. Most divers today feel a jacket BC is superior to a front-mounted one.

▶ Figure 4.21 Desirable BC features.

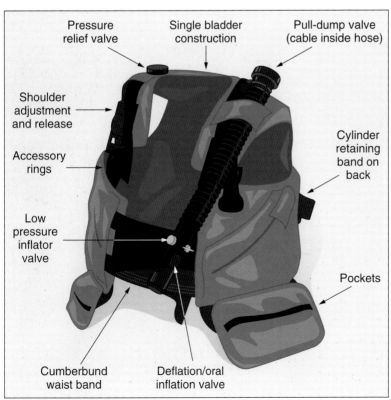

Pressure relief valve

Single bladder construction

Pull-dump valve (cable inside hose)

Shoulder adjustment and release

Accessory rings

Cylinder retaining band on back

Low pressure inflator valve

Pockets

Cumberbund waist band

Deflation/oral inflation valve

Buoyancy Compensator Features

In its simplest form, a BC is a bladder with attachments. The bladder may be coated material that comprises the BC itself or a separate bladder inside a fabric shell. The seams of a BC bladder may be glued or electronically welded depending on the type of material (see figure 4.21).

Buoyancy Compensator Selection

When selecting a BC, consider your physical characteristics, where you plan to dive, and the type of diving you plan to do. Some BCs provide more buoyancy than others. A cold-water wet suit diver needs more lift than a warm-water diver wearing a thin exposure suit. A large amount of lift is not necessarily desirable.

If you are a large, strong individual, the size and bulk of a BC may not be much of a consideration; but if you are small, it may be wise to choose a small, compact BC. The length of the

BC is important. One that extends downward too far makes donning and removing your weight belt difficult. If you are short-waisted, consider an integrated weighting system.

The fit is important because a BC needs to support you in the water. The BC should fit snugly and not ride up on your body. Models that allow adjustment for a custom fit are desirable. Renting and using different types of BCs will aid you in making a selection. Talk to experienced divers and diving professionals and observe BC trends in your area.

Care and Maintenance

An investment in a BC is not modest. But, like most diving equipment, your BC will provide years of service if you take care of it. You need to rinse your BC inside and out after use, especially after use in a swimming pool or in the ocean. Chlorine in pool water and salt crystals that form from seawater are harmful to your BC. Drain the water from your BC after use, fill the BC about one-third full with fresh water, swish the water around, and then drain the bladder. Rinse the inflator assembly thoroughly, and leave the BC fully inflated until it dries. Inflation tests the airtight integrity of the bladder and valves. If the BC does not remain firm for at least an hour, take it to a professional repair facility. Anytime your BC fails to function properly, obtain the services of a professional repairperson. It is hazardous to attempt BC repairs without special training, tools, and parts.

SCUBA CYLINDERS

A scuba cylinder stores compressed air at high pressure. The container must be strong and free of corrosion. Scuba cylinders (also called tanks) are made of either aluminum or steel. Each type has advantages and disadvantages. Figure 4.22 shows examples of various steel and aluminum tanks.

▶ Figure 4.22 Scuba cylinders are made from steel or aluminum.

Steel Cylinders

Steel scuba cylinders come in various sizes with various pressure ratings. Common sizes are 50, 71.2, and 94.6 ft³ (1,416, 2,016, and 2,679 L). The pressure to which the cylinders may be filled, or "working pressure," ranges from 1,800 to more than 4,000 psi (122 to 272 ATM).

Some compressors pump air only to 2,500 psi (169 ATM). When you cannot get air at a pressure higher than 2,500 psi (169 ATM), a steel tank may be more desirable than an aluminum tank. A steel 71.2 ft³ (2,016 L) scuba tank filled to 2,250 psi (153 ATM) contains about 5 ft³ (141.6 L) more air than an 80 ft³ (2,266 L) aluminum tank filled to the same pressure. This is because the aluminum tank must be filled to 3,000 psi (203 ATM) to obtain 80 ft³ (2,266 L).

The main disadvantage of a steel cylinder is that it can rust, which can render a tank unsafe and unusable. Do not allow water inside a scuba cylinder. The high-pressure atmosphere has a large amount of oxygen to fuel corrosion. You can keep the inside of a steel scuba tank dry, but the outside is exposed to moisture. Galvanizing inhibits rust on the outside of steel tanks, but the inside may not be galvanized because it affects air purity. Painting a galvanized finish may improve the appearance of a cylinder, but paint alone is inadequate because cracks or chips in the paint allow moisture to reach the steel. The tank will begin to rust unless there is a galvanized coating beneath the paint.

Another disadvantage of a steel scuba tank is that it has a rounded bottom because of the manufacturing process. The tank will not stand by itself unless you place a rubber or plastic boot, called a "tank boot," on the end of the cylinder. The boot makes the base of the tank flat so it will stand. Some boots have flat sides to help keep a tank from rolling when you lay the cylinder on its side. Moisture and salt trapped between the tank boot and the cylinder can cause corrosion. Boots with internal ridges to drain any water—the preferred type of boot—are self-draining.

Aluminum Cylinders

Aluminum alloy cylinders also come in various sizes with various pressure ratings. Common sizes are 50, 63, and 80 ft^3 (1,416, 1,784, and 2,266 L). The working pressure for aluminum cylinders is 3,000 psi (203 ATM).

Aluminum corrodes, but the oxide that forms arrests the corrosion process—a significant advantage over the corrosive process of rust in steel tanks. Rust is an accelerating process, but corrosion in an aluminum cylinder is a self-arresting process.

The bottom of aluminum cylinders is flat. You do not need a tank boot on the cylinder to allow it to stand by itself, but many divers put boots on aluminum tanks to protect the tank and objects struck by the bottoms of the cylinders.

Aluminum cylinders also have drawbacks. Aluminum is softer than steel, so aluminum tanks dent and gouge more easily than steel tanks. Also, brass cylinder valves control the flow of air, and an electrolytic action between the dissimilar metals of a cylinder and a valve can cause the valve to seize in the aluminum cylinder threads unless you have the valve removed periodically and coated with a special compound. Valve seizing seldom is a problem with steel cylinders.

Aluminum cylinders do not need to be galvanized. You may paint them to improve appearance, but do not bake the paint finish. Temperatures hotter than 180° F (82.2° C) reduce the strength of an aluminum cylinder and can cause the tank to explode when filled. If you would like your cylinder painted, have it done by a professional tank painting service.

Cylinder Markings

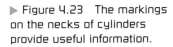

▶ Figure 4.23 The markings on the necks of cylinders provide useful information.

Several rows of markings are on the neck of a scuba cylinder, and the markings provide useful information about the cylinder. You should be able to determine the meaning of several of the marks. Figure 4.23 shows an example of cylinder neck markings.

The first row of marks on U.S.-manufactured tanks identifies the government agency sanctioning the manufacture of the tank, the type of tank metal, and the working pressure. The first letters in the row identify the government agency, such as DOT (Department of Transportation) CTC/DOT, (Canadian Transportation Commission and the Department of Transportation), or ICC (the old Interstate Commerce Commission). The next letters in the first row identify the type of metal. 3A and 3AA are designations for steel cylinders. 3AL, E 6498, and SP6498 are designations for aluminum cylinders. The final figures in the first row—the important ones for you to remember—are numbers indicating the working pressure of the cylinder in psi.

The second row of markings includes the serial number of the tank (which you should record for identification purposes), letters or numbers identifying the manufacturer of the cylinder, and the date (month and year) of the tank's first pressure test.

U.S. regulations require compressed gas cylinders to be pressure-tested before being put into service and every five years thereafter. The date of the first pressure test is part of the second row of cylinder markings, but subsequent test dates may be stamped anywhere on the neck of the tank. A registered symbol between the date and year of a pressure test identifies the facility that did the testing.

When you take your scuba tank to an air station to have it filled, the facility will examine the tank markings to determine whether the cylinder test date is current and note the pressure to which the tank may be filled.

Cylinder Selection

The main criteria for the selection of diving equipment—fit and comfort—apply to scuba tanks as well. A small person should use a small tank. Larger divers may use and require larger tanks because they have larger lungs and use more air.

The material from which a tank is made affects its capacity, size, and working pressure. Although steel is heavier than aluminum, aluminum tanks are larger and heavier than steel tanks with similar capacities. Because aluminum is not as strong as steel, the walls of an aluminum tank are thicker than the walls of a steel tank of approximately the same capacity. The higher the pressure rating, the greater the capacity of a tank of a given size. Modern high-pressure steel scuba tanks are high-capacity cylinders, but they are quite heavy. Good sizes for small divers to consider for an initial scuba tank are 50 ft^3 and 63 ft^3 (1,416 and 1,784 L). Popular sizes for divers of average size are 71.2 and 80 ft^3 (2,016 and 2,266 L).

Another important factor you should consider when selecting a scuba tank is the buoyancy of the cylinder, which is determined by the volume and weight of the tank. Aluminum tanks are more buoyant than steel tanks. High-capacity tanks have a greater change in buoyancy than smaller cylinders as you use air from them. The change in buoyancy between a full and an empty tank can vary by more than 8 lb (3.6 kg) (see table 4.4).

Table 4.4 Cylinder Size, Working Pressure, and Buoyancy

Capacity (ft)	Working pressure (psi)	Buoyancy (lb) from full to empty
Aluminum 50	3,000	−2.7 to +1.3
Aluminum 63	3,000	−2.3 to +2.7
Steel 71.2	2,250	−2.0 to +3.5
Aluminum 80	3,000	−2.0 to +3.8
Steel 76	2,400	−6.5 to −0.1
Steel 80	3,500	−7.4 to −1.0
Steel 102	3,500	−7.6 to +0.5

Some tanks are negatively buoyant whether full or empty, but most tanks sink when full and float when empty. Buoyancy for tanks varies so much that you should select a tank used most often for diving in your area or try diving with several different tanks to determine which one is easiest to manage.

Multiple-tank scuba units are for specialty applications. As a beginning diver, you do not need double or triple scuba tanks. A single tank is adequate for most diving activities.

Cylinder Accessories

Fabric or plastic sleeves can help protect the exterior of your scuba cylinder. Some sleeves have places to attach various items so the wearer can reach the items easily. Tank bands vary. Some allow you to attach a small, backup scuba cylinder to your main cylinder. There are additional accessories to help you carry or transport your scuba cylinders. Tank boots, which were mentioned previously, are a desirable cylinder accessory.

Care and Maintenance

Scuba tanks are high-pressure vessels. They are strong, but you should handle them with care. Exterior damage can render your scuba tank useless. Avoid throwing scuba tanks or allowing them to roll about on the deck of a boat or in the trunk of your car. Secure cylinders for transportation or storage. Unless you are holding a scuba cylinder, do not leave it standing in an upright position, especially at a dive site. But do store your scuba tanks in an upright position because any moisture inside will settle to the bottom where inspectors can detect it with relative ease. Rinse the outside of your cylinder with clean, fresh water after use, and pay special attention to the tank boot area of steel tanks.

Corrosion can ruin a cylinder rapidly, and pieces of corrosion can damage a tank valve or scuba regulator. One way to prevent moisture from entering a tank is to have air in the tank. Water can get into an empty scuba cylinder while you're diving, so avoid using all the air in your tank. Moisture may enter an empty tank if you store it with the valve open. Store your scuba cylinder with a few hundred pounds (about 20 ATM) of pressure inside. A low pressure keeps moisture out but provides little oxygen to aid corrosion if there is moisture in the tank.

The filling process can force water into the tank. A water trap in an air compressor is supposed to remove moisture from air, but if the moisture-removal system does not function properly, water may be pumped into your tank along with air. The filling hose attachments for scuba tanks can get wet, and water inside the filling attachments may be forced into your cylinder. Using a quality air station is important.

The diving industry requires an annual visual inspection of scuba cylinders. The examination consists of an external inspection, the removal of the valve from a cylinder, an internal inspection using a special light, the replacement of the valve, and the attachment of a decal indicating the inspection date. Most air stations require a current visual cylinder-inspection sticker on a tank before they will fill it. When you handle your scuba tank, listen for sounds of anything moving inside the cylinder. If you hear anything, have the tank visually inspected.

Government regulations specify that compressed gas cylinders must be pressure-tested every five years in the United States. Some countries require pressure testing every year or two. The test is a hydrostatic test because it takes place in water. An inspector fills a scuba tank with water and submerges it in a closed container that is completely filled with water. The inspector applies pressure to the scuba tank hydraulically, and the tank expands slightly from the pressure. The expansion displaces water from the container holding the scuba tank. The inspector measures the expansion and then releases the pressure. The tank must return to within 10 percent of its original volume within a specified period of time. If the tank is too brittle to expand and contract correctly, the inspector condemns it.

You may transport a scuba tank on airplanes only if it is completely empty and the valve is open—a situation that is not good for scuba tanks. Do not transport your cylinder by air. Diving destinations have tanks readily available, so there is no need to take a tank on a dive trip.

▶ Figure 4.24 K-valves (left) and J-valves (center) control the flow of air from the cylinder. DIN-valves (right) withstand greater pressure than other types of valves.

CYLINDER VALVES

Cylinder valves control the flow of a liquid or gas. Four types of valves are available for scuba tanks: the simple valve, the reserve valve, the high-pressure valve, and the multiple-cylinder valve. Because multiple tanks are for advanced specialty diving activities, this section addresses only the simple, the reserve, and the high-pressure valves. Figure 4.24 shows examples of valves.

The Simple Valve

A simple valve is an on-off valve that operates like a faucet. You turn the valve handle counterclockwise to open it and clockwise to close it. The first catalog of diving equipment listed this type of valve as item "K," and the valve has been identified as a **K-valve** ever since.

The **valve seat** is a soft-sealing surface. You can damage the seat with excessive closing pressure.

Valves for scuba tanks have several features, one of which is a snorkel tube that extends from the bottom of the valve into the scuba cylinder. The valve snorkel prevents moisture or particles from entering the valve when you invert the tank. Another standard feature of tank valves is a thin, metal disk called a **burst disk**. If a tank is overfilled, or the heat from a fire causes the tank pressure to increase to a hazardous level, the disk will burst and vent the tank to prevent an explosion. The disks corrode over time, and occasionally a burst disk will rupture. The failure makes a loud noise and the tank hisses loudly, but the situation is not dangerous. If the burst disk in your tank valve ruptures, you need to have the valve serviced professionally. Manufacturers rate burst disks for various pressures, and the correct disk must be used. Keep the burst disk pressure rating in mind if you want to change a valve from one scuba tank to another. A valve with a low-pressure burst disk will rupture if you use it on a tank with a higher pressure rating.

There are two types of outlets for scuba tank valves. The traditional outlet is nearly flush with the surface of the valve and surrounded by a soft, circular ring called an **O-ring**. The ring forms the high-pressure seal between the valve and the scuba regulator, so the ring

K-valve—Simple type of cylinder valve that operates like a faucet

J-valve—A reserve valve that restricts the flow of air at a specified tank pressure

must be clean and free of nicks or cuts. A newer type of threaded outlet with a recessed O-ring seal is a **DIN-valve**, which withstands higher pressures than a traditional O-ring valve. Tank pressures in excess of 3,000 psi (204 ATMs or Bars) require a DIN fitting.

The Reserve Valve

A **J-valve** (the valve was listed as item "J" in the first equipment catalog) maintains a reserve of air to permit a normal ascent. The need for a reserve valve was much more important years ago. Until the introduction of **submersible pressure gauges** (SPGs) for scuba tanks, it was difficult to estimate how much air remained in a cylinder. Divers ran out of air at depth unless they had and used a J-valve. All divers today use SPGs to monitor the amount of air in their tanks.

A J-valve is a spring-loaded reserve valve. Pressure in the tank holds the spring-loaded valve open so air can flow through the valve until the tank pressure is insufficient to overcome the force of the reserve valve spring. At this point, a pressure of 300 to 600 psi (20 to 40 ATM), the spring begins to close the reserve valve and restricts the flow of air. The diver senses the increased breathing resistance and must open the spring-loaded valve manually by turning the reserve lever on the valve. Activation of the lever removes the restriction to airflow (see figure 4.25).

▶ Figure 4.25   Tank valves.

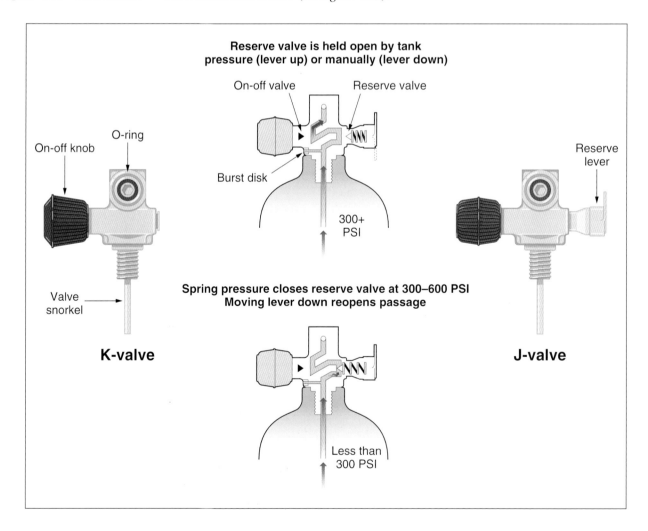

76

The reserve lever on a J-valve creates problems. If the lever is in the incorrect position (down), the valve will not maintain a reserve. If you fail to put the reserve lever in the up position before a dive, or if the lever is bumped during your dive, you might rely upon a reserve of air that will not be available. During the filling process, the reserve lever of a tank with a J-valve must be in the reserve position (down). If the lever is in the up position when the operator applies high-pressure air to the tank valve, the seat of the reserve valve will be damaged. Because J-valves cost more than K-valves to purchase and service, and because of the problems just mentioned, the J-valve's popularity has declined steadily over the years.

Valve Protectors

A protective cap is a desirable accessory for a tank valve. The cap helps prevent loss of the O-ring, helps keep dirt out of the valve, and can help prevent physical damage to the high-pressure sealing surface around the valve opening.

Care and Maintenance

Cylinder valves are made of soft metal and have thin areas, so physical abuse can ruin them. Protection of the valve is one reason why you should secure scuba tanks when you store them and why you should not leave them standing unattended. A tank that rolls about or falls over can damage the valve and render it inoperable.

When you open a tank valve, turn it slowly, open it all the way, then close it one-half turn. If the you leave the valve fully open and something strikes the handle, the valve seat will be damaged more than it would if the valve were closed slightly. When you close the valve, avoid excessive force, which shortens the life of the valve seat.

Although rinsing your tank valve after use is beneficial, soaking the valve by inverting your scuba tank in a container of warm water is better than rinsing. Water remains in the valve opening after rinsing or soaking. Open the valve momentarily to blow the water from the opening. If you leave the water in the opening and have the tank filled before the water evaporates, moisture will be forced into the tank.

Have your tank valve serviced annually by a professional. Also have your valve professionally serviced when it fails to operate easily or when the burst disk needs to be replaced. Valves receive partial servicing (lubrication) during the annual visual cylinder inspection of your scuba tank. The large O-ring that seals the valve to the scuba tank can be replaced at the time of the visual inspection. But partial servicing of your valve during a tank inspection is not the annual servicing of the valve. In a complete valve servicing, a qualified repair technician completely disassembles the valve, cleans the parts, replaces various parts, and then reassembles and tests the unit.

SCUBA REGULATORS

The function of a regulator is to reduce high-pressure air to a breathable level. Most scuba regulators use two **stages** of pressure reduction. The first stage of a regulator attaches to the valve of a scuba cylinder and reduces the high pressure to an intermediate pressure of about 140 psi (9.3 ATM). The first stage of the regulator connects via a hose to the second stage, which contains the mouthpiece. The second stage reduces the pressure from the intermediate level to the surrounding pressure. A scuba regulator is a

Scuba Wise

If you want to avoid dive accidents, use familiar, correct-fitting, well-maintained dive equipment the way that it is intended. As I look back over 34 years of dive experience, I can recall many instances in which divers got into trouble because they did not follow the essential equipment safety procedures summarized in the previous sentence. Diving allows us to explore an alien environment using life-support equipment. Modern scuba equipment is manufactured well, but you must take care of it and have it serviced periodically to keep it functioning properly. Would you consider going into outer space with life-support equipment that was not carefully maintained and serviced? We go into inner space when

we dive. Our life-support equipment is just as vital to us as an astronaut's.

Equipment problems while diving do arise, but equipment failure is rarely the primary cause of an accident. Problems cause anxiety and stress. A diver experiencing stress from environmental factors and fears may panic from the added stress that a minor equipment problem might pose. Learning to manage yourself and handle your equipment helps you reduce stress, avoid panic, and prevent an accident. One of the most important rules of accident-free diving is to have good, familiar equipment that is in good condition and used properly.

▶ Figure 4.26 Scuba regulator nomenclature: 1—first stage, 2—dust cover, 3—low-pressure hose, 4—low-pressure inflator hose, 5—console, 6—high-pressure hose, 7—primary second stage, 8—extra second stage.

demand system; it delivers air only when you demand it by inhaling. A demand system differs from a constant-delivery free-flow system, which commercial divers use. Scuba regulators are highly reliable and have a fail-safe design, which turns a demand system into a free-flow system in the event of a component failure. Figure 4.26 provides more information about scuba regulator nomenclature.

First Stages

The first stages for scuba regulators are either balanced or unbalanced. Changes in tank pressure affect the performance of a balanced first stage only slightly. With an unbalanced first stage, the performance of the regulator changes as tank pressure changes, so a balanced first stage is desirable.

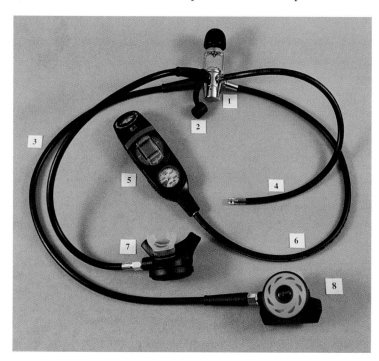

The two main types of regulator first stage valves are diaphragm and piston (see figure 4.27). A diaphragm first stage has a diaphragm that excludes water and dirt from the working parts inside. A bias spring combined with water pressure pushes the valve open. Tank pressure closes the valve when the first stage pressure equals intermediate pressure plus water pressure. A diaphragm valve has more parts than a piston first stage, so it is more expensive to manufacture and service. The diaphragm valve's exclusion of water and dirt from the mechanics allows high performance for longer periods of time than does a piston valve.

Piston first stages have an open, simple design with few moving parts. Water pressure in direct contact with the piston combines with the force of a bias spring to open the piston valve. Tank pressure causes the piston to move and the valve to close when the first stage pressure equals intermediate pressure plus water pressure. Piston first stages are easier and less expensive to service than diaphragm first stages. But dirt, salt crystals, and mineral deposits that accumulate inside a piston regulator can affect its performance. Each type of first stage has advantages and disadvantages, so either type is acceptable. A diaphragm-piston regulator combines the diaphragm and piston concepts. The diaphragm excludes water and dirt and transfers pressure to a piston.

A first stage must have a means of attachment to the tank valve. A typical regulator has a yoke that surrounds the valve and mates the regulator to the tank valve. The regulator inlet, which has an inlet filter, secures to a tank with a yoke screw. Scuba regulators that operate at above-average pressures use a DIN fitting instead of a yoke screw. A DIN fitting screws directly into a DIN-valve and does not have a yoke.

There are multiple openings, called **ports**, in first stages. One of the ports is for high-pressure air measurement with an SPG. The remaining ports are for low-pressure air. A regulator should have several low-pressure ports to supply air to the primary second stage, an alternate second stage, a BC inflator, and possibly a dry suit inflator. The sizes of ports vary. The high-pressure port usually is larger than the low-pressure openings because a low-pressure hose inadvertently connected to the high-pressure port would rupture.

Some regulators feature environmental shielding by sealing special fluid inside a flexible chamber attached to the first stage. The sealed, flexible chamber transmits water pressure to the regulator, but no water, salt, or dirt can enter the first stage. Extremely cold water can cause an unshielded regulator to freeze, but the fluid in an environmental chamber will not freeze.

Second Stages

The most common second stage is shaped like a cup lying on one side (see figure 4.28). Imagine a pliable diaphragm across the top of the cup, a mouthpiece attached to the bottom of the cup, and a purge valve attached to the lower side. A lever that activates a valve

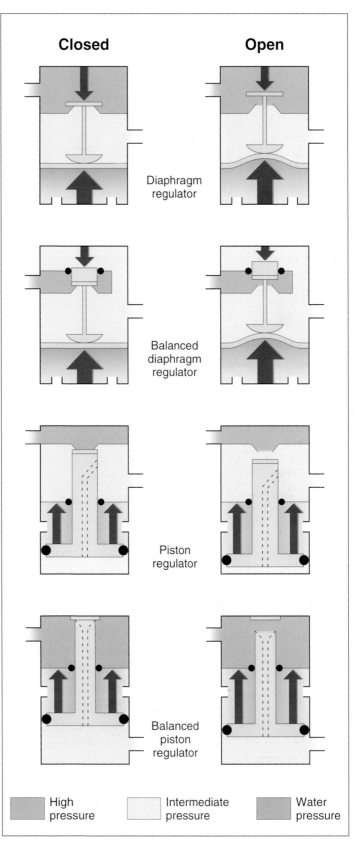

Closed **Open**

Diaphragm regulator

Balanced diaphragm regulator

Piston regulator

Balanced piston regulator

| High pressure | Intermediate pressure | Water pressure |

▶ Figure 4.27 Typical regulator first stages. Red arrows represent spring pressure. Black dots represent O-rings.

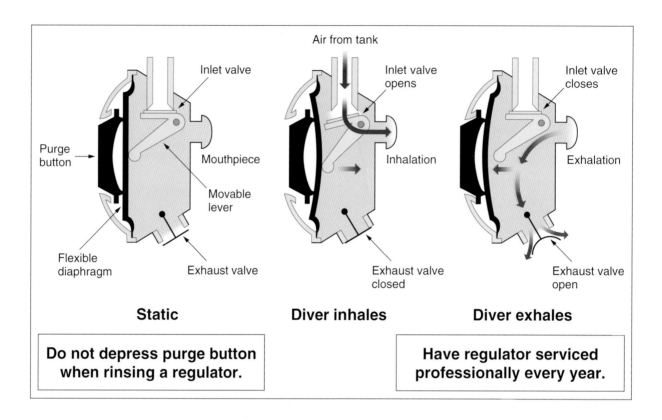

Air from tank

Inlet valve

Purge
button

Mouthpiece

Movable
lever

Flexible
diaphragm

Exhaust valve

Static

Inlet valve
opens

Inhalation

Exhaust valve
closed

Diver inhales

Inlet valve
closes

Exhalation

Exhaust valve
open

Diver exhales

**Do not depress purge button
when rinsing a regulator.**

**Have regulator serviced
professionally every year.**

▶ Figure 4.28 Regulator
operation.

inside the container is in contact with a moveable diaphragm at rest. An inhalation through the mouthpiece creates a partial vacuum inside the second stage. The pressure reduction pulls in the diaphragm, moving the lever and opening the valve, allowing air to flow from the first stage of the regulator into the second stage. When you stop inhaling, the buildup of pressure returns the diaphragm and lever to their normal positions, closing the valve and stopping the flow of air. When you begin to exhale, increased pressure inside the second stage opens the purge valve, allowing air to escape.

The two types of scuba regulator second stage valves are the downstream valve and the pilot valve. With a downstream-valve regulator, a small bias spring holds a valve closed. Inhalation moves the diaphragm, which moves a lever. The lever movement overcomes the resistance of the bias spring and opens a valve, allowing intermediate-pressure air to enter the second stage. After inhalation, air flows until the diaphragm moves outward, allowing the bias spring to close the valve. Downstream second stage valves are simple, inexpensive, and tolerate more sand and dirt than pilot valves do.

In a pilot-valve regulator, the movement of the diaphragm in the second stage opens a small valve that, in turn, opens a larger valve. When you stop inhaling from the regulator, the diaphragm returns to its normal position, and the valves close. A pilot valve delivers air up to four times easier than a downstream valve. But pilot valves are more expensive to manufacture and service than downstream valves, and you may experience a shuddering effect of air movement with a pilot valve regulator in shallow water.

All regulators have a purge, a button or area on the regulator that you depress to manually open the second stage valve. Use the purge to test the regulator, expel water and debris from inside the second stage, and relieve the pressure in the regulator after you close the tank valve.

The location of the exhaust varies. Some regulators have the exhaust valve at the bottom of the second stage, some have the exhaust at the side, and some have it in the front. The position of the exhaust affects the bubble pattern and the clearing of water from the regulator when it has water inside and you place it in your mouth. Some regulators direct exhaust bubbles by means of an exhaust tee. You will learn more about regulator positioning for clearing in chapter 5.

A regulator may be right-handed, left-handed, or bidirectional, referring to the direction from which the regulator hose must come when the regulator is in your mouth. For example, the hose must come from the right side when you are using a right-handed regulator. The hose can come from either side when using a bidirectional regulator. The directional configuration is important only for knowing how to orient the regulator when you place it in your mouth. Figure 4.29 shows directional configurations.

Some second stage casings feature strong, light, durable materials that do not bend or corrode as metal does. Several types and styles of mouthpieces are available. Use a soft, comfortable mouthpiece that does not cause jaw fatigue. A repair technician can replace mouthpieces quickly and easily.

Regulator Accessories

A regulator hose is flexible but has rigid metal connectors crimped on the ends. The points where the hose and the metal meet are stress points because the hose fibers strain against an unyielding surface. To prevent the breakdown of the hose fibers at the stress points, use hose protector sleeves. At a minimum, equip all regulator hoses with hose protectors at the first stage end of each hose.

Padded regulator bags help provide protection when you are transporting or storing your regulator. The bag should be large enough to accommodate the regulator and all its hoses without bending the hoses sharply.

Adapters allow you to use DIN-fitting regulators on standard cylinder valves. Use protective covers for the threads on DIN fittings.

Purge depressors are a feature on some regulators and an accessory for regulators that do not have them. A purge depressor depresses the purge partially to remove bias spring pressure from the second stage valve when you are not using the regulator, thus extending the life of the valve seat.

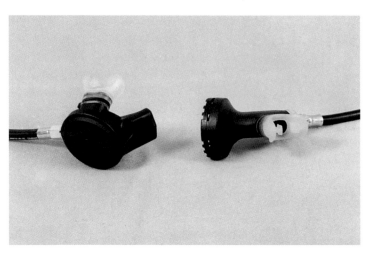

▶ Figure 4.29 Scuba regulators have different configurations.

Colored second stage covers allow you to color-coordinate your regulator with your other equipment. Other, previously mentioned accessories include various mouthpieces and hose adapters.

Regulator Selection

It takes effort to inhale and to exhale through a scuba regulator. The effort is needed to overcome resistance to breathing; good regulators have minimal breathing resistance. Compare the performance data for various regulators and select one that breathes easily over a wide range of tank pressures. A wide range of performance implies a balanced first stage.

Choose a widely used and easily serviced regulator. You want a regulator that can be serviced by facilities anywhere you happen to be and that uses readily available parts.

The type of diving you do should affect your selection. If you plan to do most of your diving from shore, you should avoid a pilot-valve second stage, which sand and dirt can affect adversely. Diaphragm first stages may be a better choice if most of your diving will be from shore.

If you do not have a scuba tank, you might consider purchasing the tank and regulator at the same time so you can match the fittings of the regulator and the cylinder valve. If you will be diving in water that is near freezing, you should select an environmentally shielded regulator.

Care and Maintenance

Your regulator is a precision instrument; it requires care and maintenance to ensure the best possible performance. Keep sand and dirt out of your regulator. Do not allow salt crystals to form inside. Soak your regulator in clean, fresh, warm water as soon as possible after diving in the ocean. You need to remove salt before it dries. If you cannot soak your regulator, at least rinse it. A combination of soaking and rinsing is best. Follow these rules when rinsing or soaking a regulator:

- *Keep the inside of a first stage dry.* The purpose of the dust cover on the first stage is to exclude water and dust. Develop the habit of replacing the dust cover and securing it in place with the yoke screw any time you do not have the regulator attached to a tank. Make certain the dust cover is in place before you rinse or soak a regulator.

- *Allow low-pressure water to flow gently through the second stage and also into the openings on the first stage.* High-pressure water can force dirt and grit into crevices where it will cause damage. Gentle pressure washes the dirt away.

- *Do not depress the purge button when you rinse the second stage unless you have the regulator pressurized.* If you do not pressurize the regulator and you depress the purge valve with water inside the second stage, you open the second stage valve and allow water to flow through the hose into the first stage.

When the regulator has dried thoroughly, lay it flat for storage. For prolonged storage, place the regulator in a plastic bag to help protect it against the harmful effects of smog. Do not bend the hoses sharply because the bending damages hose fibers. Replace hoses that are cut, bulging, or leaking.

You can avoid most problems with your regulator by having it serviced annually. Have your regulator serviced even if it seems to be functioning properly. Failure to invest in regular service can affect your safety and shorten the life of your regulator.

ALTERNATE AIR SOURCES

Several equipment options can help if you run out of air underwater. (But remember, running out of air is due only to sheer negligence.) Your best option is an **alternate air source** (AAS), which is a source of compressed air other than your primary scuba regulator. An AAS also is valuable if your primary source of air begins free-flowing or leaking during a dive because you can switch to the AAS and make a normal ascent. The two primary types of AASs are extra second stages and backup scuba units. Extra second stages allow two divers to share air without passing a single mouthpiece back and forth. Backup scuba units are fully redundant scuba systems that provide an independent source of air in an emergency. You are not dependent on a buddy to provide air when you are equipped with a backup system. Extra second stages are less expensive than backup scuba units but do not provide the benefits of an independent scuba system.

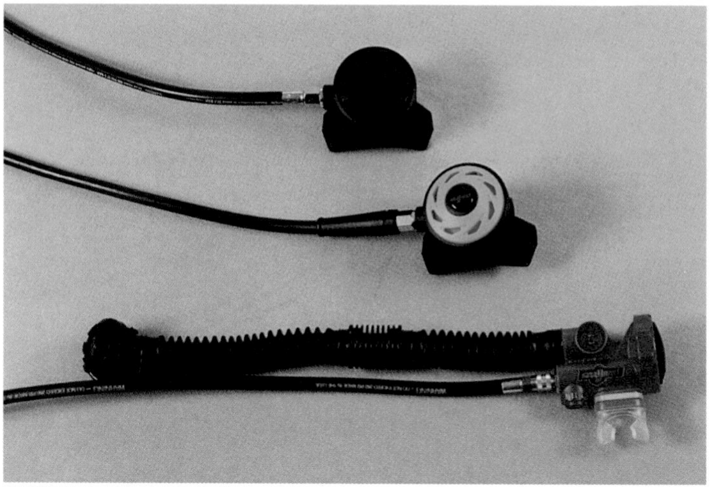

Extra Second Stages

The two types of extra second stages are an extra second stage for your regulator or a BC low-pressure inflator that has an integrated regulator second stage (see figure 4.30). An extra second stage, or **octopus**, should meet the following criteria:

▶ Figure 4.30 A primary second stage (top), an extra second stage (center), and an integrated second stage (bottom).

- The first stage of the regulator should be capable of meeting the air flow demands of two second stages.

- The hose on the extra second stage should be several inches (7 to 10 cm) longer than the primary second stage hose.

- The extra second stage should attach to your chest area in such a way that your buddy can remove it quickly and easily. Do not allow the extra second stage to dangle.

- The attachment device should cover the extra second stage mouthpiece opening to prevent the regulator from free-flowing and to keep dirt and debris from getting inside.

- The extra second stage should be brightly colored for easy identification.

There are two ways to integrate a regulator second stage into a BC low-pressure inflator. Quick-release hose fittings on the regulator second stage can allow it to be fitted in series in the low-pressure hose leading to the inflator assembly, or the BC inflator mechanism can have a built-in regulator second stage. Both types of extra second stages have advantages and disadvantages. An integrated second stage requires one less hose on your regulator because a single hose provides air for both the extra second stage and the BC inflator. When you must share air and you have an integrated second stage, you must breathe from the integrated second stage because the hose is too short for your buddy to use. With an extra second stage, you or your buddy can use either air source. Extra second stages integrated into the BC inflator may leak air. To stop a leak, you must disconnect the low-pressure air, thereby losing the functions of the low-pressure inflator and the extra second stage.

Backup Scuba Units

There are two types of backup scuba units: a **pony tank** is a small (about 13 to 20 ft³ or 368 to 567 L) scuba cylinder with a separate, standard regulator. You clamp a pony tank

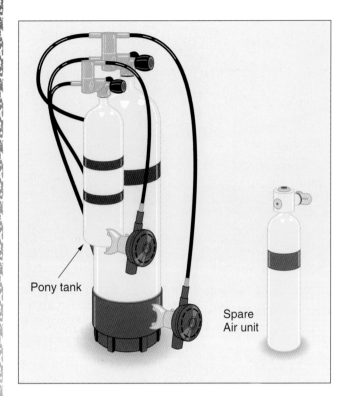

to the side of your main scuba cylinder. A **Spare Air unit** is a smaller (2- to 4-ft³ or 57 to 113 L) scuba cylinder with a special regulator integrated directly into the valve. A pony tank provides an adequate supply of air for many situations, but a Spare Air unit provides only enough air to permit an ascent from shallow depths. On the other hand, a Spare Air unit is small and light, whereas a pony tank is bulky and heavy (see figure 4.31).

Care and Maintenance

AAS equipment should receive the same care and maintenance as your primary scuba equipment. Some divers attempt to save money by having only their primary scuba equipment serviced annually. This is false economy. AAS equipment needs servicing just as much as primary scuba equipment does.

INSTRUMENTATION

You move in three dimensions in water the way a pilot does in air. Instruments are important safety requirements for flying. A pilot needs information about altitude, direction, time, and the amount of fuel remaining. Similarly, you need information about depth, direction, time, and the amount of air remaining. The minimum instrumentation you need includes a depth gauge, an underwater timer, a submersible pressure gauge (SPG), and a compass. You may also find it helpful to have a dive computer.

▶ Figure 4.31 Pony tank and Spare Air unit.

Depth Gauges

To tell how deep you have descended, you can use one of four types of depth gauges: **capillary gauge**, **Bourdon tube**, diaphragm gauge, and electronic gauge. Manufacturers calibrate depth gauges in feet of seawater (FSW). The gauges do not indicate the correct depth in fresh water, but they indicate the equivalent seawater depth if you use them starting at sea level in fresh water or if they adjust for altitude pressure changes. The FSW reading of gauges in fresh water is acceptable because tables for time limits at various depths are based on sea level depths. Table 4.5 compares the four types of depth gauges.

A capillary depth gauge is a simple instrument. It is a hollow, air-filled, transparent plastic tube sealed at one end and placed around a circular dial. The open end of the tube aligns with zero on the gauge dial. A capillary gauge uses the principle of Boyle's law. Water pressure compresses the air inside the tube during descent. The position of the air-water interface inside the tube relative to markings on the dial indicates the depth. At 2 ATM, the air column in the tube compresses to one-half its original length.

A Bourdon tube is a thin metal tube formed into a spiral. The tube may be open to the water or closed and placed inside a housing filled with oil. Oil-filled Bourdon gauges are more popular than open-tube gauges. Pressure on an open-tube gauge tries to straighten the tube and increases the coil diameter. The straightening produces a spiral movement

Caution:

Do not attempt to lubricate or service scuba equipment. Improper servicing can cause equipment failure.

Table 4.5	Depth Gauges		
Type	**Accuracy**	**Advantages**	**Disadvantages**
Capillary	Accurate only to depth of about 40 ft (12 m)	Rugged, inexpensive	Can clog with debris or air bubbles
Bourdon tube	Plus or minus 1% to 2% of full scale	Accurate	Can be damaged by reduced pressure at altitude
Diaphragm	Very accurate	Can adjust zero setting for pressure changes at altitude	Expensive
Electronic	Reading accurate within ±6 in. (15 cm)	Gauge may zero itself to compensate for changes in atmospheric pressure	Must have sufficient battery power; expensive

of the tube, which is linked mechanically to a needle to indicate the depth. Water pressure causes the coil of a closed-tube gauge to decrease in diameter. The coil movement, linked mechanically to a needle, indicates the amount of pressure exerted on the gauge.

The accurate but expensive diaphragm gauge uses elaborate mechanics to connect a thin, movable diaphragm to an indicating needle. Electronic depth gauges, also accurate and expensive, use a pressure sensor (transducer), electrical circuitry, a display, and a battery to indicate depth.

A maximum-depth indicator is a desirable feature for all depth gauges. As you will learn in chapter 6, you must know the depth of a dive for planning purposes. A digital depth gauge retains the maximum depth you attain. The instrument displays the information until the next dive or for 12 or more hours following a dive, then resets automatically. Many modern depth gauges with needle displays have a thin indicating wire that the gauge needle pushes along the dial face. When the needle retreats, the wire remains at the highest point reached on the dial. You can reset the indicating wire by turning a screw on the dial face. You must remember to reset the maximum-depth indicator before each dive when you use a needle-display gauge.

Underwater Timers

You can use either an automatic or a manual underwater timer to keep track of time during a dive. Either type may indicate time with hands on a dial or with a digital display. Pressure activates automatic timers, which start timing at a depth of about 3 to 5 ft (1 to 1.5 m) and stop timing when the depth is less than that. Automatic timers are better than watches because you do not have to remember to start or stop the timing of your dive, although you have to reset some watch-type automatic timers before a dive. Waterproof watches that you can use as underwater timers usually feature a rotating **bezel**, a movable ring that you can set to indicate elapsed time. Digital watches are accurate, but they have small buttons that can make them difficult to operate. The best timers are electronic automatic timers, which can keep track of how long you dive, how long you are at the surface between dives, and how many dives you make. You do not have to remember to reset or activate anything when you use an electronic automatic timer.

Dive Compasses

Rarely can you see more than 100 ft (30 m) underwater, so a navigational aid can be valuable. If you dive without a directional reference, you can end a dive a long distance from your planned exit point. A dive compass can help you avoid long surface swims or swims through thick surface canopies of underwater plants. You can use a compass to navigate beneath the canopies, where there are passages through the plants. A compass also is useful for relocating a precise area underwater and as a surface navigation device if fog reduces visibility.

Two types of compasses are card types and needle types. Both are mechanical. Magnetic deposits in the earth near the North Pole attract either a magnetized disk or a magnetized needle to provide a directional reference. Metal and magnetic forces—ferrous metal, magnets, or electrical motors—can deviate the compass card or needle from its correct alignment if the influence is in close proximity to a compass.

lubber line—A reference line on a compass that indicates the direction of travel

Diving compasses contain liquid to dampen the swinging of the needle or disk. To be useful for diving, a compass needs a reference line, called a **lubber line**, to indicate the direction of travel relative to the needle reference. A rotating bezel with bracketing index marks that allow you to mark the needle position for a specific direction is also desirable.

You view some compasses from the top and some from the side. Side-reading compasses display a selected course in a window on the side of the instrument. You look across a top-reading compass. You will learn how to read and use a compass in chapter 5.

Submersible Pressure Gauges (SPG)

An SPG is equivalent to the gas gauge for a car and is just as essential. You can use either a mechanical or an electronic SPG to measure cylinder pressure. A mechanical SPG is a high-pressure Bourdon tube. High-pressure air from the cylinder passes through the regulator first stage, through a high-pressure hose, and into a Bourdon tube inside a housing at the end of the high-pressure hose. The pressure tries to straighten the spiral tube, which moves a needle on a dial to indicate the tank pressure. Physical shock can damage a mechanical SPG.

An electronic SPG has a pressure sensor (transducer), circuitry, a battery, and a display. It is a form of a high-pressure depth gauge. The display may be digital or graphic. Either a symbol or psi (or ATM) in numbers may indicate the amount of air in your tank. If the electronics get wet, or if the battery dies, an electronic SPG will not function.

You should retain at least 300 to 500 psi (20.4 to 34 ATM) in your tank at the end of a dive. Mechanical SPGs typically have a red area on the dial for the first 500 psi (34 ATM). When you dive, you should monitor your air supply and make sure that you surface before the needle gets into the red area. Electronic depth gauges usually warn of a low supply of air by blinking the display.

An SPG has a **blowout plug** to relieve pressure in the housing in the event of a high-pressure leak. Identify the blowout plug on your SPG, and do not place anything over the plug that will prevent it from functioning. If the plug cannot come out to release high pressure inside the SPG housing, the face of the instrument could explode.

Instrument Consoles

You can purchase diving instruments individually or in combination. It is convenient to combine several gauges into a display unit called a **console**. An instrument console attaches to the high-pressure hose coming from your regulator first stage. When you have your instruments in a console, your arms are free of gauges and dive preparations are quicker.

The two types of instrument consoles are mechanical and electronic. A mechanical console contains an SPG and a depth gauge. Some also contain an underwater timer, a compass, and a thermometer. The instruments usually feature luminous displays, which are easy to read in low light.

With an electronic console, all instrument information except direction is in a single display. (There is only one electronic underwater compass, and it is a separate instrument.) If one gauge fails in a mechanical console, the remainder can still function; but when an electronic console fails, all the information provided by the unit is lost. Electronic displays are difficult to read in the dark unless they feature some type of illumination. Figure 4.32 shows various diving instruments.

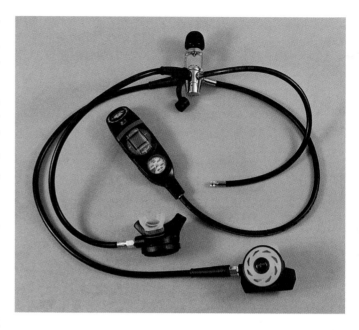

▶ Figure 4.32   Divers use many instruments to monitor their activity underwater.

Dive Computers

A dive computer is an electronic instrument with a pressure sensor, electronic circuitry, a battery, and a display. A programmed computer inside the instrument uses pressure and time information to calculate continuously the uptake of nitrogen by various compartments that have different half-times. When the absorption by any one of the compartments reaches a selected level, the device indicates that you are approaching a time limit, after which a direct ascent to the surface will no longer be possible. Upon reaching a time limit, the computer indicates a minimum depth—a **ceiling**—that you cannot exceed during ascent. You risk DCS unless you wait until the computer indicates that sufficient outgassing has occurred to allow you to continue your ascent. A dive computer provides extremely accurate time and depth information. Other common features are a low battery warning, a rapid ascent warning, a dive log mode, a dive-planning mode, and flying-after-diving information. Additional information about dive computers is in chapter 6.

Care and Maintenance

Physical abuse can damage instruments, so protect your instruments from shock. Secure your console instead of allowing it to swing freely.

Heat or prolonged exposure to hot sun can cause oil in a liquid-filled gauge to expand and break the seal on the housing encasing the instrument. If you break the seal, you have to have the gauge repaired. Hot water may cause an underwater timer to expand, break a seal, and allow water inside. Do not subject diving instruments to high temperatures. Have air leaks in SPGs repaired at the first opportunity. Have your depth gauge tested for accuracy from time to time by a professional repair facility or compare your gauge with an extremely accurate instrument, such as a digital depth gauge. Follow all manufacturer recommendations. Reduced pressure at elevations above sea level can damage some instruments. Unless an instrument is designed for use at altitude, pack it in an airtight container for flying. Soak and rinse instruments with clean, fresh water after use.

ceiling—The minimum depth that a diver cannot rise above without the risk of DCS

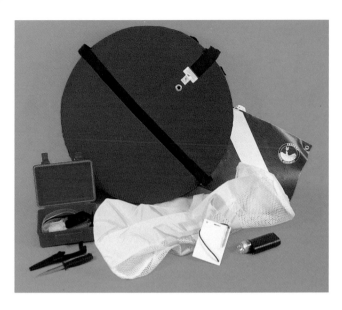

▶ Figure 4.33 Divers must carry a dive knife, and other equipment can also be helpful.

Give special attention to pressure-sensing areas to prevent them from becoming clogged with dirt or salt crystals.

DIVE KNIVES AND ACCESSORY EQUIPMENT

This section addresses some additional equipment you should have and some you may want to have. Figure 4.33 shows examples of dive knives and some dive accessories.

Dive Knives

Do not consider a knife optional equipment or an accessory. Line and cords in water can cause entanglements, so it is important to have a knife that will allow you to cut yourself or your buddy free.

The many designs of dive knives include large knives and small knives. A small knife positioned where you can reach it easily is better than a large knife that you cannot reach. The most important feature of a dive knife is an effective cutting edge. Good blades are corrosion resistant and hold a sharp edge; serrated blades cut line more effectively than straight blades.

Some knives are multipurpose tools designed for prying, digging, pounding, and measuring in addition to cutting. If you use a knife as a diving tool, then also have a small, separate dive knife.

A dive knife comes with a sheath, which has some means to lock the knife in place inside the sheath. Make sure the sheath lock is positive to prevent losing a knife. You may attach a small knife to your leg, your arm, your console, or your BC. Wear a large knife on the inside of your leg and secure it with straps that stretch to compensate for exposure suit compression.

To prevent corrosion, rinse your dive knife after diving. Inspect the edge for sharpness, remove any rust, and coat the blade with grease.

Accessory Equipment

You are likely to need several small, but important, items of accessory. These items include a gear bag, a dive flag and float, dive lights, dive kits, dive slates, signaling devices, and a diver's first aid kit.

Gear Bags You need so much equipment for diving that you also need a means to carry it. Gear bag designs feature multiple compartments, padding, novel ways for carrying or moving, sealed fabric edges, and various fabrics. The bags may be simple or complex. The type for you depends on your needs and on how much you want to invest. Be sure to get a bag with webbing handles that completely surround the bag to provide full, durable support. No matter what your budget, you will need a gear bag for your equipment.

Dive Flags and Floats In many areas, local law requires use of a dive flag while diving. In the United States, the traditional dive flag is a red flag with a white diagonal stripe. The flag usually is vinyl, mounted on a fiberglass staff, and stiffened with a wire so it will stand out from the staff at all times. In addition to the red-and-white flag, use the international Alpha flag, a swallow-tailed blue-and-white flag, when diving from a vessel. The Alpha flag is a general dive flag in countries other than the United States (see figure 4.34).

Unless you are diving from a boat, you need a float to support your dive flag. Some flag-staffs have a float attached to them. There are attachments to secure a dive flag to an inner tube and flag-holding canvas coverings for inner tubes.

Dive Lights A dive light can increase your diving enjoyment. Light levels are low under-water, and a light restores color to objects at depth and allows you to peer under ledges and into holes. You will see and enjoy much more when you have and use a dive light.

The many types of dive lights available include large, powerful, rechargeable lights, and small lights that use disposable batteries. Consider a small dive light initially. A large light is for night diving, which is an advanced activity. A small light is easy to carry, useful for day dives, and useful as a backup light for night diving. Many of today's small dive lights are bright and compact (see figure 4.35). Maintain your dive light according to the manufacturer's instructions.

Dive Kits Two equipment kits are recommended: a dive kit and a "save-a-dive" kit. The dive kit contains items you use frequently for diving. The save-a-dive kit contains items you may need to salvage a dive. The items that you might include in each are listed in the sidebar on the next page. Because the items in your dive kit are small and get wet, you may wish to keep them isolated in a container so you can find them easily. Once you get yourself and your equipment to a dive site, you don't want a minor equipment problem to keep you from diving. A broken strap, a missing O-ring, or a torn mouthpiece are examples of problems that can stop you from diving unless you have spare parts.

Keep items for a save-a-dive kit in a waterproof box. Do not mix wet items from your dive kit with dry items in your save-a-dive kit.

Dive Slates You need to record and refer to information around and in the water when you dive. Plastic slates are better than paper because water does not affect the slates. Dive slates include checklist slates, reference slates, logbook information transfer slates, and writing slates. All types are of value. You probably will have several slates when you become an experienced diver. Initially, you should have an equipment checklist, a dive planning slate, and an underwater writing slate.

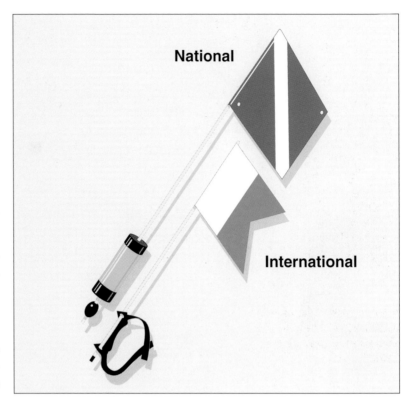

▶ Figure 4.34 Dive flags.

▶ Figure 4.35 A dive light is a useful accessory.

Equipment Kits

Dive Kit

- ☐ Defogging solution for your mask
- ☐ Wet suit shampoo
- ☐ Sunscreen
- ☐ Lip balm
- ☐ Seasickness medication

Save-a-Dive Kit

- ☐ Mask strap
- ☐ Fin strap
- ☐ Snorkel keeper
- ☐ Tank valve O-rings
- ☐ Quick-release buckle
- ☐ Weight keepers
- ☐ Regulator mouthpiece
- ☐ Crescent wrench
- ☐ Screwdrivers
- ☐ Cable ties
- ☐ Twine
- ☐ Duct tape

Signaling Devices   Long-range signaling devices are invaluable if you become adrift, especially in areas where currents are strong. A whistle is more effective than shouting to gain attention, so you should have a whistle readily available. The sound from a whistle does not require much energy to produce, and it travels well over water.

A small diver's air horn, powered by low-pressure air, works with as little as 50 psi (3.4 ATM) of tank pressure and produces a sound that can be heard up to a mile away. The device is so loud you must point the horn away from yourself to avoid hearing damage.

You can get long, bright, thin, inflatable safety tubes that fit easily into your BC pocket. Inflate a safety tube at the surface to make yourself easier to spot in the water.

You can use a signal mirror to flash sunlight long distances over water. Other forms of signaling devices for divers are flashlights, strobe lights, and waterproof flares. The greater the chance of being caught in a current, the greater your need for signaling devices.

Diver's First Aid Kit   Diving takes place in remote areas, and because it is a physical activity, someone may be injured. It is a good idea to be prepared for an emergency. You should have a first aid kit at the dive site. The items helpful in a standard first aid kit are listed in the following sidebar. Chapter 7 addresses the use of the first aid items.

SPECIALIZED EQUIPMENT

Other specialized equipment for scuba diving includes Nitrox equipment, mixed-gas equipment, and rebreathers. This equipment permits highly experienced divers with specialty training to obtain longer dive times. The risks associated with the use of specialized equipment make training and adherence to the rules pertaining to equipment use absolutely essential.

First Aid Kit

- ☐ Rescue breathing mask
- ☐ Seasickness medication
- ☐ Isopropyl alcohol
- ☐ Hydrogen peroxide
- ☐ White vinegar
- ☐ Baking soda
- ☐ Analgesic and antiseptic ointment
- ☐ Hot packs
- ☐ Eyewash

- ☐ Tweezers
- ☐ Bandage scissors
- ☐ Penlight
- ☐ Coins for emergency phone calls
- ☐ Emergency contact information for diving emergencies
- ☐ Diving first aid book
- ☐ Space blanket
- ☐ Pen and small notebook

SUMMARY

Diving involves a great deal of equipment. You are beginning to understand the equipment you need to have, how to select it, and how to care for it. You will learn more about equipment from your instructor, from retailers, from magazines, and from other divers. Get good equipment, and give it the best care possible. Diving is not enjoyable if you have constant equipment problems.

Diving Skills

5

Diving requires many skills, and you must repeat them correctly until you can execute them automatically. When you have mastered the skills of diving, your enjoyment can begin because you will be able to devote more attention to things of interest. The skills introduced to you in this chapter are the basic skills of skin diving and scuba diving.

By the end of this chapter, you will be able to

- *prepare, assemble, don, adjust, inspect, and disassemble your equipment for skin and scuba diving;*
- *demonstrate 13 standard skin and scuba diving hand signals;*
- *explain how to test and control buoyancy;*
- *explain how to clear water from a mask and from a snorkel;*
- *explain how to descend, swim with fins, and ascend when skin and scuba diving;*
- *explain how to handle, remove, and replace skin and scuba diving equipment;*
- *describe various entry and exit techniques for skin and scuba diving;*

- *explain how to use dive flags;*
- *explain the buddy system and lost buddy procedures;*
- *explain how to use a compass for underwater navigation;*
- *explain how to prevent and manage seasickness, dizziness, stress and panic, overexertion, coughing, cramps, entanglement, loss of buoyancy control, loss of air supply, and dive emergencies;*
- *explain how to rescue a nonbreathing diver and the first aid procedures for an injured scuba diver; and*
- *define the following terms: flutter kick, scissors kick, modified frog kick, dolphin kick, diver's push-ups, open-valve ascent, contact descent, noncontact descent, buddy line, compass heading, compass course, reciprocal compass course, flaring, and buddy breathing.*

You will learn most of the diving skills in controlled conditions, and when you have developed the basic skills, you will apply them in open water. (Open water is any body of water representative of dive sites in the local area.) When you can demonstrate the skills of diving in open water, you will be ready to receive your diving certification.

PREPARING TO SKIN DIVE

Skin diving is breath-hold diving underwater. This section discusses the skills of skin diving, many of which apply to scuba diving.

Preparing Equipment

Be ready to start your lesson when you come to your first water session. Prepare your mask, snorkel, and fins in advance. Clean your mask lens thoroughly so it will not fog. Adjust the mask strap so it is snug but not tight. Attach the snorkel to the mask strap on the left side, and adjust the snorkel so it is comfortable in your mouth. If your fins have heel straps, adjust them so they are snug but not tight. Complete all adjustments before your first water session.

Inspect your skin diving vest or BC by inflating it, making sure it does not leak, and then deflating it. Put it on, reinflate it, and adjust the strap(s) so it will stay in position in the water. You may need to use a strap that runs between your legs and attaches to the front and back of the flotation device to keep it from riding up when you are in the water. If the flotation device has a CO_2 detonator, inspect the CO_2 cartridge and detonator.

Your instructor will suggest an initial amount of weight for your weight belt. Adjust the length of the belt at the buckle end so the excess strap at the opposite end does not exceed 6 in. (15 cm). Allow 2 in. (5 cm) for each two-slot weight you thread onto a belt. Distribute the weight on both sides of the belt so you will be balanced in the water. Lock the weights in place with weight retainers.

Mark your personal equipment with your initials so you can identify it. You can use special paint or markers (available at dive stores) or colored tape. Pack your equipment in a gear bag. Place the items you will don last, such as your fins, on the bottom. Place the items you will don first, such as your exposure suit, on the top.

Donning Equipment

Don your exposure suit pants or legs first, then your boots, and then the top part of your suit. Donning a snug-fitting wet suit is easier if you wet the inside of your suit with a mixture of water and mild shampoo or if you wear a spandex suit as an undergarment. Place the ends of the legs of your wet suit over the tops of your boots so water can drain from your suit when you exit from a dive. If the boots are outside the legs of your wet suit, water from the suit will balloon your boots when you get out of the water. If you become warm while donning the exposure suit, cool yourself before proceeding with your preparations. For open-water diving, don a cold-water hood before donning your wet suit jacket so the shirt of the hood will be underneath your jacket. (Figures 5.1 through 5.5 illustrate the process of equipment donning.)

Don your skin diving vest or BC next. Place a skin diving vest over your head, and then secure the straps. Inflate the vest fully to make sure the adjustment will not be too tight. The straps should be as snug as possible without being uncomfortable or interfering with breathing.

Don your weight belt after the skin diving vest so it will be clear of the vest straps.

▶ Figure 5.1 Getting into your exposure suit.

Grasp the free end (the end without the buckle) of the weight belt in your right hand and grasp the buckle end with your left hand. Pick up the belt, step through it, pull it into position across your back, bend forward so gravity will support the weight of the belt, and then tighten the belt and secure the quick release. Always wear the weight belt with a right-hand release, even if you are left-handed, so that a rescuer will know how to release your belt in an emergency. If you always hold the free end of the belt in your right hand when donning it, you always will have a right-hand quick release.

Don the remainder of your skin diving equipment—mask, snorkel, and fins—at the water's edge or, if it is calm, in the water. Defog the mask, place it on your forehead, and pull the strap over the back of your head using both hands to position the strap. Position the

▶ Figure 5.2 Strapping on your BC.

▶ Figure 5.3 Donning your weights.

▶ Figure 5.4   Adjusting your mask.

▶ Figure 5.5   Putting on your fins.

mask on your face, clearing any hair from beneath the sealing edge of the mask. Reposition the split strap so it lies flat and so the split is above and below the crown of your head. You don your snorkel when you don your mask. Check the adjustment of the snorkel when your mask is in place.

Stabilize yourself when donning fins so you don't lose your balance and fall. Hold on to your buddy or to an object for support, or sit at the water's edge. Hold the side of a fin, bend one leg into a "figure 4" position, push the fin onto your foot, and pull the strap or heel pocket into place. Repeat the process for the other fin. Avoid walking with fins. If you must walk a few steps while wearing fins, shuffle your feet while walking backward. If you try to walk forward, you can lose your balance or damage your fins.

Inspecting Equipment

After you have donned your equipment, inspect it for completeness, correct positioning, and adjustment. When you are satisfied with your equipment, inspect your buddy's while he or she inspects yours. Inspect from head to toe. You may be able to see something that your buddy could not see, or vice versa. Develop the habit of inspecting each other's equipment before every dive.

SKIN DIVING SKILLS

There are three categories of skills for diving: skin diving skills, scuba diving skills, and problem management skills. This section introduces skin diving skills.

Skin Diving Hand Signals

You cannot talk with a snorkel in your mouth and your face in the water, so you use hand signals as a primary means of communication. You need to learn and use the standard hand signals shown in figure 5.6. You will learn additional hand signals for scuba diving. Display hand signals clearly and deliberately when you send them, and acknowledge all hand signals you receive.

Using a Skin Diving Vest

You inflated and deflated your skin diving vest as part of your diving preparations. You need to learn how to deflate and inflate the vest in the water. To deflate the vest, position your body so the exhaust port is the highest point. Hold the deflation valve open while you sink lower in the water. The water pressure helps force the air from the vest. You may have to hold the collar of the vest down with one hand to remove the air from that area. When you have vented all the air, close the valve. Get your buddy to confirm that all the air is out of your vest.

It is easier to inflate the vest in the water with your head underwater instead of above water. Take a breath of air, duck your face beneath the surface, insert the oral inflator into your mouth, open the valve, exhale into the vest, and close the valve. Repeat this process until you have the desired buoyancy.

If your vest has a CO_2 detonator and you choose to use it to quickly inflate the vest, grasp the activation cord and pull it downward firmly and then pull it from side to side. If your vest has CO_2 inside, avoid inhaling the gas, which is harmful to your lungs in strong concentrations. If you use a CO_2 cartridge to inflate your vest, remove and replace the cartridge at the first opportunity. It is unwise to leave an expended cartridge in the vest because rust particles inside the cartridge may damage your vest.

Testing Buoyancy

Your buoyancy should be neutral at the surface. If you are "light," you will have to struggle to descend and remain underwater. If you are "heavy," you will tire quickly at the surface and sink while swimming underwater. It is important to adjust your buoyancy so it is correct.

If you are wearing an exposure suit, you need weights to offset the buoyancy of the suit. With all equipment in place, position yourself in chest-deep water. Exhaust all air from your skin diving vest. Take a full breath, hold it, lift your feet from the bottom, and remain motionless while you slowly count to 10. If you sink, remove some weight and try again. If you exhale half your fully inflated lungs and still can't submerge, you need to add weight until you can. When your weighting is correct, you will remain at the surface while holding a full breath and will sink when exhaling. Adjust your weighting until your buoyancy is neutral.

▶ Figure 5.6 Skin diving hand signals.

1. Descend   2. Ascend   3. Stop

4. Okay a.   4. Okay b.   4. Okay c.

5. Something's not right   6. Emergency

Clearing the Mask

If you get water in your mask while skin diving, simply pull the bottom of your mask away from your face slightly when you are at the surface and let the water run out. You will learn how to clear water from a mask underwater when you learn to use scuba equipment.

Using the Snorkel

Stand in the water and lean forward with the snorkel in your mouth. Place your face in the water and inhale gently. If you inhale forcefully at first, you may inhale water. When you are sure the tube is clear, you may breathe more forcefully through your snorkel. When you descend beneath the surface, the snorkel tube may fill with water. As described in chapter 4, self-draining snorkels will drain nearly all the water from the tube when you surface.

If your snorkel is not the self-draining type, you will have to blast the water from the tube with a strong, sharp exhalation. To do this, blow hard into the snorkel to force the water out. Inhale cautiously after exhaling. If a little water remains in the tube, you can breathe past it if you inhale gently. After you fill your lungs again, expel the remaining water with another forceful exhalation.

If you have a simple snorkel without valves, you can clear the tube while ascending by using the displacement method. Begin by looking up to invert the snorkel; then exhale a small amount of air into the tube. As you ascend, the air expands according to Boyle's law and displaces the water in the tube, which will be clear of water when you reach the surface. The tube is inverted at this point, however, so when you turn it to an upright position, water will flow into the tube unless you exhale while rolling your head forward at the surface. Continuous exhalation prevents water from entering the tube. When you use the displacement method, which is easier than the blast method, you may take a breath the moment you reach the surface. Figure 5.7 shows the displacement method.

Learn to keep the snorkel in your mouth when you are in the water. Avoid the temptation to remove the mouthpiece and shake the water from your snorkel. You do not have to remove the

▶ Figure 5.7 Displacement method of clearing a snorkel.

a

b

mouthpiece when you can clear your snorkel proficiently. When your hands are occupied, you will not be able to remove and replace the snorkel to clear it.

Using Fins

Fins provide large surfaces that you can push against the water for propulsion. The strong muscles of your legs can push the fins against the resistance of the water. The blades of the fins need to push the water the way a broom sweeps a floor. A broom will not sweep if you move it up and down, and your fins will not provide propulsion if you move them lengthwise in the water. You must kick them back and forth in wide, sweeping kicks. Small fins allow short, quick kicks, but larger fins require wider, slower kicks. Moving efficiently, not speedily, is your objective when wearing fins.

▶ Figure 5.8　Flutter kick.

The most common fin kick is the **flutter kick**, which is an up-and-down kick that you can do facing down, up, or to the side. Your fins need to be underwater to provide propulsion. It is easier to keep your fins submerged at the surface when you are on your back or on your side instead of your stomach. Move your legs up and down from the hip while bending your knees only slightly. Extend your legs almost fully throughout each stroke and use wide, slow kicks. Keep your hands at your sides or extend them in front. Do not use your hands and arms to swim. Figure 5.8 shows the flutter kick.

The **scissors kick**, shown in figure 5.9, is a resting kick that is similar to a flutter kick. While lying on your side, slowly extend one leg (either leg) backward while you extend the other leg forward, then pull your legs together quickly. Hold a streamlined position with your toes pointed while you glide through the water. When you come to a stop, repeat the stroke. Extend your legs almost fully throughout the stroke.

▶ Figure 5.9　Scissors kick.

A **modified frog kick** is useful because it uses different muscles from the flutter or scissors kicks. Changing kicks is helpful if you become tired or develop leg cramps. The modified frog kick is different from a swimmer's frog kick. Assume a facedown position with your fins perpendicular to the bottom, rotate your ankles and point the tips of the fins outward, slide the fins tip first in an outward direction, and then pull the bottoms of the fins together quickly in a wide, sweeping arc. Extend your legs almost fully throughout the stroke, hold the final position with your feet together, point your toes, and glide (see figure 5.10). When you come to a stop, repeat the stroke.

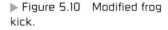

▶ Figure 5.10　Modified frog kick.

The **dolphin kick** is also useful for a change of pace. Hold both feet together continuously. Exert force against

▶ Figure 5.11   Dolphin kick.

the water with a wavelike up-and-down motion of your body. To begin, straighten your body, extend your fins with your legs together, bend your shoulders forward, and pull your feet slightly backward. Next, lift your shoulders, thrust forward forcefully with your hips, and then pull down with your fins. When you see this kick demonstrated, you will be able to learn it by imitation. If you lose a fin, you can use the dolphin kick to propel yourself. Cross your legs and put the leg without a fin behind the one that has a fin. Figure 5.11 shows what the dolphin kick looks like.

Surface Dives

You need to be able to dive down to see the beautiful world beneath the surface. The initiation of a skin dive beneath the surface is a surface dive. The principle of a surface dive is simple: you raise part of your body above the water and point yourself straight down; the weight you have above the water drives you downward. Once you are submerged, you start swimming to continue your descent.

There are several types of surface dives: pike, tuck, and feet-first (see figure 5.12). You do the pike dive while moving forward at the surface. Bend forward at the waist and make the trunk of your body vertical in the water. Next, quickly lift your legs out of the water to a vertical position. The more of your legs you can lift out of the water, the farther your surface dive will push you under the water. For shallow dives, you can do the pike dive by lifting only one leg.

When you have learned the pike dive, you will be ready for the tuck dive, which is similar. Do the tuck dive from a stationary position. Begin in an upright position in the water, pull your knees to your chest, and sweep backward with your arms to roll yourself forward in the water. When you are inverted, extend yourself fully into a vertical position. The procedure is a coordinated movement you must do quickly to get your legs above water. When you get your legs extended, the remainder of the dive is the same as the pike dive.

Use a feet-first dive in areas where surface plant growth is dense because you are less likely to get entangled. Begin in a stationary, upright position and use a strong scissors kick to propel yourself up and out of the water as far as possible. Pull your arms downward to your sides for added lift. When you reach the highest point, point your toes downward and hold your arms to your sides. The weight of your body will push you below the surface. When your downward momentum ends, do a tuck dive to invert yourself, then continue your descent.

Descents, Underwater Swimming, and Ascents

To prepare to descend, vent all air from your flotation device. Pre-equalize your ears using an ear-clearing maneuver at the surface so that it will be easy to clear them while you descend. Hyperventilate three times, inhale as fully as possible, and don't exhale until you return to the surface.

Initiate your descent with a good surface dive. Equalize the pressure in your ears and mask every couple of feet during your descent. Use wide, slow, powerful kicks to propel yourself to your desired depth, and then relax as much as possible.

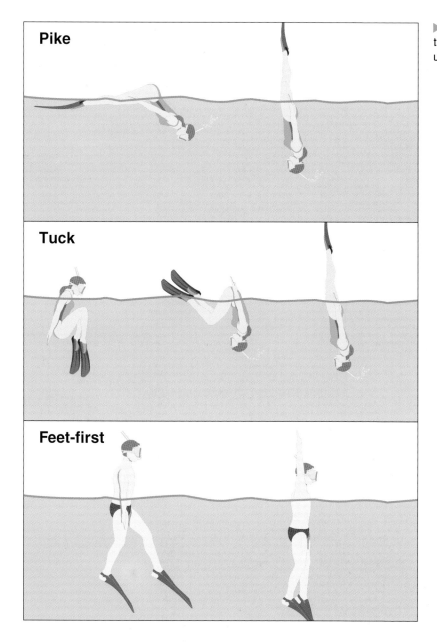

Pike

Tuck

Feet-first

▶ Figure 5.12   You can use a pike dive, tuck dive, or feet-first dive to descend underwater.

Swimming underwater sounds simple, but some people have trouble controlling direction. Your head is your rudder. Pull your head backward while swimming face down and you will go up. Bend your head forward and you will go down. Bend your trunk to the left or right to turn. With practice, you can go in any direction you choose without using your hands.

The three rules for ascents are to reach up, look up, and come up slowly. Extend one arm over your head for protection and look up to avoid obstructions and determine when the surface is near. A slow ascent is better than a rapid ascent because swimming rapidly uses more oxygen. Make one or two revolutions during your ascent to check your surroundings. Figure 5.13 shows a skin diver ascending.

Alternate breath-hold dives with your buddy. Make sure your buddy knows where you are at all times.

Handling Equipment

Occasionally you may need to remove, adjust, and replace skin diving equipment while you are in the water. You should be able to handle your equipment easily with training and practice.

To remove, adjust, and replace your mask, begin by inflating your skin diving vest. Because you will make the adjustment above water, use buoyancy to reduce the effort. After you make the adjustment, replace your mask using the four-step procedure for donning the mask described earlier in this chapter.

You may need to adjust a fin strap or remove sand or gravel from your fins while diving. The fins are easier to remove, adjust, and replace than the mask is. You do not need as much buoyancy to work with your fins because you can look into the water and make the adjustment underwater. In fact, too much air in your skin diving vest can be a nuisance. Keep your face in the water, breathe through your snorkel, and work with one fin at a time.

You may need to tighten, adjust, or replace your weight belt. The weights may slip or the belt may fall off. To tighten or replace your weight belt, you need to get the belt across the small of your back while you are in a facedown position breathing through your snorkel. If you try to replace or tighten the belt in an upright position, you will have a constant fight with gravity. When you are in the correct, facedown position, gravity becomes your ally while you secure the buckle. To get the belt into position across your back, begin in an upright position while holding the free end of the weight belt against the outside of your right thigh. Lean back into a horizontal, faceup position momentarily, then roll to your left to a facedown position while continuing to hold the free end of the belt against your right thigh. At this point, the belt will be draped across the backs of your thighs. Clear your snorkel so you can breathe. While holding the free end of the belt in your right hand, reach down with your left hand, grab the buckle end, and pull the belt into position across your back.

Removing Equipment

Your equipment helps you adapt to the underwater environment. Develop the habit of keeping it in place while in the water. You may need to defog your mask or make an adjustment, but other than that you should wear your equipment continuously. Avoid the tendency to prop your mask on your forehead when you are at the surface. Mask propping is a sign of distress and a good way to lose your mask and snorkel. If you must remove your mask while in the water, pull it down around your neck where it will be secure.

The removal of fins varies with bottom conditions at dive sites. In some areas, you may remove your fins in waist-deep water and wade out of the water. In other areas, you need to wear your fins until you are clear of the water. There are several ways to remove fins. When you prepare to climb a boat ladder, hold the ladder continuously while using the "figure 4" position to remove each fin. If the boat has a platform at the rear, swim onto the swim step and remove your fins while in a kneeling position. When you remove fins in waist-deep water or on land, use your buddy for support. On steep beaches, you may

▶ Figure 5.13 Extend your arm for protection when ascending.

choose to crawl from the water. Your buddy can remove your fins while you are on your hands and knees. Your buddy then crawls ahead of you, and you remove your buddy's fins. When you stand up, you exchange fins.

Weight belt removal also varies. When you can walk or climb out of the water, wear your belt. When you remove a weight belt, lower it gently instead of dropping it. You may cause damage or injury if you develop the habit of dropping your weight belt. If you must pull yourself onto a dock or into a small boat, remove your belt first and hand it up.

Keep your skin diving vest in place until you are clear of the water. Remove your skin diving vest, then your wet suit. Remove your wet suit by turning it inside out. Be sure to remove your boots before your wet suit pants. You will need assistance from your buddy for a pullover jacket or a jumpsuit.

PREPARING TO SCUBA DIVE

Nearly all the skills of skin diving are embodied in scuba diving, but you'll need to learn many additional skills for scuba diving. In this section, you are introduced to the preparatory skills of scuba diving; the next section covers basic and postdive skills. The more familiar you become with the skills by studying them, the better you will be able to develop them when you do them. Learn skills correctly from the outset so you develop correct habits for your diving safety.

Packing Equipment

It is inconvenient to get ready to dive and discover that something is missing or not right. You can (and should) take steps to prevent equipment inconveniences. Begin by using a checklist when you pack your diving equipment so you will be sure you have everything you need (see the diving equipment checklist in the appendix). After taking inventory, inspect your equipment as you pack it. If you have not used your equipment for a while, assemble it and test it first. Make sure everything works properly.

Pack your equipment in your gear bag except for your weight belt, tank, and BC. When you carry your equipment, put your BC on your tank, and carry the tank on your back, your gear bag in one hand, and your weight belt in the other hand (see figure 5.14). Equipment-carrying devices can reduce the work of moving your diving equipment.

Assembling Equipment

Today's backpacks are part of the BC and have one or more bands to secure the scuba cylinder. Many of the bands are made of webbing, which stretches when wet. Soak a fabric tank band in water for a couple of minutes before securing it around a scuba tank. The soaking softens the webbing and allows it to stretch when you tighten the band. A dry fabric belt may allow the tank to slip when the band gets wet and stretches. A tank that slips from a pack can be a hazard.

Orient your backpack with the opening of the tank valve facing the backpack. Stand the tank up with the valve handle facing to your right.

▶ Figure 5.14 Proper way to carry equipment.

Slide the tank band over the tank with the tank between you and the pack. Tighten the band so the valve opening points directly toward the pack.

The height of the tank band on the tank varies with the type of backpack. Generally the top of the pack will be even with the base of the tank valve. After you attach the pack and before you attach the regulator, don the scuba tank and check the height adjustment by slowly tilting your head backward. If your head hits the tank valve, the tank is too high in the pack. Reach over your shoulder for the tank valve. If you cannot touch it, the tank is too low in the pack. Adjust the height as needed. When you become familiar with the correct height adjustment, you will not need to test it before completing the assembly of the scuba unit, but you should check it before entering the water.

Tighten the band as much as possible before securing it and test the tightness by grasping the tank valve with one hand and the top of the pack with the other hand. Try to move the pack up and down on the tank. If there is movement, the band needs to be tighter.

Attach the regulator assembly to the scuba tank. The tank valve should have a valve protector or a piece of tape over the valve opening. Remove the cover or tape (put the tape in a trash container or in your gear bag). Loosen the regulator yoke screw, and remove the dust cover. If your regulator second stages have purge depressors, release the purges. Expel any water or dirt from the valve by opening the tank valve slightly and momentarily before you attach the regulator to the tank.

Your regulator has several hoses. Orient your primary second stage hose toward the same side of the tank as the handle of the tank valve so that the hose will come over your right shoulder. When you orient the hose this way, the other hoses orient automatically as long as they are untangled and can hang freely.

Carefully seat the inlet opening on the regulator on the valve outlet and turn the yoke screw or DIN fitting until it is snug but not tight. Tighten the fittings with your fingers and thumb. (See figure 5.15 for an example of regulator attachment.)

Attach various regulator hoses to the scuba unit. It is easier to attach the low-pressure hose to the BC before you pressurize the hose. Attach your instrument console to the BC, but do not attach your extra second stage yet.

Turn on the air. Hold the SPG with the front facing away from you and others so it will not cause an injury if it fails when pressurized. The SPG blowout plug should prevent an explosion from occurring, but holding the gauge is a good precaution. Open the tank valve slowly in a counterclockwise direction. Open the valve all the way; then close it one-quarter turn. You will feel the hoses stiffen under pressure. Listen for leaks in the system. If the regulator free-flows, cover the mouthpiece opening with your thumb to stop the flow. If air leaks from the tank valve seal, turn the air off, remove the regulator, and inspect the seal. You may have to replace the O-ring. Solve all air leakage problems before you use the scuba unit.

▶ Figure 5.15 Your regulator and hoses should look this way if attached correctly to the cylinder.

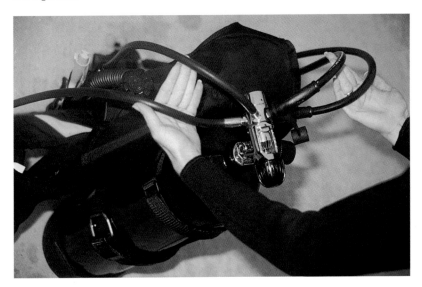

Scuba Wise

People are creatures of habit, and habits are the result of repetitive actions. If you repeat an action correctly enough times, you form a good habit. On the other hand, if you repeat an action incorrectly enough times, the habit created will be bad. Divers need good habits to avoid accidents, but sometimes they fail to take the time to develop the habits. I watch divers on charter boats and at dive sites when they prepare to dive and notice that they fail to inspect their equipment adequately, plan their dive properly, or follow many of the practices outlined in this chapter. Usu-ally they know what to do, but because they have physically bypassed many steps every time they go diving, they have a habit of skipping important items. How safe is a pilot if he or she ignores the preflight checklist? Taking the correct action requires concentration initially, but when repeated until the action becomes a habit, the process becomes automatic. We can make complex processes simple when we repeat them. I strongly encourage you to take the time to form good diving habits. If you will, I assure you that the odds of being injured are extremely small.

Testing the unit is the final step. Use your SPG to make sure the tank is full. Reset instruments in your console as needed. While looking at the SPG, depress the regulator purges momentarily to test the second stages and clear them of any debris; then breathe deeply through each second stage several times. The tank pressure reading should remain constant while you breathe from the regulator. If the pressure reading drops when you inhale, you have not opened the tank valve sufficiently. Do not open a valve partially to check the pressure of a tank. When you have finished testing the regulators, attach the extra second stage to the BC. Depress the low-pressure inflation valve on the BC for one or two seconds to make sure the valve functions correctly. When you have completed the assembly and testing of the unit, lay it on its side with the regulator and instruments on top.

Equipment assembly procedures are the same for both new and experienced divers. Always assemble and test your scuba equipment before you suit up. Practice will help you recall the assembly procedures.

Donning Equipment

With skin diving equipment, you don the weight belt after the skin diving vest, but with a jacket-type BC, you should don the weight belt before the scuba unit.

A good way to don a scuba unit out of the water is for your buddy to hold the system and help you into it. Once your arms are through the shoulder straps, bend forward and balance the unit on your back while you secure the waistband. Place the regulator hoses over your shoulders while you fasten the waistband so the hoses will not be trapped beneath the waistband. Some dive boats have vertical tank racks on seats to allow you to sit while donning the system. Do not sit on the deck or ground to don a scuba tank, however, because the tanks of other scuba divers may strike you in the head.

Some divers prefer to don the scuba unit in the water—a good practice if you dive from a small boat or have a minor back problem. Put the scuba unit into the water first. To don a jacket-BC unit the way you would don a coat in the water, inflate it fully, sit on it, put your arms through the arm holes, and slide off and into the unit. Or you may don your scuba unit over your head. Maneuver the tank in front of you with the valve facing you and the backpack facing up. Place the regulator in your mouth and keep the primary second stage hose between your arms. (If you place your right arm inside the loop of the hose, it will wrap around your arm when you try to lift the tank over your head.) Place your forearms completely through the armholes just past your elbows, and begin to lift the scuba unit over your head. Rather than lifting the unit, push yourself down in the water and duck beneath the scuba unit. Lower the tank into position on your back. Use your left hand to pull your snorkel clear of your BC as the tank lowers into position. When the tank is in place, lean forward and secure the waistband.

BAG Method of Inspecting Equipment

Buoyancy (B)

- [ ] The weight system is in place.
- [ ] The quick release is accessible.
- [ ] The weights are free to drop.
- [ ] The weight belt has a right-hand release.
- [ ] You know how to operate the weight system release.
- [ ] The BC is operational.
- [ ] The low-pressure inflator functions.
- [ ] The deflator valve functions.
- [ ] The CO_2 mechanism (if there is one) functions.*

Air supply (A)

- [ ] The tank is full, and the tank valve is open all but one-quarter turn.
- [ ] All regulator hoses are oriented correctly and free for use.
- [ ] The primary and secondary second stages function.
- [ ] The alternate air source is secured in such a way that it will not free-flow, and you can locate it easily.

General (G)

- [ ] Your buddy's equipment is complete.
- [ ] The equipment is correct from head to toe.
- [ ] Remember that you can see things your buddy cannot see.

* To inspect the CO_2 mechanism, unscrew the cartridge and examine it to ensure that it has not been used. While the cartridge is removed, examine the firing pin to make sure it moves freely when you operate the firing arm. Return the firing arm to the unfired position, and replace the cartridge.

Inspecting Equipment

When you have donned your scuba equipment and the remainder of your diving equipment, inspect all your equipment to make sure it is positioned, adjusted, and functioning correctly. Your buddy should do likewise. Then inspect each other's equipment.

The three areas of equipment inspection are buoyancy, air supply, and general. The acronym "BAG," which uses the first letter from each area, is a handy memory jogger. Specific checks for each area are listed in the sidebar titled "BAG Method of Inspecting Equipment."

Equipment inspections are important. Solving problems is easier before you enter the water than afterward. It does not take much time to inspect each other's equipment, but the practice can save a lot of time. Make predive inspections a habit.

BASIC SCUBA DIVING SKILLS

To be a scuba diver (and enjoy diving with minimum risk of injury), you need to learn the proper procedures for entering and exiting the water, controlling your buoyancy, descending and ascending, monitoring your instruments, and coordinating with a buddy. This section provides a helpful introduction to these skills, but you must learn them by doing. You will learn the skills in pool-like conditions and then apply them in open water.

Entry Techniques

The four basic types of water entries for divers are wading, seated, feet-first, and backroll. You need to learn when to use which type and the procedures for each. The objective of any entry is to get into the water the easiest way possible without injuring yourself or losing any equipment. After you enter the water and are under control, switch from your regulator to your snorkel if you are going to swim or remain at the surface.

You can make open-water entries from the shore or from a boat. Shore entries may be wading entries, or you may enter from an artificial structure such as a dock, pier, or jetty. There may be surf. Bottom conditions can range from smooth and soft to rough and firm. The bottom may slope gradually or steeply, and there may be holes and drop-offs. There may be plants, animals, and rocks in the entry area. The conditions vary greatly, and so do the entry techniques. A good entry technique for one location will be inappropriate for another. It takes experience and knowledge of the area to determine an effective entry procedure.

Some general techniques are good to keep in mind when making wading entries at an open-water site. A wading entry sounds simple, but keep in mind that diving equipment affects your center of gravity, your mobility, and your peripheral vision. You must walk backward when wearing fins.

If there is little or no surf, you may be able to wade in, don your fins, and begin your dive. Breathe through your regulator and have your BC inflated partially. Shuffle your feet to detect holes and rocks and to chase away bottom-dwelling creatures. When the water reaches your thighs, lie down in the water and start swimming (see figure 5.16). In some areas with muddy bottoms, do not wade because you can sink deeply into the mud and lose a fin when you try to extract your foot. When the bottom is firm and the water is calm, you can wade into the water without your fins and don them in the water. It is helpful to have information about the bottom conditions of a dive site.

In most areas where there is surf, don your fins before you enter the water and do not remove them until you are clear of the water after the dive. Time your entry to coincide with small waves. (See wave sets in chapter 7.) Keep all equipment in place and breathe through your regulator. Deflate your BC because you want to duck beneath breaking waves when they are higher than your waist. If you inflate your BC, you will be unable to duck beneath the waves and a large wave could lift and toss you. Hold your mask with one hand at all times; spread your fingers and curl them over the top of the mask so you can see. Keep your knees bent and shuffle sideways into the waves to minimize your profile to the moving water. Stop moving just before a wave hits you, allow the wave to pass, then resume your shuffling until the water is deep enough to swim. Allow incoming waves to pass over you, and move through the surf zone quickly.

▶ Figure 5.16 Wading in.

To enter the water from a commercial dive boat, you can enter from the side or from a water-level platform at the back of the boat. Have all equipment in place, breathe from your regulator, and hold your mask securely. Have any specialty items, such as a camera, handed to you after you are in the water or retrieve them from an equipment line. When entering from the side of a boat, note the direction of boat movement. Wind will cause an anchored boat to swing from side to side. If you enter the water on the side of the boat when the boat is moving in that direction, the boat may pass over you after you enter.

You can do a controlled-seated entry from a dock, swimming platform on a boat, or any surface where you can sit close to the water, which may be only a few feet deep or too deep to stand in. With all equipment in place, turn and place both hands on one side of yourself on the surface on which you are seated, lift yourself slightly, move your body out over the water, and lower yourself into the water. A controlled-seated entry is a simple, easy, controlled entry. See figure 5.17.

Use feet-first entries when the distance to the water is too high for a seated entry, such as when entering from a commercial charter boat. There are two types of feet-first entries: giant stride and feet-together.

Use the giant stride entry, shown in figure 5.18, when the distance to the water is about 3 to 5 ft (0.9 to 1.5 m) and you want to remain at the surface during the entry. Stand at the entry point with your equipment in place and your BC partially inflated. Observe the point of entry and make sure the area is clear. Hold your mask firmly with one hand, spreading your fingers so you can see. Look straight ahead while stepping out with one leg. The

▶ Figure 5.17 Entry from a seated position.

entry is a step, not a hop or a jump. If you step out as far as you can, your trailing leg follows automatically. Keep one leg extended forward and the other leg extended backward until you hit the water; then pull your legs together quickly to stop your downward momentum. As soon as you stabilize at the surface, turn and signal that you are "Okay," and then move away from the entry point so the next diver may enter.

Use the feet-together entry when the distance to the water is too high for a giant stride entry and when you are concerned about discomfort from the impact with the water. The

▶ Figure 5.18 Giant stride.

procedures are the same as for the giant stride entry except that after you step out from the entry point, you bring your legs together before you hit the water. A feet-together entry submerges you. After you bob back to the surface and stabilize, signal the next diver and clear the entry area. See figure 5.19.

A seated backroll entry can be done from either a seated or a squatting position. This entry is shown in figure 5.20. Use the seated backroll entry from a low, unstable platform, such as a small boat. Use a backroll entry when the distance to the water is too high for a seated entry and the platform is too unstable for you to stand. To do a seated backroll, sit with all equipment in place and your back to the water. Move your bottom to the very edge of the surface on which you are sitting. Have someone make sure the entry area is clear. Hold your mask with one hand and your mask strap with the other hand. If you do not hold the mask strap, the force of the water may wash it up over your head and your mask may fall off. Lean backward to begin the entry. Hold your knees to your chest as you roll backward to avoid clipping your heels on the edge of the seat surface. You are likely to do a backward, disorienting somersault in the water with this entry. You can reorient yourself when you bob back to the surface.

A squatting backroll is used when there is no suitable surface on which to sit. The thin side of a small, rocking boat is a good example of an unsuitable seat. For a squatting backroll entry, prepare yourself while sitting on an adequate seat immediately adjacent to the entry area. Make sure the entry area is clear, then stand partially, turn your back to the entry area, and literally sit down into the water. Pull you knees to your chest as you enter so you do not catch your heels. See figure 5.21.

Surface Snorkeling With Scuba Equipment

You'll want to use your snorkel for surface swimming so you can conserve the air in your tank. When snorkeling while wearing scuba equipment, inflate your BC partially. If you put too much air into your BC, the weight of the scuba tank will roll you sideways if you are swimming facedown. You can also swim on your back or side; these positions allow your kick to be wider than when swimming facedown, and the tank weight will not be a factor. If you swim on your back, you can breathe without the snorkel. Swim alongside—not behind—your buddy. Move slowly and steadily, pacing yourself. Rest if you feel short of breath and before beginning your descent.

▶ Figure 5.19 Feet together entry.

Recovering and Clearing the Regulator

When you are in the water wearing scuba equipment, you need to recover your regulator second stage from behind your right shoulder when you get ready to use it. The second stage will have water inside, and you must clear the water before you breathe. If you start with the regulator in your mouth, you need to place the regulator in the water. The task is more difficult than it sounds because if you place the second stage in the water with the mouthpiece facing up, the regulator free-flows. Place the second stage in the water with the mouthpiece facing downward to prevent free-flow.

▶ Figure 5.20 Seated backroll.

▶ Figure 5.21 Squatting backroll.

There are two ways to recover the regulator second stage from behind your shoulder. The most popular technique is the sweep method. Lean to the right side so gravity swings the second stage away from you. Reach back with your right hand until you touch the bottom of your scuba tank, and then extend your arm and sweep it forward in a large arc. The hose will lie across your arm, where you can retrieve the second stage easily.

The second method of recovering the second stage is the over-the-shoulder reach. Reach back toward your regulator first stage with your right hand while lifting the bottom of your scuba tank with your left hand. Grasp the second stage hose where it attaches to the first stage and follow it down to the second stage end. Some divers find this recovery method difficult or impossible.

Clearing the regulator can be as simple as exhaling into it. As long as the exhaust valve is at the lowest point, the water inside the second stage will be displaced. If the exhaust valve is not at the lowest point when you exhale, only part of the water may be exhausted, and you may inspire some water when you inhale. To avoid choking on inhaled water, find out where the exhaust valve is on your regulator, be sure to make it the lowest point when you clear your regulator, and inhale cautiously after clearing the regulator.

Another method to clear a regulator second stage—the purge method—uses low-pressure air to clear the water from the chamber. If you insert the mouthpiece into your mouth and depress the purge, you may blow water down your throat. There are two ways to prevent getting water in your throat. One way is to depress the purge lightly as you place the bubbling regulator in your mouth, and use back pressure from your lungs to keep water out of your mouth and throat. The other method is to place the regulator into your mouth, block the opening with your tongue, and depress the purge momentarily to clear the chamber. Either method is acceptable. If you are purging the regulator while placing it in your mouth, release the purge the moment the regulator is in place to avoid overinflating your lungs.

Snorkel-Regulator Exchanges

You need to be able to switch from breathing from your snorkel to breathing from your regulator and vice versa. When you prepare to descend for diving, you exchange your snorkel for your regulator; when you surface after a dive, you exchange your regulator for your snorkel. Do both exchanges with your face in the water. Take a breath, exchange one mouthpiece for the other, and clear the new breathing device.

BC Inflation and Deflation

You should be familiar with the three ways to inflate a BC and the two ways to deflate one.

The easiest and most common means of inflation is the low-pressure inflator, which adds air to the BC in short bursts. Inflating the BC for several seconds can cause serious buoyancy control problems if the inflator valve sticks. By adding air a little at a time, you will have better control of your buoyancy.

If your low-pressure inflator or your integrated second stage develops a problem while you are diving, you may need to disconnect the low-pressure hose. When you disconnect the hose, the low-pressure inflator no longer functions, so you will have to control buoyancy by orally inflating the BC. The mouthpiece of a buoyancy compensator usually is more elaborate than the mouthpiece of a skin diving vest. To help exclude water from a BC, the mouthpiece has a purge so the water inside may be cleared before you open the valve to the BC. To clear the BC mouthpiece and inflate the BC, follow these procedures:

1. Insert the mouthpiece into your mouth.
2. Exhale a small amount of air into the mouthpiece to clear it.
3. Keep the mouthpiece in your mouth.
4. Depress the manual inflator-deflator valve.
5. Exhale into the BC.
6. Repeat the procedure until you achieve the desired amount of buoyancy.

You may use the same bobbing technique at the surface that you learned for the skin diving vest (see page 97), but oral inflation procedures are different underwater. To inflate a BC orally underwater, follow these steps:

1. Grasp the inflation valve with your left hand and your regulator second stage with your right hand.
2. Take a breath.
3. Insert the BC mouthpiece into your mouth.
4. Clear the mouthpiece.
5. Exhale most of the air in your lungs into the BC.
6. Save enough air to clear the regulator, which fills with water when you remove it from your mouth.
7. Repeat the procedure until you achieve the desired amount of buoyancy.

The third method of BC inflation is with a CO_2 detonator, an optional feature many diving professionals consider neither necessary nor desirable. If you choose to equip your BC with this option, take care of the mechanism and know how to operate it.

You can deflate your BC with the manual inflator-deflator valve or with a dump valve. If you do not use a dump valve, you must open the deflator valve at the lower end of the BC hose and hold it higher than the highest point of the BC. A dump valve is more convenient than the deflator valve. Note that you can deflate your BC only when the exhaust port is the highest point. Air will not escape if you try to deflate a BC in a horizontal or inverted position, so you need to be in an upright position to deflate your BC.

Buoyancy Testing

There are similarities between buoyancy testing for skin diving and buoyancy testing for scuba diving, but there also are some important differences. Buoyancy varies more when you're scuba diving than when you're skin diving, and the volume of air in your lungs varies more when scuba diving. You dive deeper, so suit compression affects your buoyancy more. As you use air from your scuba tank, your buoyancy changes. You need to sense buoyancy changes quickly to maintain control of your buoyancy.

Your initial buoyancy test for scuba diving can be the same as your buoyancy test for skin diving. Begin by testing your BC at the surface. Inflate it fully, then deflate it. Make sure the low-pressure inflator and all deflation valves function correctly. With your regulator in your mouth and your BC completely deflated, relax and breathe slowly. When your lung volume is high, you should remain at the surface with your eyes just below the interface. If you sink with your lungs full of air, you need to remove some weight. When you exhale completely, you should sink. If you cannot sink after a complete exhalation,

diver's push-ups—Buoyancy evaluation where, when weighted properly, a full inhalation will raise the shoulders while the fin tips remain on the bottom and an exhalation will cause the shoulders to sink

you need additional weight. Test your buoyancy while you are close to your point of entry and correct any buoyancy problems before you attempt to dive.

As you descend in open water, you may need to add air to your BC to maintain neutral buoyancy. Strive to maintain a neutral state of buoyancy continuously. Add air to your BC in small amounts, and test your buoyancy by stopping all motion and observing what happens. If you are sinking, inhale and add air to your BC. If you are rising in the water, exhale and release air from your BC. With experience you will know when to add air to or vent air from your BC and how much air to add or release.

To evaluate your state of buoyancy on the bottom, assume a rigid, facedown position with your arms at your sides. If your buoyancy is correct, a slow, full inhalation will raise your shoulders while your fin tips remain on the bottom, and a slow, complete exhalation will cause your shoulders to sink. Some people call this buoyancy evaluation **diver's push-ups** (although you do not use your hands). If you do not rise with a full inhalation, add a small amount of air to your BC and try again. Figure 5.22 shows a diver doing diver's push-ups.

As a scuba diver, you want enough weight to get down at the beginning of a dive and enough weight to allow you to remain in control when you ascend at the end of the dive. The precise weight for scuba diving is the amount you need to hover at a depth of 15 ft (4.6 m) with 300 psi (20 ATM) of air in your tank and no air in your BC. The amount may overweight you slightly at the beginning of a dive. Test your buoyancy at a depth of 15 ft (4.6 m) at the end of a dive to see if you need to make an adjustment for your next dive.

Controlling Buoyancy

No skill identifies a scuba diver's ability as much as buoyancy control. The ability to finely control buoyancy is important for safety, for enjoyment, and for the welfare of the environment. When your buoyancy is out of control, a hazard exists for both you and the environment around you.

With your buoyancy adjusted to the point at which you can pivot on your fins on the bottom while inhaling and exhaling, push yourself about 2 ft (0.6 m) off the bottom and remain motionless. You may or may not remain in a horizontal position, but that is not important. Maintain your depth by controlling your average lung volume, but remember to breathe continuously. If you are sinking, keep more air in your lungs. If you begin rising, reduce the amount of air in your lungs. With practice, you will be able to hover motionless just off the bottom.

To demonstrate mastery of hovering, assume a vertical position in the water. Cross your legs at the ankles, grasp a wrist with the opposite hand, and remain motionless. Find an eye-level reference and develop the ability to hover motionless while upright in the water. Pay attention to the buoyancy effects of breathing. Once you master hovering in both horizontal and vertical

▶ Figure 5.22 Successfully performing diver's push-ups indicates good buoyancy control.

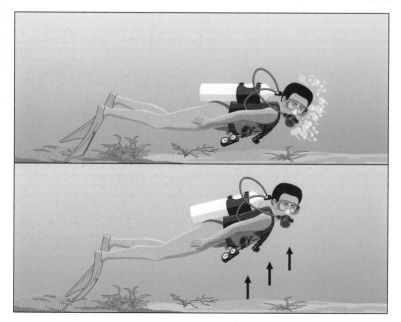

positions, you will realize several benefits. Your air will last longer, swimming will not tire you as much, you will need fewer buoyancy adjustments, and you will do less damage to the diving environment. Once you can hover, your buoyancy control will continue to improve with practice until you become a highly experienced diver.

Another useful skill for maintaining neutral buoyancy is a BC venting technique called an **open-valve ascent**. When you ascend, air in your BC expands and affects your buoyancy. You must release the expanding air to maintain control of buoyancy. If you vent the air from time to time, your buoyancy will be in a constant state of change: you may not release enough air, or you may release too much. The open-valve ascent is a better alternative. Hold the BC inflator-deflator valve just below the level of your shoulder, point the mouthpiece of the inflator-deflator valve downward, and open the deflator valve. Air will not escape because the opening is lower than the exhaust port on the BC. While you hold the mouthpiece downward and the deflation valve open, raise the inflator-deflator slowly until air just begins to bubble from the mouthpiece. Bubbling occurs when the mouthpiece and the exhaust port on the BC are at the same level. If you hold the inflator-deflator valve at the bubbling level while ascending, the expanding air inside the BC will bubble out through the open valve and your buoyancy will remain constant. If you need to release additional air to control buoyancy, raise the inflator-deflator slightly; if you need to decrease the amount of air you release, lower the assembly slightly.

Using the Dive Flag

You should display the appropriate dive flag or flags when diving. Some areas require you to use a flag, but authorities in all areas encourage use of a dive flag. Follow these conventions when you use a dive flag: display the flag only when divers are in the water, and surface within 100 ft (30 m) of your flag—the closer the better. The flag does not guarantee your safety from boaters, who are supposed to give the flag a berth of at least 100 ft (30 m), but it does serve as a signal to many boaters who recognize that the flag means there are divers in the vicinity. Figure 5.23 shows divers using a dive flag.

If you support your flag with a surface float, you will need to tow your float to the area where you dive. In areas lacking underwater plants, you may be able to tow the float while you dive. In areas with plants, you need to anchor the float to keep it from drifting away, and you must navigate back to the flag at the end of your dive. Tow a surface float behind you when entering through surf, and push it ahead of you when exiting through surf.

Descending

Scuba descents are different from skin diving descents. You will need to learn several procedures. You usually descend head-first as a skin diver, but scuba divers descend feet-first. A feet-first descent allows better control of buoyancy, provides better orientation, allows buddies to maintain contact during descent, helps prevent the swallowing of air, and allows easier equalization of air spaces.

open-valve ascent—A method for maintaining neutral buoyancy during an ascent by keeping the BC inflator-deflator valve open while holding the valve in a special way

▶ Figure 5.23 Surface as close as possible to a dive flag.

Descending involves several procedures, which seem complex at first but become a routine with practice. The process of descending includes preparing to descend, initiating the descent, and completing the descent.

1. Preparing to descend
   - Check your instruments. Orient yourself at the surface and set a reference on your compass. Be sure your underwater timer and depth gauge are zeroed.
   - Confirm that your buddy is ready to begin.
   - Exchange your snorkel for your regulator.
   - Pressurize your ears slightly to begin the equalization process.
   - Hold your BC deflator valve in your left hand.
   - Give or acknowledge the signal to descend.

2. Initiating the descent
   - Begin the descent by venting your BC. It is better to do this with the dump valve than by holding the deflator valve above your head. Hold the inflator-deflator valve in your left hand throughout the descent so you can add or release air from your BC at any time. Exhale fully to help get started downward.
   - Breathe shallowly for the first 10 ft (3 m).
   - Equalize your ears about every 2 ft (0.6 m) for the first 15 ft (4.6 m). If you experience equalizing problems, ascend a few feet to reduce the pressure, equalize again, and redescend. Exhale some air into your mask to prevent a mask squeeze.
   - Keep your fins still while you descend so you do not stir up silt on the bottom.
   - Control your rate of descent by the average amount of air you keep in your lungs. When you begin sinking while your lungs are full, add a short burst of air to your BC to regain neutral buoyancy.

3. Completing the descent
   - Remain with your buddy throughout the descent.
   - Avoid contact with the bottom.
   - Hover above the bottom, level off to a swimming position, agree on a direction with your buddy, and begin your dive.

Two types of descents in open water are the **contact descent** and the **noncontact descent**. A descent that you control by maintaining contact with a line or the slope of the bottom is a contact descent, which you should do whenever possible. A descent made vertically in water without any physical contact is a noncontact descent, which is more difficult to control than a contact descent.

Clearing the Mask

Above the surface, water inside a mask will run out if you pull the bottom of the mask away from your face. Water inside a mask underwater also flows out the bottom of the mask if you displace the water with air. It is easy to put air inside the mask—just exhale lightly through your nose. A long, light exhalation is better than a short, forceful one because a strong exhalation blows air past the seal of the mask and does not displace water effectively.

To clear a mask while scuba diving, you need to develop the skill of breathing through your mouth with your nose exposed to water. With concentration and practice, you can master this skill quickly. Try inhaling through your mouth and exhaling through your nose first, and then try inhaling and exhaling through your mouth. If you feel any water going up your nose, exhale immediately to keep the water out.

To clear a mask that has a purge valve, seal the mask against your face, tilt your head downward to make the purge the lowest point in the mask, and exhale through your nose until the mask is clear of water.

To clear a mask without a purge, hold the top of the mask against your forehead, take a breath, and start exhaling slowly. When the level of the water is below your eyes, tilt your head back while continuing to exhale and the remainder of the water will flow out the bottom of the mask. You must be exhaling when you tilt your head back or water will run up your nose. Bubbles from the bottom of the mask indicate when you have cleared all the water from your mask. It may sound like it takes a long time and a lot of air to clear a mask, but with practice you will be able to flood and clear your mask several times after a single inhalation. Clearing requires only a few seconds.

To practice clearing a mask, you will need to flood it with water. This is not difficult, but a few tips make it easier. If you will exhale lightly while tilting the mask forward on your face to break the seal at the top, the mask releases from your face easily, and the air escapes at the highest point. When you reseat your mask to begin clearing it, be sure to hold back any strands of hair with one hand while you reseat the mask with the other. Hair under the mask causes leakage. If you are wearing a hood, make sure that the hood is clear of the mask before attempting to clear water from the mask.

Buddy Diving

You should always dive with a companion, using the **buddy system**. A buddy provides reminders and assistance and sees things that you might not see. Buddies inspect each other's equipment, provide feedback based on observations, and work as a team. Dive buddies should remain close enough to each other that each can immediately assist the other in an emergency. The more turbid the water and the greater the depth, the closer buddies should remain to each other. During your training, you should strive to remain within touching distance of your buddy at all times; learn to keep track of your buddy. Maintaining contact with a dive buddy in open water is not difficult when you follow a few standard procedures.

Agree upon a position relative to each other and maintain that position as much as possible. That way, your buddy will know where to look for you, and you will know where to look for your buddy. The best dive team configuration is side by side; the least desirable is for one diver to be behind the other.

Agree on a direction of movement. Divers should maintain that direction until both agree to proceed in a different direction. When you follow this practice, there are fewer directions to consider when you and your buddy become separated.

Confirm your buddy's position every few seconds. If you scan the areas ahead from side to side while swimming, you should get a glimpse of your buddy each time you turn your head in the direction of your buddy.

When visibility is poor, physical contact can keep you and your buddy together. Holding hands is appropriate. Or you can use a short line—a **buddy line**—to keep in contact with each other.

If you become separated from your buddy underwater, look for your buddy for up to one minute. If you are unable to locate your buddy, ascend slightly and turn in a circle while looking for bubbles. The visibility often is better a few feet above the bottom than it is on the bottom. If you do not see your buddy's bubbles, ascend to the surface and wait for your buddy, who is supposed to duplicate your procedure. When you have reunited at the surface, descend again and continue your dive. Obviously it is better to remain together underwater than to surface to reunite.

If you are unable to relocate your buddy underwater, and if your buddy does not surface promptly, look at your surroundings to mark your position so you will know the approximate location where your buddy was last seen. If someone is overseeing the diving operations, notify the person that your buddy is missing so a search can be initiated. If you are alone, try to locate bubbles that could indicate your buddy's position.

Underwater Swimming

When you swim along the bottom, your fins can raise a cloud of silt that harms the environment and reduces visibility. Silting is more of a problem when you are overweighted because the excess weight angles your fins toward the bottom when you swim (see figure 5.24). The first step in reducing silt is to weight yourself properly. In areas where the bottom silt is thick, add air to your BC to make yourself slightly buoyant underwater. The buoyancy forces you to swim at a slight downward angle and keeps your fins' thrust directed upward. Another way to reduce silt is to remain far enough from the bottom to keep from disturbing it. Finally, consider changing your kick if you boil up silt with your kick strokes.

When you kick something while swimming, you must overcome the tendency to want to get away from whatever you kick. Your kicks are strong and can damage the environment or another diver. As soon as you feel something with a fin, stop kicking, look back to see what you have hit, and maneuver yourself clear before proceeding.

▶ Figure 5.24 Overweighting causes divers to stir up silt.

Navigation

To find your way underwater, you can use natural navigation and compass navigation. You can best determine your relative position with a combination of both types of navigation.

With natural navigation, you use natural surroundings to determine where you are. Light, shadows, plants, formations, water movement, depth, and other indicators can help you navigate. As you move, note your surroundings. Ask yourself which way you are going relative to the movement of the water, to sand ripples on the bottom, to the depth contour, and to the angle of the sun. By noting natural aids to navigation, you can find your way underwater.

A dive compass increases the accuracy of navigation. (See figure 5.25 for an example of a dive compass.) You need to be able to set a direction (called a **compass heading**) and determine which way you are going relative to the directional reference you have set. Your compass should have a reference line, called a lubber line, that you point in the direction of travel. The north-seeking needle or card of the compass establishes a position relative to the lubber line as long as you hold the compass in a level position. Many dive compasses have index marks on a movable bezel. You set the index marks to indicate the heading.

To go in the direction set on the compass, you must hold the compass so the lubber line is directly in line with the centerline of your body. If the lubber line points to one side, you will not be on course even though the north reference is at the correct point on the dial.

A **compass course** is a series of headings that leads to a destination. There are many types of compass courses. One frequently used course is the **square compass course** To navigate a square course, set your initial heading and proceed in that direction for a given distance, which may be measured by time, tank pressure, or fin kicks. Stop, turn 90 degrees to the right while continuing to keep the lubber line aligned with the centerline of your body. Note the relative position of north on the compass, and proceed in the new direction the same distance you did on the first leg of the course. Stop again, and turn another 90 degrees to the right. Note the position of north on the compass, which should be opposite your initial heading. Proceed along the third leg of the course the same distance as before. Stop once more, turn again 90 degrees to the right, note the relative position of north, and follow the new heading back to your starting point.

Divers also frequently follow a **reciprocal compass course**—an out-and-back course. Set the initial heading on the compass. Then at the midpoint of the dive, turn 180 degrees until north on the compass is directly opposite the original heading, and follow the reciprocal heading back to your starting point.

If you do not know precisely where you are when the end of a dive is near, it may be wise to surface, find a reference for your exit, and set a compass heading that leads directly to the end-of-dive location. Be especially careful if you surface more than 100 ft (30 m) from your dive flag.

A compass provides correct directional reference information when it is not affected by nearby objects. Metal objects, other compasses, and electrical fields within a couple of feet of a compass can cause the compass reading to deviate from its correct reading. Keep metal, magnets, dive lights, and other compasses away from your compass to help ensure accuracy.

Monitoring Your Instruments

Most diving instruments are passive; that is, they do not provide information unless you look at them. Some instruments emit an audible beep (one dive computer talks), but most require observation to provide information. Develop the habit of checking your instrumentation frequently while diving so you can control your depth, dive time, and

▶ Figure 5.25 A dive compass.

square compass course—A series of headings that allows the diver to travel in a square pattern so that the dive ends where it began

reciprocal compass course—A course where the diver moves in a given heading for a given distance and returns to the origination point by reversing the direction of travel

direction and avoid running out of air. You should be able to accurately estimate your tank pressure at any time during training. If you cannot estimate the pressure within 300 psi (20 ATM) at any time, you need to monitor SPG more frequently.

When you are planning to dive in open water, look at your instruments when you assemble your equipment. Look at your instruments again when you inspect your equipment, again before you descend, and again while you descend. Refer to your compass for directional reference before you begin moving underwater. Monitor your gauges every few minutes while diving, and compare your air pressure with your buddy's several times during a dive. At any given time during a dive, you should be able to estimate accurately your depth, your dive time, your direction, your tank pressure, and your buddy's tank pressure. If you cannot do this, you need to improve your instrument monitoring skills.

Scuba Diving Hand Signals

Scuba divers use several hand signals that are not used for skin diving. The scuba signals relate to air supply. Learn and use the standard hand signals described in figure 5.26. Remember to display hand signals clearly and deliberately and also to acknowledge them.

Normal Ascents

Scuba ascents are different from skin diving ascents, but there are a few similarities. The procedures you need to learn become automatic with practice and experience.

To initiate an ascent, one member of a buddy team gives the ascent signal, which the other acknowledges. Always obey the ascent signal. Prepare to ascend by noting your time, depth, and remaining air. Locate and hold your BC inflator-deflator assembly in your left hand. Begin the procedures for the open-valve ascent described on page 113.

Begin ascending slowly with your buddy while breathing continuously. Monitor your depth gauge and keep tabs on your buddy. The maximum rate of ascent is 0.5 ft/s (.15 m/s), which is quite slow. Some instruments warn you when your rate of ascent is too rapid. You need training, practice, and awareness to avoid exceeding the maximum rate of ascent.

Stop and decompress (outgas) for 1 to 3 minutes at a depth of 15 ft (4.6 m) to help prevent DCS. The procedures for decompression are described in chapter 6. As you ascend, look up and around. Extend one hand above your head for protection against overhead obstacles. Make one full rotation to view the surrounding area as you near the surface.

When you reach the surface, make another rotation to view the area, then inflate your BC to establish buoyancy. Exchange your regulator mouthpiece for your snorkel.

Handling Equipment

There will be situations when you need to remove, adjust, and replace scuba equipment while you are in the water. You may need to remove equipment to exit the water onto a boat, to make an adjustment, or to free the equipment from an entanglement. With training and practice, you should be able to handle your equipment easily.

▶ Figure 5.26   Scuba diving hand signals.

| 1. Low on air | 2. Out of air | 3. Give me air |

Removal of the scuba unit is easy because it is similar to removing a coat. Open the releases, slip your left arm free, swing the scuba tank forward under your right arm, hold the scuba unit with your left hand, and pull your right arm free. It is easier to free your left arm if you insert your hand and wrist through the arm hole of the BC first and remove it hand-first than it is to try to pull your arm through first. If you are at the surface in water too deep to stand when you want to remove your scuba unit, remove your weight belt first and place it on a surface float or support station. Replace the scuba unit in the water according to the in-water donning procedures presented on pages 105-106.

Exit Techniques

The technique you will use to exit the water depends on the situation. To exit from shallow water in a swimming pool, begin by removing your weight belt, tank, and fins (in that order). Carefully place the equipment on the side of the pool; then climb out by using the ladder or lifting yourself up onto the edge of the pool. See figure 5.27.

To exit from the deep end of a swimming pool, as shown in figure 5.28, begin with your BC inflated partially. If you exit on a ladder, grasp the ladder with one hand and remove your fins with the other; maintain contact with the ladder at all times. Place your fins on the edge of the pool or slide the heel straps over your wrists; then climb the ladder to exit the water. Clear the exit area at once, and take your fins with you.

To exit from deep water without a ladder, begin by carefully placing your weight belt out of the water. Remove the scuba unit and use one hand to trap the regulator hose against the surface onto which you will exit. Use your other hand to remove your fins and place the fins out of the water. Place both hands on the exit edge. With the regulator hose trapped under one hand, lower yourself to about chin level in the water while you extend one leg forward and one leg backward. Move upward and pull your legs together forcefully in a strong scissors kick to provide upward momentum. Pull with your arms until you are far enough out of the water to push downward and lift yourself from the water. See figure 5.29. Immediately after your exit, turn around and pull your scuba unit from the water carefully.

▶ Figure 5.27 Exiting from shallow water in a pool.

▶ Figure 5.28 Exiting from the deep end of a pool.

▶ Figure 5.29 Exiting from deep water without a ladder.

119

▶ Figure 5.30   Exiting onto a boat with a ladder.

▶ Figure 5.31   Surf exit.

If you are exiting onto a boat that has a ladder, keep your tank on and use the ladder exit technique. Maintain contact with the ladder at all times when you are in the water. If the boat has a platform at the rear, you usually swim onto the platform, remove your fins, and then stand on the platform and board the vessel (figure 5.30).

Techniques for wading exits in open water vary with the environment. Usually it is a good idea to wear all your equipment until you are clear of the water. Shuffle your feet along the bottom while moving backward.

Surf exits require training and practice. Stop outside the breaking waves and evaluate the surf. Approach the surf zone with your regulator in your mouth and your BC deflated. Hold your mask continuously in the surf zone. Follow a breaking wave, and allow additional waves to pass over you until the water is only a couple of feet deep. See figure 5.31. If the surf is mild, you can stand at that point and back out of the water. If the surf is strong, swim until you can crawl; then crawl clear of the water.

When you are clear of the water, work with your buddy to remove your fins. The buddy system is in effect all the time, not just while you are in the water.

Disassembling Equipment

The first step in disassembling your scuba equipment is to turn off the air by turning the valve in a clockwise direction. Release the pressure in the hoses by depressing the purge on the regulator second stage. Keep the purge depressed until you bleed all the air from the system. Next, disconnect all hoses from the scuba unit—the low-pressure inflator, the extra second stage, and the SPG. Loosen the yoke screw and remove the regulator from the tank. Dry the first stage dust cover thoroughly and replace it. Loosen the tank band and remove the BC from the scuba tank.

MANAGING PHYSIOLOGICAL PROBLEMS

If you do everything you are trained to do as a scuba diver, you can avoid problems. But it is not a perfect world. If you fail to pay attention or forget to do something, a problem may occur. Good divers can deal with nearly any problem. This section introduces you to proven ways of dealing with potential diving difficulties. Do not be overly concerned about the problems presented. You can prevent them, but knowing how to deal with them helps reduce your apprehension.

Difficulties affecting your physiology include seasickness, dizziness, stress and panic, overexertion, coughing, and cramping. When you have one of these problems, your body sends messages that something is wrong. You need to know the messages and the physical actions you can take to help your body overcome physiological difficulties.

Seasickness

It is best to prevent seasickness (see chapter 3) because taking medication after you are seasick is usually ineffective. If you do get seasick, you are likely to vomit. Vomiting underwater can be dangerous because of involuntary gasping that can cause you to choke. Only you can determine your degree of nausea. If you throw up or feel you are on the verge of doing so, do not dive. If you feel queasy, getting into the water may help you overcome the feeling. Some divers who feel slightly nauseated find that they feel better if they get into the water quickly and dive. After that first dive, they are fine for the remainder of the day.

Surface if you feel nauseated while diving. If you must vomit underwater, do not vomit through your regulator. Hold the second stage against one corner of your mouth and depress the purge fully while you vomit. You should get air instead of water if you gasp. When you have finished throwing up, place the second stage in your mouth, clear it, and resume breathing. The purge method should be a last resort.

If you are seasick and have to throw up while aboard a boat, do it over the rail on the side of the vessel opposite the wind. Do not use the rest room, or head, as it is called on a boat. The best remedy is to get to land, rest until you feel better, take seasickness medication, and return to the vessel. If you are ill from motion sickness, and if the dive boat has a dinghy and there is land nearby, request to be taken to shore for a while.

Dizziness

The absence of visual clues in a weightless environment can cause temporary dizziness. Visual references can help you prevent disorientation (see chapter 3). Injury, temperature changes, and pressure changes affecting the inner ear also can cause a whirling feeling called vertigo, which may be more difficult to overcome than dizziness caused by disorientation.

To cope with either dizziness or vertigo, first seek a fixed visual reference. If possible, make physical contact with something solid for a point of reference. If there is nothing to see or to grasp, close your eyes and hug yourself. In most cases, dizziness will pass in a minute or two. If you then move slowly and keep your head still, you should be able to surface. A good buddy will recognize your difficulty and assist you.

Stress and Panic

Stress is the perception that a substantial imbalance exists between environmental demand and response capability, and it occurs under conditions in which failure to meet the demand is perceived as having serious consequences. Stressors are conditions or attitudes that cause stress. Dive stressors, which may be internal or external, include cold, illness, exhaustion, injury, fears, equipment problems, loss of air supply, buddy separation, depth, darkness, currents, and disorientation. Stress is not always bad. Moderate stress can cause a feeling of exhilaration, improve performance, and lead to positive condition called eustress. Excessive stress causes anxiety, decreases performance, and leads to a negative condition called distress.

Knowledge and appraisal of a situation affect your reaction to stress. Training, experience, and your predisposition toward a situation affect your knowledge and appraisal. Thus, your perception of the circumstances are determined by what you know and are able to do, by what you have done, and by any inherent fears about the circumstances that you might have.

The problem with stress in diving is that it can lead to panic—a sudden, uncontrolled, irrational reaction to a perceived danger. Divers who panic often perish. We must manage stress to prevent panic. Dr. Tom Griffiths, who has researched stress, says, "The most critical factor in the progression of panic after stress increases is whether or not a problem arises." Divers who can recognize and manage stress can overcome problems and are far safer than those who cannot cope with the effects of stress.

Two common components of stress are the physiological and the psychological. Anxiety causes involuntary physiological changes. When stress leads to anxiety, your breathing and heart rates increase, your nervous system becomes more active, and your awareness decreases. These factors decrease your performance and increase your anxiety. Then heightened anxiety begins the cycle again. Unless you interrupt the cycle, anxiety will escalate until you panic. Psychological difficulty is every bit as critical as the physical problems. Frank Pia, a chief lifeguard, says, "Much of the distress that a person experiences when difficulty arises stems from what the person tells himself about the situation." You can be exhilarated by a situation or allow it to cause anxiety and distress. Pia continues, "The difference between panic and a heightened physiological state is the thought process."

Michael J. Asken, who has written books about stress, encourages the use of Task-Relevant Instructional Self-Talk (TRIST). You determine your emotional state when in distress by what you tell yourself. Asken says that in a stressful situation, "Success is not achieved by focusing on the outcome, hoping for a good outcome, or even telling yourself that the outcome will be okay. The most effective self-talk involves imagining that your instructor is sitting on your shoulder guiding you through your response."

With these concepts in mind, you can recognize and manage stress. The first steps are to sense your breathing rate and your self-talk when a problem occurs. If your breathing rate is fast and you are having negative thoughts about the situation, it is time to break the stress cycle. Stop all physical activity, establish buoyancy, and breathe deeply. Divers in distress usually have an adequate supply of air! As you gain control of respiration, you will be able to think more clearly. Take control of your thoughts before they take control of you. Imagine that you are telling someone else how to deal with this situation. Assess your options, determine the best course of action, and then take deliberate action. As you begin to overcome the difficulty, your confidence will increase and your physiological condition will begin to return to normal. Figure 5.32 shows how to break the stress cycle that leads to panic.

▶ Figure 5.32 The panic cycle and how to break it.

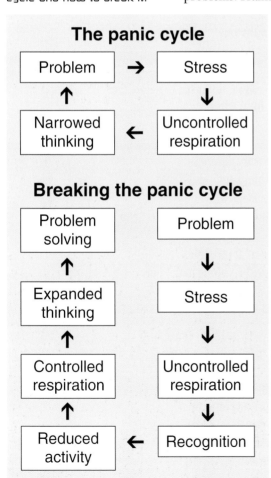

The panic cycle

Problem	→	Stress
↑		↓
Narrowed thinking	←	Uncontrolled respiration

Breaking the panic cycle

Problem solving		Problem
↑		↓
Expanded thinking		Stress
↑		↓
Controlled respiration		Uncontrolled respiration
↑		↓
Reduced activity	←	Recognition

Now you can understand why some divers are thrilled by the same situation that causes other divers to panic. Remember that stress is simply a matter of perception and that you can change your perception with training and experience. You can also learn to manage difficult situations by imagining them vividly in your mind. Your body cannot distinguish the difference between an actual event and one that you imagine. As you learn to solve problems in your mind, you can learn to recognize and manage stress.

Overexertion

If you work too hard while using scuba, the equipment may not be able to supply enough air to meet your respiratory needs. You experience a sudden feeling of suffocation, and you may suspect your equipment has malfunctioned. It is unlikely that scuba equipment will cease to function suddenly in a way that restricts airflow. More likely than not, overexertion is causing the feeling that you cannot get enough air. You manage overexertion similarly to the way you manage stress. Stop all physical activity and exhale deeply; you should overcome your respiratory problem within a minute or two.

Coughing

When water strikes your larynx, a reflex coughing action tries to clear the foreign matter from your airway. When you cough while in water, you may inhale additional water, which can complicate the situation. You need to overcome the reflex as quickly as possible. The best way is to swallow hard three times in rapid succession. If you must cough, try to do so through a regulator so you will inhale air rather than water if you gasp. You can lose buoyancy as you expel air when coughing, so you may need to establish positive buoyancy if you cough excessively.

Cramps

When your muscles get cold or when circulation to your muscles is inadequate, cramping may occur. A cramp is a sudden, strong, involuntary, persistent, painful muscle contraction. Divers tend to get cramps in the lower legs and the feet. To remove a cramp, stretch the affected muscle and rub it to increase circulation. Pounding a cramped muscle is ineffective and causes tissue damage. If you experience a cramp in your leg or foot in the water, you may be able to release it by grasping the tip of your fin and pulling it toward you. Buddies can and should assist one another with cramp removal. Figure 5.33 shows a diver releasing a cramp with a buddy's help.

▶ Figure 5.33 Rubbing and stretching a cramped muscle can help release a cramp.

MANAGING PHYSICAL PROBLEMS

Potential physical diving difficulties include entanglement; loss of buoyancy control; loss of air supply; and a distressed, injured, or incapacitated buddy. As with physiological problems, you can overcome these problems, but you should be able to avoid them. It is much better to prevent problems than to deal with them.

Entanglement

You probably will encounter fishing line, nets, wire, string, and rope in water, and these items may entangle you. Underwater plants can also entangle divers in some areas. Streamlining your equipment to minimize places where things can get caught helps reduce the chance of entanglement. Being aware also helps. When you encounter something that can entangle you, swim around it or push it beneath you and swim over it. Avoid swimming beneath things that could cause entanglement. The area of your tank valve and regulator first stage is one of the easiest places to become entangled and also one of the most difficult areas to free from entanglement.

If you become entangled underwater, stop. Then try to examine the problem without turning because turning often compounds the problem. If you can reach the entanglement, free yourself. If not, signal your buddy to help you get free. If you can see what you are doing, you may use your dive knife to cut yourself free. Trying to cut yourself free from something in the area of your tank valve would be an obvious mistake. If your tank is entangled, you can't reach the entanglements, and your buddy is not nearby to lend assistance, remove your scuba unit, free it from entanglement, and put it back on.

Loss of Buoyancy Control

You can lose control of buoyancy underwater if you lose weights, if a low-pressure inflator on your BC or a dry suit sticks, or the cartridge on your BC accidentally detonates. You can take steps to prevent loss of buoyancy control. Check your weight system from time to time while diving to make sure it is secure. Inspect your low-pressure inflators before each use, and have them serviced at the first sign of unusual operation. Don't opt for a CO_2 detonator on your BC.

If your weights fall off while underwater, immediately maneuver yourself into an inverted position, swim down forcefully, and retrieve the weights. If you are successful, you will be able to avoid an uncontrolled ascent; if you are unsuccessful, you will float to the surface. Your rate of ascent will depend on how buoyant you are without your weights, the type of exposure suit you are wearing, the amount of air in your BC at the time, the depth, and the amount of surface area you can expose to the direction of motion. You learned about resistance to movement, or drag, in chapter 2. The greater the cross-sectional area of an object moving in a given direction, the greater the resistance to movement in that direction. If you lose control of buoyancy and your ascent is uncontrolled, you can slow your rate of ascent by **flaring**—arching your back, extending your arms and legs, and positioning your fins so they are parallel to the surface. Flaring is the method recommended to slow a buoyant ascent. Figure 5.34 shows a diver in the flaring position.

Unless you care for your BC inflator carefully and have it serviced annually, the inflator valve will stick eventually. If your low-pressure inflator sticks in the open position, the

flaring—A method of slowing an uncontrolled ascent by arching the back, extending the arms and legs, and positioning the fins so they are parallel to the surface

first action you should take is to hold your BC deflator valve in the open position. Modern BCs vent air faster than the low-pressure inflator admits air. If the inflator valve remains stuck, disconnect the low-pressure hose. If an uncontrolled ascent results, flare to slow your rate of ascent.

CO_2 compresses more than air. If your BC has a CO_2 detonator and it misfires underwater, the resulting buoyancy will depend on the pressure (depth), the water temperature, and the size of the cartridge. If your detonator activates accidentally, vent the gas from the BC and flare if an uncontrolled ascent results.

Loss of Air Supply

You are unlikely to have air supply difficulties if you have your regulator serviced annually, if you maintain your regulator properly, and if you monitor your SPG. Potential problems are a regulator that free-flows, low air pressure, and no air to breathe. There are ways to deal with each of these difficulties.

▶ Figure 5.34 Flaring is an appropriate way to slow a buoyancy ascent.

Sand, dirt, and freezing weather conditions can cause regulator free-flow. If free-flow occurs, your best course is to switch to your extra second stage. You also could use your buddy's extra second stage. If there is no source of air except the regulator that is free-flowing, you can breathe from it by pressing your lips lightly against the mouthpiece, taking the air you need, and allowing the excess air to escape. Look down while you breathe from the regulator to keep the escaping air from causing your mask to leak.

You are supposed to end a dive with at least 300 psi (20 ATM) of air in your tank. If you are inattentive and breathe nearly all the air from your cylinder while diving, it will become difficult to get air from your regulator. Divers often refer to the situation as being "out of air," but, in reality, they are out of air only at the depth at which breathing is difficult. As you ascend, the lower ambient pressure allows you to obtain additional air from your tank. When breathing becomes difficult and your tank is nearly empty, use your buddy's alternate air source (AAS) or ascend while continuing to breathe shallowly through your regulator.

In the rare event that you should completely lose your primary source of air while underwater, you have five ascent options. Figure 5.35 shows the order of preference for ascent options.

An extra second stage assisted ascent—an octopus-assisted ascent— closely approximates a normal ascent. You ascend while breathing from your buddy's extra second stage. When you require air underwater, get your buddy's attention and give the signals for "out of air" and "give me air," if possible. If your buddy's extra second stage and primary second stage are similar, your buddy will hand you or you may take the extra second stage. If your buddy has an extra second stage integrated into the BC low-pressure inflator, your buddy will hand you the primary second stage and breathe from the integrated second stage. If you are unable to gain your buddy's attention, take the extra second stage, begin breathing, and then signal your buddy that you have no air. After you establish a breathing rhythm, grasp each other's right forearm and ascend normally.

BE AWARE CHECK YOUR AIR

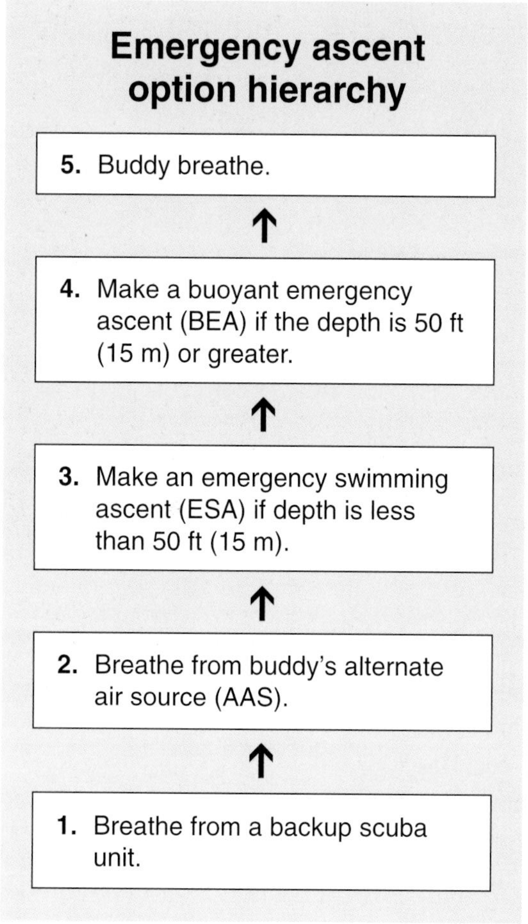

Emergency ascent option hierarchy

5. Buddy breathe.

4. Make a buoyant emergency ascent (BEA) if the depth is 50 ft (15 m) or greater.

3. Make an emergency swimming ascent (ESA) if depth is less than 50 ft (15 m).

2. Breathe from buddy's alternate air source (AAS).

1. Breathe from a backup scuba unit.

▶ Figure 5.35 Loss-of-air-supply flowchart.

An emergency swimming ascent (ESA) is a scuba ascent you do using only the air in your lungs. The ascent rate of an ESA is faster than a normal ascent but not rapid. Retain your regulator in your mouth and try to breathe from it from time to time. Do not hold your breath, or you risk a lung overexpansion injury. If you exhale too much air, you will have a strong urge to breathe. The key to a successful ESA is to exhale enough air so your lungs remain at a comfortable volume. When you do an ESA correctly, you can ascend 50 ft (15 m) easily without an overwhelming desire for air. If the depth is 50 ft (15 m) or more, establish buoyancy by discarding your weights to initiate a buoyant emergency ascent (BEA). Swim for the first portion of the ascent, but allow yourself to drift up when buoyancy can replace swimming. Flare during the last 15 ft (4.6 m) of a BEA and keep your lungs at a comfortable—but not maximum—volume.

Buddy breathing—the sharing of a single regulator second stage by two divers—is the least desirable loss-of-air option because it jeopardizes the safety of two people. You and your buddy should practice buddy breathing at the surface before beginning a dive if buddy breathing is a loss-of-air option for the dive. Buddy breathing by two divers who are not proficient with the skill can result in disaster, but proficient buddy breathers can make a loss-of-air situation a mere nuisance.

Initiate buddy breathing with the "out-of-air" signal followed by the signal for "give me air." Your buddy holds the regulator second stage in the right hand and grasps your shoulder strap with the left hand. Your buddy extends the second stage toward you and holds it in such a way that you have access to the purge. You grasp the wrist (not the regulator) of the donor with your left hand and your buddy's shoulder strap with your right hand. Guide the second stage into your mouth and push your lips against the mouthpiece to make a seal instead of inserting the mouthpiece into your mouth. By not putting the mouthpiece into your mouth to breathe, you can exchange the regulator quickly and reduce mask leakage caused by facial movements. Take several quick breaths initially; then pass the regulator back to your buddy. Exhale a small amount of air continuously when you are not breathing from the regulator. The exhalation helps prevent a lung overexpansion injury during ascent. After the initial contact, you and your buddy each take two breaths before passing the regulator. Do not inhale fully when buddy breathing because full breaths cause buoyancy problems or a lung injury. A medium inhalation is adequate because you receive air every few seconds. Do exhale normally to reduce your urge to breathe (see figure 5.36.)

As soon as you and your buddy establish a breathing rhythm, you should swim to the surface, holding on to each other throughout the ascent. Blow bubbles continuously when the regulator is not in your mouth. Remember to control your buoyancy.

Skills for loss-of-air situations require proficiency, so they must be learned well and renewed periodically. Discuss the procedures for a loss-of-air situation with your buddy and agree on the options you will use. You should both be familiar with the signals, positions, and techniques.

ASSISTING YOUR BUDDY

You have read about many ways in which you can assist your buddy and how your buddy can assist you, so you should realize the importance of the buddy system while diving.

In addition to helping your buddy handle entanglements, cramps, equipment problems, and loss-of-air situations, you may need to provide assistance if your buddy is incapacitated from exhaustion, illness, or an injury.

A buddy who becomes excited at the surface needs assistance in regaining control. Help such a buddy establish buoyancy, calm down, and breathe slowly and deeply. When the situation is under control, you may be able to help your buddy resolve the difficulty that caused the excitement.

▶ Figure 5.36   Air sharing requires good skills and cooperation.

If your buddy becomes exhausted at the surface, provide assistance with the bicep push or the fin push. Both pushes are illustrated in figure 5.37. Use the bicep push when your buddy can help and the fin push when your buddy is too exhausted to help at all. Monitor your buddy and offer encouragement while you provide assistance.

▶ Figure 5.37   The bicep push and fin push are ways to assist an exhausted buddy.

MANAGING EMERGENCIES

Diving accidents occur when divers do not exercise good judgment or when they fail to follow recommended practices. If you do what you are supposed to do, the chances of your becoming the victim of a diving accident are extremely small. But you may have to render aid to someone else who violates safety rules. This section identifies the aid you should be capable of providing.

Training and Preparation

Three types of emergency preparedness training are recommended for all divers: first aid, cardiopulmonary resuscitation (CPR), and diving rescue techniques. You can get first aid and CPR training from various public service organizations. You'll learn some diving rescue techniques in your entry-level course, but you should complete a rescue specialty course.

Emergency preparedness includes having emergency equipment and information available. Emergency equipment desirable at a dive site includes

- a diving first aid kit,

- an oxygen delivery system,

- a blanket (if appropriate), and

- drinking water.

You may not have all the emergency equipment yourself, but you can determine whether it is available aboard a boat or as part of an organized dive.

Have a means of communication—a telephone, cellular phone, CB radio, or marine radio—to summon assistance. Have contact information for local emergency medical assistance and for the emergency treatment of divers at the dive site. Have phone numbers and radio frequencies for local emergency support services. Examples of numbers to have include the U.S. Coast Guard, paramedics, hospital, ambulance, sheriff's office, recompression facility, and the International Diver's Alert Network (IDAN). The Diver's Alert Network has a 24-hour emergency number to assist with the coordination of diving accidents. You should be an IDAN member and know the IDAN emergency number, which is (919) 684-8111.

Rescues

An unconscious diver underwater may drown unless rescued immediately. Illness, drugs, and blows to the head can cause loss of consciousness. If you discover an unconscious diver underwater, make the diver buoyant and get him or her to the surface immediately. You need not concern yourself about expanding air if the diver is not breathing because an unconscious person exhales automatically regardless of head position. Do not concern yourself about the diver's decompression status; he or she can be treated for bends but will die after 4 minutes without air. Do not jeopardize your safety when attempting to rescue another diver.

A nonbreathing diver needs air quickly and must get it at the surface. This is where your CPR and diving rescue techniques training are invaluable. Open the victim's airway. Often this is all an unconscious person needs to be able to breathe. To open the airway, tilt the head. Turn the person's head to the side to drain water from the mouth and throat. Vomiting is common, so be prepared for it. Clear vomitus from the victim's mouth and throat at once or the person may inhale it.

A person who is not breathing requires rescue breathing and medical assistance. Call for help. While keeping the victim's airway open, lightly pinch the victim's nostrils to seal them. Seal your mouth over the other person's and fill the person's lungs with air until the chest rises gently. Give the victim one breath every 5 seconds or two breaths every 10 seconds while swimming to safety. A gurgling sound from the victim indicates water or vomitus in the airway. If water flows into the victim's mouth, roll the person to the side and drain the fluid before continuing rescue breathing. The preferred method of in-water artificial respiration is with a rescue-breathing mask, which you can carry in the pocket of your BC. Figure 5.38 shows a person doing rescue breathing using such a mask.

You probably will not be able to detect a pulse in the water, so don't bother trying. You cannot administer CPR in the water; you must remove the victim from the water and position him or her on a firm surface.

First Aid

There are some aspects of first aid that standard first aid courses do not teach. This section addresses the basics of those aspects, but you need additional study and training—which you can obtain in rescue-specialty and oxygen administration courses.

▶ Figure 5.38 Rescue breathing with a breathing mask.

We have addressed the most important aspects—breathing and circulation—of first aid. Nothing is more important than attending to basic life support. The next priority for any serious diving injury is treatment for shock. Lay an injured diver who is breathing on the side, keep the person warm (but avoid overheating), and administer sips of water if he or she is conscious. When you suspect an air embolism, DCS, or near drowning, have the person breathe oxygen in the highest possible concentration. Keep any diver who has been unconscious in the water or who has symptoms of DCS lying down until the patient can be evaluated at a medical facility. Monitor the patient continuously.

You should be able to recognize signs and symptoms that indicate a serious diving illness. In addition to unconsciousness, the following signs and symptoms indicate an injury that requires the prompt administration of oxygen and medical treatment:

- Sudden, extreme weakness
- Numbness
- A "pins and needles" sensation
- Inability to do simple motor skills
- Paralysis
- Unequal pupils

A few venomous marine animals can inflict life-threatening wounds (see chapter 7). The wounds can cause pain, weakness, nausea, shock, mental confusion, paralysis, convulsions, depression or arrest of breathing, and even cardiac arrest. Fortunately, such wounds are rare. Venomous injuries are either punctures or stings.

First aid for venomous puncture wounds involves removing all foreign matter from the wound, applying hot packs to the injured area for half an hour, and keeping the injured area below the level of the heart. Obtain medical attention.

First aid for a venomous sting includes killing any stinging cells that are in contact with the skin, removing any residue, cleansing the area, applying an analgesic ointment for pain relief, and obtaining medical attention. Vinegar is a good solution to apply to all stings to neutralize stinging cells initially.

You may not recall the first aid procedures in the event of an accident, so it is a good idea to have a diving first aid book to help you identify an injury and administer the appropriate first aid.

Managing Accidents

If a serious diving accident occurs, and no supervisory personnel are available to take charge, you have to manage the situation to the best of your ability. Summon help, but do not leave a seriously injured diver unattended. Enlist the aid of others. Try to locate the injured diver's identification and medical information. Write down what happened, the person's dive profile, his or her symptoms, times, and so forth. Pin the information in a conspicuous place, and send it with the injured diver to the medical facility. Accompany the patient to the medical facility, if possible.

SUMMARY

The skills of diving range from simple skin diving procedures to complex scuba skills to problem management. You need to learn the skills correctly the first time, practice them until you can do them easily, and renew them frequently to keep yourself proficient. You also need to be trained and prepared to handle a diving emergency.

Dive Planning

6

First you learn the theory of diving, then the skills of diving, and then you apply what you have learned. Your training objective is to qualify to dive without supervision, which involves planning your underwater excursions.

By the end of this chapter, you will be able to

- list at least nine factors that affect dive planning;

- explain the why, who, where, when, how, and what of advance dive planning;

- explain the steps of short-term dive planning and preparation;

- explain the on-site planning procedures for a dive;

- list at least five methods of obtaining area orientations for scuba diving;

- use dive tables to plan repetitive dives that do not require decompression;

- explain the dive-planning procedures for cold or strenuous dives, variations in ascent rate, multi-level dives, omitted decompression, diving after required decompression, going to altitude after diving, exceeding maximum time when doing precautionary decompression, and a repetitive dive RNT that exceeds the ADT of the previous dive;

- define the following terms: residual nitrogen, repetitive dive, surface interval time, maximum dive time, decompression stop, letter group designation, precautionary decompression stop, residual nitrogen time, actual dive time, equivalent dive time, adjusted maximum dive time, emergency decompression, limiting line, dive profile, step dive, spike dive, multilevel dive profile, sawtooth dive profile, and contingency plan;

- explain contingency planning for scuba dives; and

- compare the advantages and disadvantages of dive computers.

In this chapter, you will learn about all phases of dive planning—advance planning, short-term planning, on-site planning, and postdive planning. You will also learn about area orientations and how to do dive profile planning. An essential part of dive planning is to schedule your time and depth to avoid DCS.

DIVE-PLANNING FACTORS AND PHASES

A well-planned dive increases enjoyment and satisfaction and decreases the risk of injury. A poorly planned dive can be disappointing, embarrassing, and discomforting. After you read this chapter, you will understand the significance of the expression, "Plan your dive, and then dive your plan."

Dive-Planning Factors

Many factors affect your plans for a dive or a dive trip. Keep the following considerations in mind when you are looking ahead to a dive outing:

- Health and fitness are important. Illnesses, required medications, and recent operations probably disqualify you from diving. If your health is not normal, consult a diving physician. If you have any doubt, refrain from diving until you are in good health. Try to prevent motion sickness if you are prone to it.

- Climate is a big factor affecting dive planning. If you dive close to where you live, dive planning is easier than if you intend to dive thousands of miles away. A difference in climate usually means a big difference in diving conditions, which means a difference in your equipment requirements.

- When you travel many hours to a diving destination, the distance affects your planning. Allow a day to rest and recover from travel before you dive. After two or more days of repetitive diving, wait one full day before flying home.

- Weather affects diving conditions significantly. Storms and sudden changes in the weather can make diving dangerous. Know the weather forecast, and reschedule your dive if the weather forecaster predicts poor weather. Know the expected wind speed, air temperature, and water conditions.

• Seasonal changes affect water movement, water visibility, air and water temperatures, entry and exit areas, and the presence of certain types of animals. You should know what to expect at a dive site at different times of the year. It helps to know the visibility, water temperatures, tides, surf, surge, currents, bottom composition, silt conditions, plants, and animals.

You need to be physically and mentally fit for diving. Fitness for diving implies that you

• are well rested,

• are well nourished,

• have the physical strength and stamina to meet the requirements of the environment and the activity,

• are qualified for the activity,

• are not apprehensive about your plans,

• are not goaded into doing something you are not prepared to do, and

• do not allow pride to affect good judgment.

Your objective for the dive affects your planning. Different diving activities require different plans and different equipment. The planning of an underwater photography dive is not the same as the planning of a dive in which you intend to hunt for game.

You must know and observe laws, regulations, and customs. Some areas have laws that require use of a dive flag. Obey fish and game regulations. Some diving professionals discourage taking any living thing from an area. You need to know the behavior expected of you. It is better to know the expectations in advance than to be embarrassed at the dive site.

Etiquette is important. Will early diving activities be offensive to homeowners adjacent to the dive site? Will the parking of vehicles at a site irritate people? Be considerate of others who may be in the area where you intend to dive. Consider the impact of noise, the changing of clothes, and dive site access; also consider your impact on those fishing nearby. Then make your plans reflect good etiquette.

Advance Planning and Preparation

The first phase of dive planning is the determination of why, who, where, when, how, and what.

WHY—Determine the objective of the dive. What do you want to do? Take photos? Explore? Look for artifacts?

WHO—Determine with whom you want to dive. Select a buddy who is interested in your dive objective.

WHERE—Determine a primary and an alternate site.

WHEN—Determine the best time to dive. The water usually is calmer in the morning in most areas than it is in the afternoon. Tidal currents and height may be factors affecting when to dive.

HOW—Decide how to reach the dive site. Who will drive? What are the directions?

WHAT—Determine what the equipment needs are for the dive. Who will bring the float and flag? How many tanks do you need? Are there any special needs for the intended activity?

Advance preparation may include

- making reservations,
- paying deposits,
- buying or renting equipment,
- having equipment serviced or repaired,
- getting tanks filled,
- obtaining a fishing license or permit,
- buying film for photography, and
- obtaining emergency contact information.

Your preparations usually include a trip to your local dive facility. Inspect your equipment before you go. You may discover a needed repair that requires some time to complete. Identify your equipment needs early.

Short-Term Planning and Preparation

The day and evening before you intend to go diving, you need to take two actions. First, find out the weather forecast and current water conditions so you can determine whether conditions will be acceptable for your diving activities. Call your dive buddy and discuss and confirm your plans. Last-minute revisions, such as going to the alternate site, may be necessary. If you anticipate poor diving or weather conditions, reschedule the dive.

The second step of short-term preparation is packing your diving equipment and your personal items. (See the appendix for an equipment checklist.) Write down your dive plans and schedule, and leave the information with a friend. Instruct your friend to notify the authorities if you fail to return by a certain time.

Scuba Wise

Having reviewed dive accident reports for decades, I have found that the failure to adequately plan, or to carry out the plan, for a dive is a common cause of accidents and injuries. I have been able to avoid serious injury during 34 years of diving. I have had some bad experiences, however, and they occurred when I failed to plan adequately, when I attempted activities without training, or when I did not have adequate knowledge of a new dive site.

A favorite dive buddy and I were on a photo assignment in the Cayman Islands. At the end of a day, we went snorkeling in front of the dive resort. We swam offshore through a break in an offshore coral barrier reef and enjoyed an hour of viewing the beautiful and colorful animals of the area. We had not planned our exit. I suggested that we re-turn to shore by swimming directly over the barrier reef, and my buddy agreed. There were waves breaking over the reef, but I was familiar with wave action, so the waves were not a concern to me. The wave action was stronger than either of us expected, but I managed to avoid injury from the coral by holding on to dead coral between waves. My buddy, who did not know how to handle the situation, was lacerated severely by the coral. Our failure to plan our dive was the cause of his injury. If we had discussed our course and the exit procedure before the dive, his pain and suffering could have been avoided. Even a simple snorkel dive requires planning. One of the best rules of diving is, "Always plan your dive, and then dive your plan."

On-Site Planning and Preparation

When you and your buddy arrive at the dive site, determine whether the conditions are acceptable for diving. If not, go to an alternate site. If the conditions at the alternate site also are unacceptable, abort the dive.

An important step in assessing a dive site is estimating the current. Look for telltale signs such as kelp bent over from water movement, a wake around the anchor line or behind an anchored boat, or objects drifting on the surface.

Determine the velocity of moving water by measuring how long it takes a floating object to move a certain distance, such as the length of your boat. When an object moves 100 ft (30 m) in 1 minute, its speed is approximately 1 knot (1.15 mph or 1.85 km/hr). When a current exceeds about ⅓ knot (0.38 mph or 0.6 km/hr), you must pay heed because you can swim only about ¾ knot (0.86 mph or 1.4 km/hr). Plan the dive so that the current assists you to your exit point at the end of the dive. Figure 6.1 shows a table that can help you estimate current velocity.

If the diving conditions are favorable, determine the diving area. Select the entry and exit, and discuss the entry and exit procedures. Agree on the course to be followed during the dive. Agree on time, minimum air pressure, and landmarks for changes in direction. You and your buddy should know in advance approximately where you will be anytime during the dive.

An important part of your planning is the discussion and agreement about buddy system procedures. Decide who is in charge of the team, where you will position yourselves relative to each other, how you will move (steadily or start-and-stop), and what reunion procedures you will follow in the event of separation. Remember communication is much easier on land than it is underwater, so take advantage of the opportunity you have to communicate and coordinate while preparing for a dive.

Always plan for emergencies. Agree on air-sharing procedures. Discuss what to do in the event of a serious diving emergency. Know where, how, and whom to call for help. Make sure you both have access to a first aid kit and other emergency equipment. A few minutes spent coordinating procedures before an emergency can save precious seconds should an accident occur.

Scuba diving requires dive profile planning. You and your buddy need to agree on the maximum time and depth for your dive. You must limit time and depth to DCS. We will discuss dive profile planning right after area orientations, which is another important subject.

Current velocity estimation

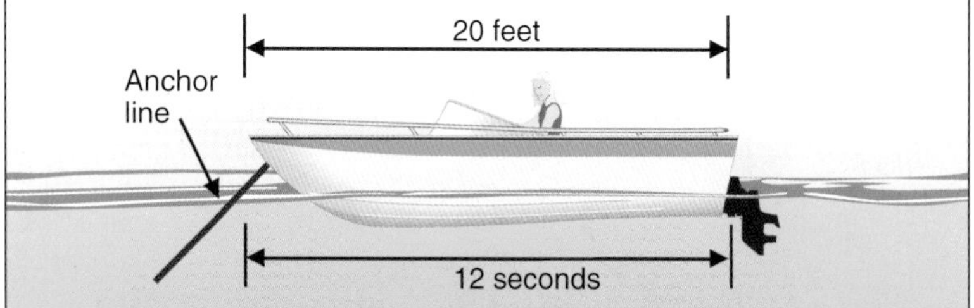

Measure how long it takes a floating object to travel 100 feet. If an object travels 20 feet in 12 seconds, it travels 100 feet in 1 minute (60/12 = 5 x 20 = 100).

Current velocity table
(time to travel 100 ft)

Time (seconds)	Speed (knots)	Time (seconds)	Speed (knots)
5	12	95	0.62
10	6.0	100	0.59
20	3.0	110	0.54
30	2.0	120	0.49
40	1.5	130	0.46
50	1.2	140	0.42
60	1.0	150	0.39
70	0.84	160	0.37
80	0.74	170	0.35
90	0.66	180	0.33

▶ Figure 6.1 You can estimate the velocity of a current if you time how long it takes a floating object to move the length of your boat.

AREA ORIENTATIONS

Area orientations have been referred to throughout this book, so by now you should understand the importance of learning about a dive site before diving there. Because orientations are vital, and because you want to be a responsible diver, you need to learn how to obtain orientations.

Area orientations may be formal or informal. A formal orientation is provided as a service by a diving professional. The professional will tell you what to look for and what to look out for in the area and will lead you on a dive. A professional dive guide will provide guidance and suggestions and point out items of interest and potential hazards. When you have completed a formal orientation, request that the professional sign and stamp your logbook. A continuing education dive course is another excellent form of formal orientation for a new area.

Formal orientations are ideal, but if you cannot arrange one, consider some or all of the following options for an informal orientation:

1. *Obtain and read books, articles, and brochures about diving in an area.* Learn as much about an area as you can before you go there.

2. *Write to dive stores in the region where you intend to dive.* Ask if you can participate in a dive class session for your orientation to the area.

3. *Write to dive clubs in the region where you intend to dive.* Ask if you can participate in a club-sponsored dive when you are in the area. Ask for contact information for several club members who dive regularly and who may be willing to allow you to go diving with them.

4. *When you arrive in a new area, find local dive sites and visit them when divers are likely to be there.* Ask the divers about the sites while they are preparing to dive or after they exit from a dive. If you have your equipment ready, you may be able to accompany them on a dive, but make sure they have experience diving at the site.

5. *Purchase a space on a diving charter boat.* When you board the vessel, tell the crew you are new to the area. Ask for advice about diving procedures and ask to be introduced to an experienced diver who can provide additional information.

When you dive with local divers, allow them to go first. Do as they say and do as they do. Procedures vary from region to region. A procedure you use in your area may be inappropriate for a different area. For example, in your normal diving environment, you may be able to enter the water without holding on to a line. But if you tried to do so in a different area, you might be swept away at once. Be humble, listen to others, and follow their example to avoid embarrassment.

DIVE PROFILE PLANNING

There are time limits for how long you can remain at various depths. These limits are determined by the amount of nitrogen absorbed by your body. You may absorb the nitrogen during one dive or a series of dives, and it takes time to eliminate nitrogen from your body. If you dive again before the excess nitrogen has had time to outgas, you add to the nitrogen already in your body and reach critical nitrogen levels faster than if you did not have excess nitrogen residing in you before the dive. You need to be aware of the effects of residual nitrogen, which is nitrogen remaining in your system from a dive made within the past 12 hours. Repetitive diving poses another planning problem. A repetitive dive is any dive made within 6 to 24 hours (depending on the dive-planning device) of a previous dive. Figure 6.2 shows how the amount of residual nitrogen in the body builds from repetitive dives. A precautionary decompression stop during ascent reduces DCS risk.

precautionary decompression stop—A 2- to 5-minute delay in ascent at 15 ft (4.6 m) made at the end of every dive to minimize the risk of DCS

Decompression experts use complex mathematical calculations and field testing to establish time limits for various depths for single and repetitive dives. The experts put the time limits on tables and calculators and program them into dive computers. You need to know how to use the dive-planning devices so you can plan your dive profile to minimize your risk of DCS. Table 6.1 shows the maximum number of minutes the major training organizations recommend for specific depths.

No dive-planning device can guarantee that you will not develop DCS. Dive tables, calculators, and computers provide information based on statistics acquired through testing. The statistical probability that a diver who adheres to the profile limits of a device will develop DCS is small. The devices assume that you are in good health, that you do not get cold during the dive, that you do not exert strenuously, and that you ascend at the correct rate.

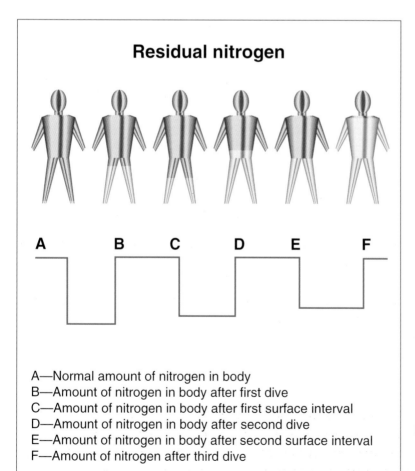

Residual nitrogen

A—Normal amount of nitrogen in body
B—Amount of nitrogen in body after first dive
C—Amount of nitrogen in body after first surface interval
D—Amount of nitrogen in body after second dive
E—Amount of nitrogen in body after second surface interval
F—Amount of nitrogen after third dive

▶ Figure 6.2 If you make a repetitive dive before allowing the excess nitrogen to leave your body, the nitrogen continues to accumulate.

Table 6.1 Dive Time Limits of Various Diver-Training Organizations (in minutes)							
	USN	YMCA	NAUI	PADI 1	PADI 2	SSI	DCIEM
30 FSW	–	–	–	–	205	205	300
40 FSW	200	150	130	140	130	130	150
50 FSW	100	80	80	80	70	70	75
60 FSW	60	50	55	55	50	50	50
70 FSW	50	40	45	40	40	40	35
80 FSW	40	30	35	30	30	30	25
90 FSW	30	20	25	25	25	25	20
100 FSW	25	20	22	20	20	20	15
110 FSW	20	13	15	16	15	15	12
120 FSW	15	10	12	13	10	10	10
130 FSW	10	5	8	10	5	5	8
140 FSW	10	5	–	8	–	–	7

Note. FSW = feet of salt water (depth). All other numbers are time limits in minutes.

USN = United States Navy;

YMCA = YMCA Scuba Program;

NAUI = National Association of Underwater Instructors;

PADI 1 = Professional Association of Diving Instructors (Dive table);

PADI 2 = PADI Recreational Dive Planner (Circular calculator);

SSI = Scuba Schools International;

DCIEM = Canadian Defence and Civil Institute of Environmental Medicine.

If you dive to the maximum time limits of any dive-planning device, you increase the likelihood of DCS. The shorter your exposure to pressure, the less the chance that you will develop the bends.

DIVE TABLES

More than 30 years ago, the U.S. Navy (USN) developed tables for dive planning. The recreational diving community adopted the military tables and has used modified versions successfully for many years. Although the tables were designed for military diving versus recreational diving, many decompression experts still consider the USN dive tables—with reduced maximum dive times—appropriate tables for recreational use. Variations of the USN tables are used widely today.

The USN tables use compartments with half-times of 5 minutes, 10 minutes, 20 minutes, 40 minutes, 80 minutes, and 120 minutes. The amount of nitrogen remaining in the 120-minute (2-hour) compartment determines the letter group designations of the tables. Because outgassing of a compartment takes 6 half-times, you can see why the USN tables define a repetitive dive as any dive within 12 hours (6 times 2 hours) of a previous dive.

The USN dive tables consist of four sets of tables:

1. No-Decompression Timetable

2. Surface Interval Timetable

3. Residual Nitrogen Timetable

4. Decompression Timetables

Modifications to the Dive Tables

Diving organizations and manufacturers have modified the USN dive tables to make them more appropriate for recreational diving. The following are some typical differences between the USN dive tables and modified USN dive tables:

letter group designation—The letter on a dive table that corresponds to the amount of nitrogen in a diver's body

• *Reduced time limits.* Dive-planning devices today include maximum time limits that are less than the no-decompression limits of the USN dive tables.

• *Reduced depth limits.* The USN dive tables provide dive planning information for depths to 190 ft (58 m). The recommended maximum depth limit for recreational diving is 130 ft (39.6 m). New divers should limit diving to depths of about 60 ft (18 m). Advanced divers qualify to dive to approximately 100 ft (30 m). Divers completing a deep diving specialty course qualify to dive to 130 ft (39.6 m). Depth in water is similar to speed on land. When you qualify for a driver's license, you may drive at speeds up to 65 mph (104.6 km/hr) or more. With experience, you probably will drive faster—but not much faster because it is dangerous. Driving at very fast speeds is hazardous and requires specialized training, special equipment, and controlled situations to minimize the risk of serious injury or death. Deep diving (beyond 100 ft or 30 m) is similar to race-car driving in many respects. Deep diving is a professional endeavor that unqualified recreational divers should not attempt.

• *Revised surface interval times* (time spent at the surface between repetitive dives). In 1983, a USN study reported a number of errors in the Surface Interval Timetable. The errors usually do not affect the type of diving that recreational divers do, but some modified versions of the tables include the corrections.

• *Combined tables.* Modified versions of the USN dive tables often incorporate information to make the tables easier to use. Table 3 (Residual Nitrogen Timetable) may include the adjusted maximum dive time (AMDT) for repetitive dives along with the residual nitrogen time (RNT). Table 1 (No-Decompression Timetable) often includes required decompression information to eliminate a separate decompression timetable.

Dive Table Use

After you learn to use the modified USN dive tables in this book (see page 143), you will be able to use most dive tables because the procedures are similar. An overview of the modified USN tables makes it easier to understand how to solve a specific dive-planning problem.

Table 1 provides three items of information: the maximum dive time (MDT) without required decompression stops for various depths, a letter group designation for various dive profiles, and the time duration for emergency decompression stops.

surface interval time (SIT)—The time spent at the surface between repetitive dives

adjusted maximum dive time (AMDT)—The amount of time a diver may spend at depth, considering the RNT and the SIT; AMDT = MDT − RNT

residual nitrogen time (RNT)—The time in minutes, converted from a letter group designation, that is equivalent to the nitrogen remaining in the body from a previous dive

maximum dive time (MDT)—The maximum time a diver may spend underwater for the deepest depth reached during a dive

Comparison of Dive Table Terms

USN Tables	Modified USN Tables
Bottom time	Actual dive time (ADT)
No-decompression limit	Maximum dive time (MDT)
Equivalent bottom time	Equivalent dive time (EDT)
Surface interval time	Surface interval time (SIT)
Residual nitrogen time	Residual nitrogen time (RNT)
	Adjusted MDT (AMDT)

actual dive time (ADT)—The amount of time a diver spends underwater

equivalent dive time (EDT)—The sum of the ADT and the RNT; ADT + RNT = EDT

Table 2 (Surface Interval Timetable) provides letter group information based on your surface interval time (SIT). You begin a surface interval with one letter group designation; as you outgas nitrogen, you acquire lower letter group designations.

Table 3 provides adjusted (reduced) dive time limits based on the amount of nitrogen in your body from a previous dive or dives.

Table 4 (Decompression Timetables) converts a letter group designation at the end of a surface interval to an amount of time at a planned depth. You add residual nitrogen time (RNT) to your actual dive time (ADT) to determine your equivalent dive time (EDT) for a repetitive dive. Use the equivalent time, which represents the total amount of nitrogen in your system, to return to Table 1 for a new end-of-dive letter group designation.

Now you are ready to learn how to plan dives using all four tables. The horizontal listings are rows and the vertical listings are columns (see page 143).

Rules for using the dive tables are simple and easy to remember.

Dive Table Rules

- When you consult the tables, use the deepest depth you attained during a dive. If you spend part of the dive at one depth and the remainder of the dive at a shallower depth, treat the dive as if you spent all the time at the deepest depth.

- Enter the tables at a depth that is exactly equal to, or is the next greater depth than, the maximum depth of your dive. The USN tables have 10 ft (3 m) increments. If the depth of your dive is 50 ft (15 m), use the 50 ft (15 m) listing. It the depth of your dive is 51 ft (15.5 m), you must use the 60 ft (18 m) listing.

- If depths shallower than 40 ft (12 m) are not on the version of the tables you use, calculate all dives shallower than 40 ft (12 m) as 40 ft (12 m) dives.

- From the times listed for a specific depth, select the time that is exactly equal to, or is the next greater than, the time of your dive. If you dive to 60 ft (18 m) for 22 minutes, use the 25-minute listing on the tables because there is no 22-minute listing for that depth.

- When the time is less than 10 minutes, add the times of the dives together and use the deepest depth of the dives when you consult the tables. Do not include the surface interval time as part of your dive time. Although the USN tables indicate a minimum surface interval time of 10 minutes, the minimum recommended time between recreational dives is 1 hour.

HKP Dive Table Instructions

1. Begin first dive at Table 1. Use exact or next greater number for all depths and times. Find end-of-dive letter group at bottom of Table 1.
2. Find end-of-surface-interval letter group at left of Table 2. Use exact or next greater time. Use the letter group to refer to Tables 3 and 4.
3. Actual dive time of a repetitive dive must not exceed the times indicated by Table 3 coordinates.
4. Add residual nitrogen time (RNT) from Table 4 coordinates to actual dive time (ADT) to obtain equivalent dive time (EDT). ADT + RNT = EDT.
5. Use EDT to return to Table 1.

Table 1—MDT and EDT Table

Time (minute)

Ft	M	15	30	45	60	75	95	120	145	170	205	250	310/5
30	9	15	30	45	60	75	95	120	145	170	205	250	310/5
40	12	5	15	25	30	40	50	70	80	100	110	130	150/5
50	15		10	15	25	30	40	50	60	70	80	100/5	
60	18			15	20	25	30	40	50	60/5	80/7		
70	21		5	10	15	20	25	30	40	50/5	60/8	70/14	
80	24		5	10	15	20	25	30	35	40/5	50/10	60/17	
90	27		5	10	12	15	20	25	30	30/5	40/7	50/18	
100	30		5	7	10	12	15	20	25	30/5	40/15		
110	33			5	10	13	15	20/5	30/7				
120	36			5	10	12	15/5	25/6	30/14				
130	39			5	8	10/5	25/10						

Group letters: A B C D E F G H I J K L

Table 2—SIT Table

(old group)	A	B	C	D	E	F	G	H	I	J	K	L
L	0:26	0:45	1:04	1:25	1:49	2:19	2:53	3:36	4:35	6:02	9:12	12:00
K	0:28	0:49	1:11	1:35	2:03	2:38	3:21	4:19	5:48	8:58	12:00	
J	0:31	0:54	1:19	1:47	2:20	3:04	4:02	5:40	8:50	12:00		
I	0:33	0:59	1:29	2:02	2:44	3:43	5:12	8:21	12:00			
H	0:36	1:06	1:41	2:23	3:20	4:49	7:59	12:00				
G	0:40	1:15	1:59	2:58	4:25	7:35	12:00					
F	0:45	1:29	2:28	3:57	7:05	12:00						
E	0:54	1:57	3:24	6:34	12:00							
D	1:09	2:38	5:48	12:00								
C	1:39	4:48	12:00									
B	3:20	12:00										
A	12:00											

HUMAN KINETICS PUBLISHERS
Box 5076, Champaign, IL 61825-5076
1-800-747-4457

ABBREVIATIONS

ADT–Actual Dive Time
MDT–Maximum Dive Time
EDT–Equivalent Dive Time
SIT–Surface Interval Time
AMDT–Adjusted Maximum Dive Time
RNT–Residual Nitrogen Time

WARNING:

NO DIVE TABLE CAN GUARANTEE AVOIDANCE OF DECOMPRESSION SICKNESS. USE THE TABLES CONSERVATIVELY.

© 1993 Dennis K. Graver ISBN 0-87322-532-5

Table 4—RNT Table

Ft	M	A	B	C	D	E	F	G	H	I	J	K
30	9	12	25	39	54	70	88	109	130	160	190	229
40	12	7	17	25	37	49	61	73	87	101	116	138
50	15	6	13	21	29	38	47	56	66	76	87	99
60	18	5	11	17	24	30	36	44	52	61	70	79
70	21	4	9	15	20	26	31	37	43	50	57	64
80	24	4	8	13	18	23	28	32	38	43	48	54
90	27	3	7	11	16	20	24	29	33	38	43	47
100	30	3	7	10	14	18	22	26	30	34	38	43
110	33	3	6	10	13	16	20	24	30	36	39	39
120	36	3	6	9	12	15	18	21		120	130	130
130	39	3	6	8	11	13	16	19				

Box: **ADT + RNT = EDT — Return to Table 1**

Group column labels (right): L K J I H G F E D C B A

Table 3—AMDT Table

	A	B	C	D	E	F	G	H	I	J	K
M (Ft)	30	60	90	120	141	162	180	196	211	225	238
A	12	14	29	43	57	69	81	93	105	113	123
B		4	14	24	33	42	51	59	67	74	
C			6	14	20	26	33	39	45		
D			3	9	14	20	25	31	36		
E			3	7	12	17	22	27	31		
F				5	9	14	18	23	17		
G				2	6	10	13	18			
H					2	5	9	12			
I						3	6	9			
J						2	6				
K							5				

Note: Repetitive dives should not exceed 80 ft (24 m).

Example 1
MDT and EDT Table

Ft	M	15	30	45	60	75	95	120	145	170	205	250	310/5
								Time (minute)					
30	9	15	30	45	60	75	95	120	145	170	205	**250**	310/5
40	12	5	15	25	30	40	50	70	80	100	110	**130**	150/5
50	15	→	10	15	25	30	40	50	60	70	**80**		100/5
60	18			10	15	20	25	30	40	**50**		60/5	80/7
70	21		→	5	10	15	20	30	35	**40**	50/5	60/8	70/14
80	24		5	10	15	20	25	30	**35**	40/5		50/10	60/17
90	27	→	5	10	12	15	20	**25**	30/5		40/7		50/18
100	30		5	7	10	15	**20**	25/5				40/15	
110	33		→	5	10	13	**15**	20/5			30/7		
120	36			5	10	**12**	15/5				25/6	30/14	
130	39		→	5	**8**	10/5						25/10	
Group		A	B	C	D	E	F	G	H	I	J	K	L

Example 2
SIT Table

		A	B	C	D	E	F	G	H	I	J	K	L
←	L												0:26
	K											0:28	0:45
←	J										0:31	0:49	1:04
	I									0:33	0:54	1:11	1:25
←	H								0:36	0:59	1:19	1:35	1:49
	G							0:40	1:06	1:29	1:47	2:03	2:19
←	F						0:45	1:15	1:41	2:02	2:20	2:38	2:53
	E					0:54	1:29	1:59	2:23	2:44	3:04	3:21	3:36
←	D				1:09	1:57	2:28	2:58	3:20	3:43	4:02	4:19	4:35
	C			1:39	2:38	3:24	3:57	4:25	4:49	5:12	5:40	5:48	6:02
←	B		3:20	4:48	5:48	6:34	7:05	7:35	7:59	8:21	8:50	8:58	9:12
	A	12:00	12:00	12:00	12:00	12:00	12:00	12:00	12:00	12:00	12:00	12:00	12:00

Use Table 1 to determine the maximum dive time (MDT) for a dive. Enter the table on the row corresponding to the depth you plan to dive, then proceed to the right to determine the MDT for the depth. The numbers in bold print indicate MDTs.

To use Table 1 to obtain a letter group designation following a dive, enter the table on the row corresponding to the maximum depth of your dive, then proceed to the right to the first number you do not exceed. Proceed downward along that column and obtain a letter group designation for the dive. For example, a dive to 50 ft (15 m) for 30 minutes assigns you to letter group "E." A dive to 45 ft (14 m) for 28 minutes also places you in letter group "E." (Remember, when you exceed a number, you must use the next larger number.)

Use the Surface Interval Timetable, Table 2, to determine a letter group designation following a surface interval. Enter the table using the letter group designation you obtained from Table 1. Move downward along the column until you find the first time (expressed as hours:minute; e.g., 1:26 is 1 hour and 26 minutes) that equals or exceeds your surface interval. Remember that whenever you exceed a number on the tables, you use the next larger number. Follow the column to the left and obtain the new letter group designation. For example, if your letter group was "E" at the beginning of a 1-hour, 58-minute surface interval, your letter designation would be group "C" at the end of the surface interval. The designation would be letter group "C" for a surface interval from 1:58 to 3:24.

Use Table 3 to determine your adjusted maximum dive time (AMDT) for a repetitive dive. Residual nitrogen in your body reduces your MDT from Table 1. Table 3 provides the reduced time limits. For example, if your letter group is "C" from a previous dive or dives and you plan to dive to 70 ft (21 m), your dive time must not exceed 25 minutes.

Use the Residual Nitrogen Timetable, Table 4, to convert your letter group designation into a time in minutes that is equivalent to the nitrogen remaining in your body from a previous dive. The amount of time varies depending on the depth of the dive you plan to make. To determine your RNT, find the column corresponding to the depth you plan to dive

Example 3
AMDT Table

60	18	5	1.						
70	21	4	9	1					
80	24	4	8	13	18	2			
90	27	3	7	11	16	20	2		
100	30	3	7	10	14	18	22		
110	33	3	6	10	13	16	20	24	
120	36	3	6	9	12	15	18	21	
130	39	3	6	8	11	13	16	19	→

ADT... Return to Table 1

M	9	12	15	18	21	24	27	30	33	36	39	
Ft	30	40	50	60	70	80	90	100	110	120	130	
												L ←
	21											K
	60	14										J ←
	90	29	4									I
	120	43	14									H ←
	141	57	24	6	3	3						G
	162	69	33	14	9	7						F ←
	180	81	42	20	14	12	5	2				E
	196	93	51	26	20	17	9	6	2			D ←
	211	105	59	33	25	22	14	10	5	3		C
	225	113	67	39	31	27	18	13	9	6	2	B ←
	238	123	74	45	36	31	22	17	12	9	5	A

Repetitive dives should not exceed 80 ft (24 m).

Example 4
RNT Table

Ft	M	A	B	C	D	E	F	G	H	I	J	K	
30	9	12	25	39	54	70	88	109	130	160	190	229	→
40	12	7	17	25	37	49	61	73	87	101	116	138	
50	15	6	13	21	29	38	47	56	66	76	87	99	→
60	18	5	11	17	24	30	36	44	52	61	70	79	
70	21	4	9	15	20	26	31	37	43	50	57	64	→
80	24	4	8	13	18	23	28	32	38	43	48	54	
90	27	3	7	11	16	20	24	29	33	38	43	47	→
100	30	3	7	10	14	18	22	26	30	34	38	43	
110	33	3	6	10	13	16	20	24					→
120	36	3	6	9	12	15	18	21					
130	39	3	6	8	11	13	16	19					→

ADT + RNT = EDT
Return to Table 1

M	9	12	15	18	21	24	27	30	33	36	39
Ft	30	40	50	60	70	80	90	100	110	120	13
	21										
	60	14									

Repetitive dive should not ...

and the row that corresponds to your letter group following your surface interval. The numbers at the coordinates indicate your RNT. For example, if your letter group was "C" at the end of the surface interval and you were planning to dive to 70 ft (21 m), your RNT would be 15 minutes.

Add your RNT to the ADT of your repetitive dive to establish the EDT. Using the EDT, reenter Table 1 and obtain a new letter group designation. For example, if your RNT is 15 minutes and your ADT is 20 minutes for a dive to 70 ft (21 m), your EDT is 35 minutes (20 plus 15) and your end-of-dive letter group is "G."

Example 5
MDT and EDT Table

Ft	M	Time (minute)											
30	9	15	30	45	60	75	95	120	145	170	205	250	310/5
40	12	5	15	25	30	40	50	70	80	100	110	130	150/5
50	15	→	10	15	25	30	40	50	60	70	80		100/5
60	18		10	15	20	25	30	40	50		60/5		80/7
70	21	→	5	10	15	20	30	35	40		50/5	60/8	70/14
80	24		5	10	15	20	25	30	35	40/5		50/10	60/17
90	27	→	5	10	12	15	20	25	30/5		40/7		50/18
100	30			5	7	10	15	20		25/5		40/15	
110	33	→		5	10	13	15	20/5			30/7		
120	36				5	10	12	15/5			25/6	30/14	
130	39	→			5	8	10/5					25/10	
		↓	↓	↓	↓	↓	↓	↓	↓	↓	↓	↓	↓
		A	B	C	D	E	F	G	H	I	J		

← L
K
← I

To determine the time for emergency decompression for a dive in excess of the MDT, enter Table 1 just as you did to obtain a letter group designation for a dive that did not require decompression. If the ADT or EDT of your dive exceeds the MDT for the depth, decompress at a depth of 15 ft (4.6 m) for the number of minutes indicated to the right of the slash for the bottom time. For example, if your EDT for a dive to 70 ft (21 m) exceeds 40 minutes but is not more than 50 minutes, you must decompress for at least 5 minutes. Following a dive requiring emergency decompression—a required delay in ascent you must take when your ADT or EDT exceeds the MDT for the dive—refrain from further diving for at least 24 hours. Plan your dive profiles so you do not exceed the MDTs and do not approach the limiting line—the point at which decompression time exceeds the precautionary 3 minutes.

Special Equipment Dive Planning

You must use special dive tables for oxygen-enriched air (Nitrox), and you learn how to use the tables when you take a Nitrox specialty course. Do not attempt specialized diving without proper training. Exceeding the 130 ft (39.6 m) depth limit by a few feet when breathing compressed air is not particularly dangerous, but exceeding the maximum depth limit (which varies with the mixture) when breathing mixed gases can cause seizures and drowning. Scuba equipment that uses a mixture other than compressed air is only for divers who have the prerequisite experience and training.

Dive Profile Terms and Rules

There are several types of dive profiles, made by plotting time and depth. Figure 6.3 shows a diagram of a standard dive profile. A square profile describes a dive to a constant depth for a given time. It is typically depicted as a profile with square corners. A multi-level dive profile is a dive that progresses from deep to shallow during a given time. When you make a dive in a series of steps, you may refer to it as a step dive. A sawtooth dive profile is a dive that progresses from deep to shallow and back to deep. Avoid this type of dive, which is depicted graphically as a sawtooth. The fourth profile is the bounce

emergency decompression—A required delay in ascent a diver must take if the ADT or EDT exceeds the MDT for a dive profile. It is a dive with a short ADT, such as a dive to free a fouled anchor. You also should avoid this profile, which is, appropriately enough, depicted graphically as a spike. Bounce-profile dives are sometimes called spike dives. Figure 6.4 shows how the four profiles are depicted graphically.

All dive-planning devices assume you dive according to certain procedures. For example, a dive-planning device assumes you do not exceed a maximum rate of ascent. The USN (or modified USN) dive tables assume a maximum rate of 30 ft (9 m) per minute. Do not exceed this ascent rate. The tables assume you ascend at the correct rate. If you ascend faster, you may get DCS, especially during repetitive dives.

Because you absorb nitrogen as pressure increases and because it takes time for you to eliminate it, you should always make your deepest dive the first dive of the day; then make each successive dive to a progressively shallower depth. If you make a shallow dive followed by a deeper dive, residual nitrogen from the shallow dive will reduce the time you may stay at the deeper depth. When making a multilevel dive, go to the deepest depth first, then ascend to shallower depths as the dive progresses.

Short exposures at depths in excess of 80 ft (24 m) affect certain tissues in the body. Subjecting these tissues to repetitive dives in excess of that depth may result in DCS. Do not make repetitive dives in excess of 80 ft (24 m).

Dive Profile Diagramming

Diagram your dive profiles when planning and recording your dives. Include planned and actual depths, MDTs, ADTs, letter group designations, and SITs. For repetitive dives,

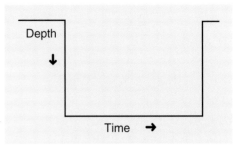

▶ Figure 6.3 Standard dive profile.

▶ Figure 6.4 Types of dive profiles.

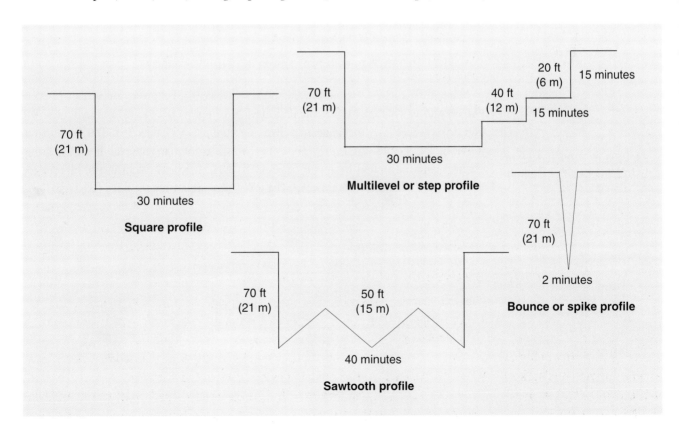

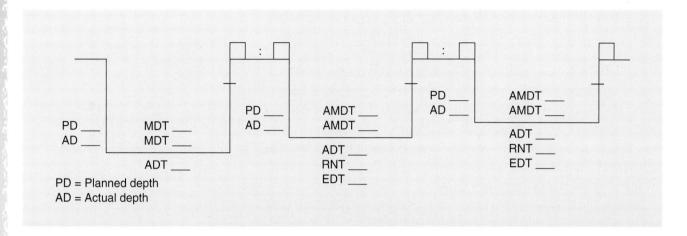

PD ___
AD ___

MDT ___
MDT ___

ADT ___

PD = Planned depth
AD = Actual depth

PD ___
AD ___

AMDT ___
AMDT ___

ADT ___
RNT ___
EDT ___

PD ___
AD ___

AMDT ___
AMDT ___

ADT ___
RNT ___
EDT ___

▶ Figure 6.5 Make photocopies of this worksheet to use as you plan your dives.

include RNTs and EDTs. A simple method for diagramming dive table problems is to use a worksheet like the one shown in figure 6.5

Try the following exercise, which combines diagramming with the dive table procedures you have learned. Use the blank diagramming worksheet in figure 6.5. If you have any difficulties, refer to the preceding section regarding use of the tables. Assume all dive times include 3 minutes of precautionary decompression. Calculate and diagram the following series of dives (the answers to the diagramming problem are in the next paragraph and in figure 6.6):

- The first dive is to 78 ft (24 m) with an ADT of 20 minutes followed by an SIT of 1.5 hours.

- The second dive is to 55 ft (16.8 m) with an ADT of 25 minutes followed by a surface interval of 2 hours.

- The third dive is to 40 ft (12 m) with an ADT of 25 minutes.

▶ Figure 6.6 An example of how to complete the diagramming worksheet.

Solution: The letter group following the first dive is "E." Following the surface interval, the letter group changes to "D." The RNT for a "D" diver at 60 ft (18 m) is 24 minutes. The EDT (ADT plus RNT) for the second dive is 49 minutes (24 plus 25). The letter group following the second dive is "H." Following the second surface interval, the letter group changes to "E." The RNT for an "E" diver at 40 ft (12 m) is 49 minutes. The EDT for the third dive is 74 minutes (49 plus 25). The letter group following the third dive is "H."

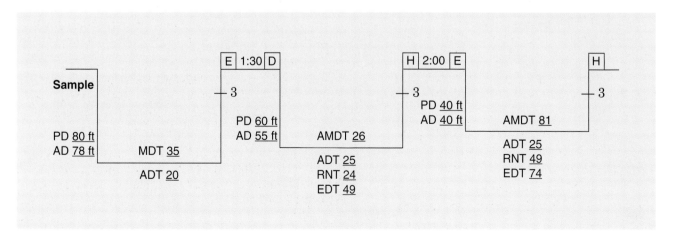

Sample

PD 80 ft
AD 78 ft

MDT 35

ADT 20

E 1:30 D

3

PD 60 ft
AD 55 ft

AMDT 26

ADT 25
RNT 24
EDT 49

H 2:00 E

3

PD 40 ft
AD 40 ft

AMDT 81

ADT 25
RNT 49
EDT 74

H

3

The following tips make dive profile diagramming easier:

- Begin by entering the maximum allowable time (MDT for the first dive and AMDT for repetitive dives) for the planned depth. ADT must not exceed the maximum allowable time.

- Enter a letter group at every upper corner of a profile except the first corner.

- Add ADT and RNT to obtain EDT for every repetitive dive. Use the recall word "ARE" to help remember that you add ADT and RNT to obtain EDT.

Planning Time and Depth Limits

Now combine the dive table procedures to plan a series of dives. Use the blank diagram shown in figure 6.5. Assume the depth of the first dive—the deepest dive—is 60 ft (18 m). The MDT, according to Table 1, is 50 minutes. Assume an ADT of 22 minutes (including precautionary decompression) for the dive. Your letter group designation following the first dive is "E." Now plan a repetitive dive to the same depth. If your surface interval is less than 55 minutes, you remain in the "E" group, your RNT is 30 minutes, and your AMDT is 20 minutes. Your surface interval should be at least 1 hour, as recommended. If you wait an hour between the first and second dives, your letter group changes to "D," your RNT is 24 minutes, and your AMDT is 26 minutes. If you want to dive for more than 26 minutes, you need to extend your surface interval to at least 3 hours and 25 minutes.

Assume you repeat the first dive. Your RNT is 24 minutes and your ADT is 22 minutes, so your EDT is 46 minutes. Your letter group following the second dive is "H."

Assume the dive site is so good that you wish to make a third dive to 60 ft (18 m). Refer to Table 3 to plan the dive because Table 3 provides the maximum allowable times for various letter group designations. There is no allowable time at 60 ft (18 m) for a diver with a group "H" designation. Only 6 minutes are allowed for a diver with a group "G" designation. Proceed up the column. If you want to dive to 60 ft (18 m) again for more than 20 minutes, you need to attain letter group "D," which allows 26 minutes of diving without required decompression. When you know the group you need to attain and your starting group, you can plan your surface interval. The Surface Interval Timetable tells you that you must wait at least 2 hours and 24 minutes to move from group "H" into group "D."

Use the tables to help you plan dives to avoid emergency decompression. There are three options for planning repetitive dives that will not require emergency decompression. If your RNT prevents you from making a desired dive, you may (1) reduce the duration of the dive, (2) reduce the depth of the dive, or (3) increase the surface interval preceding the dive.

Test what you have learned by answering the dive-planning problems. Diagram the problems. Include precautionary decompression time in all dive

Dive-Planning Problems

1. Following a dive to 71 ft (21.6 m) for 27 minutes and a surface interval of 60 minutes, what is the maximum depth to which you may dive for at least 15 minutes without emergency decompression?

2. Following a dive to 77 ft (23.5 m) for 24 minutes and a surface interval of 1 hour and 45 minutes, what is the maximum allowable time for a dive to a depth of 50 ft (15 m)?

3. Following a dive to 60 ft (18 m) for 21 minutes, what is the minimum surface interval that will allow a dive of the same duration to the same depth without emergency decompression?

Solutions to Dive-Planning Problems

1. The letter group following the first dive is "G." The letter group changes to "F" after the surface interval. Refer to Table 3. Group "F" allows 9 minutes for 70 ft (21 m), 14 minutes for 60 ft (18 m), and 33 minutes for 50 ft (15 m). The maximum depth to which you may dive for at least 15 minutes without emergency decompression is 50 ft (15 m).

2. The letter group following the first dive is "F." The letter group changes to "D" after the surface interval. The maximum allowable time without emergency decompression for a group "D" diver at 50 ft (15 m) is 51 minutes.

3. The letter group following the first dive is "E." You must have a letter group designation of "D" for a repetitive dive of 21 minutes without emergency decompression (refer to Table 3). Changing from group "E" to group "D" requires a minimum surface interval of 55 minutes.

times. Compare your answers with the solutions provided.

Special Procedures

Unusual circumstances may arise that require special procedures. The following are examples of such circumstances:

- A cold or strenuous dive
- Variations in the rate of ascent
- Multilevel dives
- Omitted decompression
- Precautionary decompression causes ADT or EDT to exceed the maximum time limits
- Diving after required decompression
- The RNT for a repetitive dive exceeds the ADT of the previous dive
- Altitude after diving

When you have finished studying this section, you should be able to describe the procedures for using the modified USN dive tables for dive profile planning for each of these situations.

When a dive is particularly cold or strenuous, use the next greater time for the dive. If the dive is cold and strenuous, use the next greater time and depth.

If you ascend faster than 30 ft (9 m) per minute, extend your precautionary decompression stop by at least 2 minutes. The faster you ascend, the more you should increase the stop time.

Consider dives to multiple levels to be square profile dives with all the time of the dive at the deepest depth of the dive. Do not attempt to extrapolate the dive tables.

If you need to decompress, but fail to do so, use the following procedure for omitted decompression. If you have no symptoms of DCS following the dive, remain out of the water, breathe oxygen in the highest concentration possible, rest, drink water, and be alert for symptoms of DCS. Wait 24 hours before diving again. If you suspect DCS, proceed at once to a medical facility for a medical examination. The USN has a procedure for in-water decompression, but diving medical experts agree that this procedure is inappropriate.

If precautionary decompression causes your ADT or EDT to exceed the maximum time limits, determine your letter group designation with the MDT limit.

After a dive that requires decompression, wait at least 24 hours before diving again.

If the RNT for a repetitive dive exceeds the ADT of the previous dive, use the RNT for planning the repetitive dive.

Ascending to altitude after diving increases the likelihood of DCS because of the further reduction in pressure. Driving into the mountains or flying after diving can cause DCS that would not occur if you remained at sea level until you eliminated the excess nitrogen.

The International Diver's Alert Network (IDAN) recommends waiting a minimum of 12 hours before ascent to altitude in a commercial jet airliner (up to 8,000 ft or 2,438 m). If you make multiple dives for several days or make dives that require decompression stops, wait for an extended surface interval beyond 12 hours before flight. The greater the interval before the flight, the less likely that DCS will occur.

IDAN does not have a recommendation for flying or driving at lower altitudes. The most extensively tested tables for altitudes are the Swiss dive tables, which use a compartment with a much longer half-time than the USN tables. A recent approach to altitude delays after diving makes the USN dive tables surface intervals equivalent to those of the Swiss tables. Converted USN minimum surface intervals in the Altitude Delay Timetable (table 6.2) specify the minimum time to attain permissible nitrogen levels for various altitudes.

Altitude is any elevation above 1,000 ft (300 m). The Altitude Delay Timetable provides recommended time delays for altitudes up to 10,000 ft (3,000 m). To use the timetable, enter the table horizontally on the top line and find your starting repetitive group. Next, find the altitude to which you wish to ascend. If you exceed a number, use the next greater one. The time at the coordinates of the desired altitude and your starting repetitive group indicate the minimum time delay recommended before ascending to the altitude selected. Note that for about half of the table no delay (0:00) is required.

Profile Contingency Planning

When you plan a dive profile, you should also plan for contingencies. You should know what to do in case you unintentionally exceed your planned depth or time or both. A

Table 6.2   Altitude Delay Timetable

	STARTING REPETITIVE GROUP										
Altitude	ABC	D	E	F	G	H	I	J	K	L	Group*
2,000	0:00	0:00	0:00	0:00	0:00	0:00	0:00	0:00	0:00	2:26	K
3,000	0:00	0:00	0:00	0:00	0:00	0:00	0:00	0:00	2:37	4:08	J
4,000	0:00	0:00	0:00	0:00	0:00	0:00	0:00	2:53	4:30	5:51	I
5,000	0:00	0:00	0:00	0:00	0:00	0:00	3:04	4:57	6:29	7:44	H
6,000	0:00	0:00	0:00	0:00	0:00	3:20	5:24	7:12	8:38	9:54	G
7,000	0:00	0:00	0:00	0:00	3:41	6:02	8:06	9:43	11:10	12:36	F
8,000	0:00	0:00	0:00	4:08	6:50	9:11	11:04	12:41	14:19	15:40	E
9,000	0:00	0:00	4:57	8:06	10:48	12:58	14:51	16:39	18:11	23:09	D
10,000	0:00	6:18	10:37	13:25	15:56	18:05	20:10	21:18	23:24	24:50	C

Note. Times represent the minimum recommended time delay before ascending to listed altitude and are USN surface interval times with a delay factor of 5.4. Altitude is in feet. Times are in hours:minutes; for example, 5:24 is 5 hours 24 minutes.

*Recommended minimum repetitive groups for indicated elevations.

▶ Figure 6.7 A contingency matrix helps you plan ahead for unexpected events.

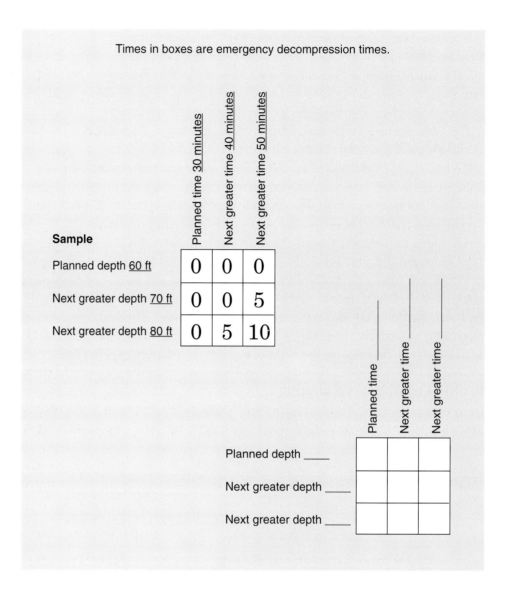

Times in boxes are emergency decompression times.

Sample

Planned depth <u>60 ft</u>

Next greater depth <u>70 ft</u>

Next greater depth <u>80 ft</u>

Planned depth _____

Next greater depth _____

Next greater depth _____

simple matrix, such as that depicted in the figure 6.7, is helpful. Prepare a contingency matrix in advance of your dives and carry it with you while diving.

USING DIVE CALCULATORS AND COMPUTERS

The benefits of a dive computer (figure 6.8) outweigh the potential problems associated with its use. Learn how to use dive tables and dive calculators so you will know how to plan a dive if you do not have dive computer. Obtain a dive computer as soon as you can.

Dive Calculators

There are circular planning devices that eliminate the mathematics required with the dive tables. Circle-shaped calculators automatically compute all calculations. Guides on the calculators help eliminate line-jumping errors that divers frequently make when using dive tables.

The calculator for the modified USN tables features simplicity and ease of use. There are only a few instructions for use, and they are printed directly on the calculator.

Dive Computers

Dive tables have 5 or 10 ft increments and require that all the time of a dive be counted at maximum depth of the dive. If the first part of your dive is deeper than the remainder of the dive, you are penalized because the tables consider the entire dive to take place at the deepest depth (see figure 6.9). At the end of the dive you receive a letter group designation that is higher than you deserve. Dive tables are used to plan dives in advance.

▶ Figure 6.8 Dive computers make time and depth determinations easy.

Dive computers use 1 ft increments for profile planning and calculate nitrogen absorption continuously. As you vary depth during a multilevel dive, you are charged only for the nitrogen you absorb. You do not incur the maximum-depth penalty of the dive tables, so your RNT is less following a multilevel dive with a dive computer compared with the same dive using dive tables. The penalty avoidance is the primary advantage of a dive computer as a dive-planning device. Dive computers provide advance planning information, but you also can carry them with you when you dive, and they provide information about your decompression status continuously. In fact, scrolling is one dive planning function of a dive computer that displays the time limits for various depths sequentially.

Regardless of the type of computer that you use, you should understand some basic principles.

First, be sure to read the instruction manual that comes with your computer. Wait 24 hours after diving with dive tables before using a dive computer. Do not exceed the ascent rate specified by the manufacturer, and do a 5-minute precautionary stop at a depth of 15 to 20 ft (4.6 to 6 m) at the end of every dive. If you exceed the rate of ascent specified for your computer, extend the duration of your precautionary stop by at least the amount of time it should have taken you to ascend to the stop depth. Do not make repetitive dives in excess of 80 ft (24 m). Keep your dive computer activated until its outgassing is complete. If your computer fails at any time during a dive at a depth in excess of 30 ft (10 m), terminate the dive immediately with precautionary decompression. If your computer fails or if you switch it off accidentally, discontinue diving for 24 hours.

If you exceed the maximum time limit for a dive, the computer will display a ceiling—the minimum depth to which you may ascend. As you decompress, the ceiling will become shallower until it indicates that you may surface. The situation is emergency decompression, which you should avoid. Wait 24

▶ Figure 6.9 The striped area represents penalty time imposed by dive table procedures.

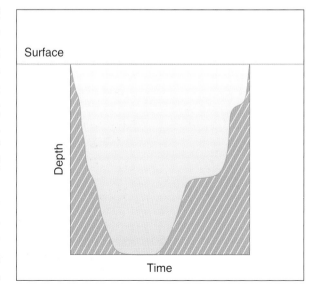

Dive Computers:
Advantages and Disadvantages

Advantages

- You avoid the maximum-depth penalty of the dive tables.
- Dive profile information is accurate.
- Dive computers may provide a stored record of the dive profile.
- Dive computers eliminate the errors made with manual dive planners.
- Additional features, such as an ascent rate indicator, are available.

Disadvantages

- Dive computers are electronic instruments that can fail.
- Dive computers are expensive to purchase and service.
- Each diver must have a separate computer.
- The mathematical model varies from one type of computer to another, so some confusion results when each diver forming a buddy team uses a different type of computer.
- Not all dive-planning information displayed by a computer may be accepted at face value. You must learn and apply the dive computer guidelines included in this section.

hours before diving again following any dive with a ceiling.

The concept of backup planning with dive tables is good for square profiles, but table planning for multilevel computer dives is not feasible.

DIVE PROFILE PLANNING RECOMMENDATIONS

Whichever planning device you use, you should follow these recommendations to minimize the risk of DCS. Limit multiple-day, multilevel dives because repetitive multiple-depth profiles make you more susceptible to DCS. After three consecutive days of repetitive diving, wait a full day before diving again. Avoid repetitive dives with short surface intervals. Use all dive-planning devices conservatively. Exercise good judgment and common sense.

Planning for the Unexpected

After you complete your plans, you need to implement them. The first rule of dive planning is, "Plan your dive, and then dive your plan." When on a dive, you and your buddy should make every effort to do as you had agreed to do before the dive. When circumstance forces change in your plans, it helps to have contingency plans. Here are some examples of possible procedure contingencies for a dive. You should have a contingency plan for what to do for any of the following situations. Know what to do if you

- surface downcurrent from a boat when you had planned to surface in front of it,
- are unable to reach or use the exit point you had selected on shore,
- end the dive a long distance from your exit location,
- exceed the MDT for a dive,
- experience a failure of your dive computer while diving, or
- ascend directly to the surface without precautionary decompression.

POSTDIVE PLANNING

After a dive, you and your buddy should reflect on your experience. How closely did the actual dive match the dive that you had planned? If there were deviations from the plan, what caused them? Could you have prevented the deviations with a different plan or approach? What changes can you make to improve the next dive? Some problems may require research, or you may need to ask the advice of a diving professional. The experience of each dive should affect your plans for future dives. Your dives with your buddy should progress more smoothly each time you dive together, and each time you visit a dive site, your dive procedures should improve. A review of each dive with your buddy and a discussion about future diving are valuable parts of dive planning. Even if you have a new dive buddy for a dive, you should plan your dives together and discuss the experience afterward. Predive discussions with a new buddy take longer than they do with a regular dive partner.

SUMMARY

The saying "If you fail to plan, you plan to fail" is true for scuba divers. All phases of dive planning are important and help ensure enjoyable and successful underwater experiences. Follow the recommended steps of planning, get area orientations when appropriate, have contingency plans, and discuss your dives with your buddy.

Dive profiles are a large portion of dive-planning. Whether you use dive tables, a calculator, or a computer when you dive, do so conservatively. No dive planning device can guarantee that you will not develop decompression sickness after diving. The deeper, longer, and more frequently you dive, the greater the risk of DCS. Make a precautionary decompression stop at the end of every dive, avoid improper profiles, and have surface intervals of an hour or more.

Diving Environment

7

Learning to dive gives you an opportunity to explore the aquatic environment, which covers more than 70 percent of the earth's surface. The underwater world is fascinating. This section introduces you to biological and physical conditions of the diving environment. You will learn about people's effect on the environment, and the environment's effect on people. You affect the underwater world more than you might imagine.

By the end of this chapter, you will be able to

- describe the aquatic food cycle and explain how the process contributes to the red tide;
- list five types of aquatic life injuries and three ways to avoid such injuries;
- list four types of pollutants and describe the effects they have on the underwater environment;
- list three actions that divers can take to help preserve aquatic life;
- list five ways to keep from damaging the environment while you are underwater;
- contrast the general diving conditions for freshwater diving and saltwater diving;
- describe the hazards of cavern diving, cave diving, and ice diving;

- explain the cause of tides and their effects on diving activities;
- explain the cause of waves and surf and their effects on diving activities;
- explain the causes of currents and their effects on diving activities;
- describe a rip current and explain how to escape from one; and
- define plankton, bloom, red tide, kelp, stipes, fronds, ciguatera, scombroid, tetrodotoxin, thermocline, reverse thermocline, overturn, upwelling, eddies, cavern, cave, sink, syphon, continental shelf, tsunami, stand, spring tide, neap tide, flood, ebb, slack water, fetch, swell, crest, trough, wave height, wavelength, wave period, wave train, rip current, drift, set, trail line, and drift dive.

INTRODUCTION TO AQUATIC BIOLOGY

The plants and animals of the underwater world are wondrous and diverse. The millions of animals in the aquatic realm range from creatures of microscopic size to those weighing tons. To appreciate, respect, and enjoy aquatic life, you need to learn certain aspects of biology. This section familiarizes you with the flora and fauna of the aquatic realm. Aquatic life fits into three categories: life forms that drift with the currents, those that swim freely and are able to move against the currents, and those that dwell on the bottom.

▶ Figure 7.1 The underwater food cycle.

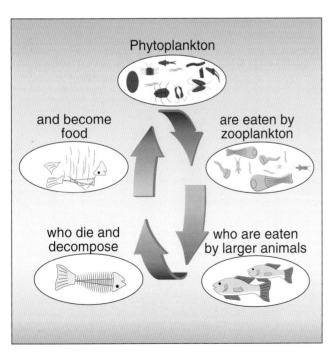

Phytoplankton

and become food

are eaten by zooplankton

who die and decompose

who are eaten by larger animals

Drifters

The drifters are called **plankton**. Animals that drift are called zooplankton; drifting plants are called phytoplankton. Plankton begins the food cycle in the waters (see figure 7.1). Small animals eat plankton, and larger animals eat the smaller animals. When the large animals die, their remains sink to the bottom and decompose. The decomposed material rises to the surface, where it becomes food for the plankton.

Warm water and nutrients cause some plankton to multiply. Overpopulations of plankton, called **blooms**, can color the water, destroy underwater visibility, and form toxins in animals that feed by filtering water. Toxin from blooms makes clams and mussels unsafe for consumption during summer months in some areas. One type of red phytoplankton often creates blooms, known as **red tide**, in the seas. Diving conditions are poor in areas affected by plankton blooms.

Another type of aquatic plant, called algae, is an important part of the aquatic world. Plants use light to produce their own food and become food for animals. They convert water and carbon dioxide (CO_2) to oxygen and carbohydrates through the process of photosynthesis. Various types of algae are found in underwater areas where light is available. Most algae grow in shallow water where light is most abundant. Thick moss drapes objects in some freshwater areas. A grasslike, green, tropical saltwater algae that provides a habitat for many forms of life is called turtle grass. Some cold, saltwater, shallow-water types of long, flowing algae, such as surf grass or eel grass, can cause you to trip if you try to walk against it. Slippery plants cover rocks and can cause you to slip and fall unless you move cautiously.

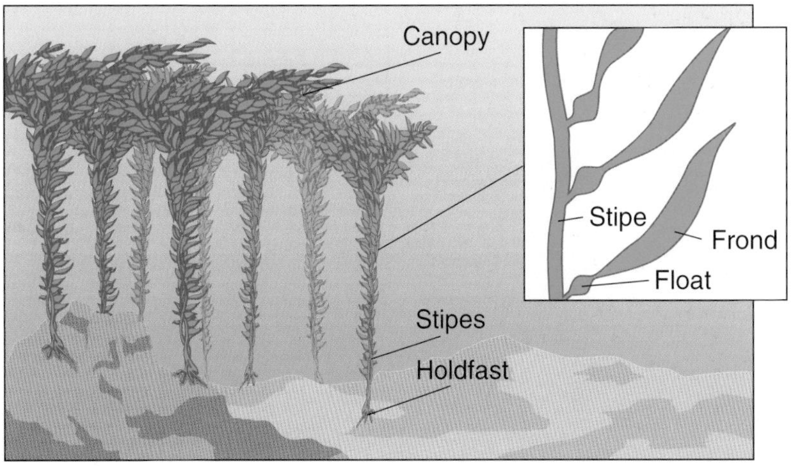

▶ Figure 7.2 A typical kelp bed.

Giant algae, called **kelp**, produce long strands, called **stipes**, in which you can become entangled, but you can learn how to avoid and how to deal with this problem. A rootlike structure, called a holdfast, anchors kelp to the bottom; numerous gas bladders, called floats, lift kelp toward the surface. What appear to be the leaves of kelp are **fronds**. Large areas of kelp, known as kelp beds, have thick canopies that blanket the surface of the water (see figure 7.2). It is difficult to swim through a kelp canopy at the surface, but it is easy to swim between the clumps of stipes beneath the surface. Underwater navigational skills are important when diving in areas where kelp is dense. Kelp "forests" are popular diving areas because they contain great quantities of life.

Swimmers

One of the rewards of diving is seeing fish. There are fish in nearly all the waters of the earth. You cannot outswim the slowest fish, so do not chase them. If you want to observe fish closely, blend into the environment. Fish will get closer to you than you could ever get to them.

Collecting for aquariums requires specialized knowledge and procedures. Most fish have an internal air bladder for buoyancy control. If taken to the surface too quickly, the air bladder expands and kills the animal. Avoid handling fish because the experience can be traumatic, as well as physically damaging, to the animal.

▶ Figure 7.3 Eating pufferfish will cause poisoning that could result in death.

Eating some types of fish can harm you. Some fish are poisonous. Types of fish poisoning include **ciguatera**, **scombroid**, and **tetrodotoxin**. Ciguatera results from eating fish that consume a certain species of algae. Ciguatera poisoning causes gastrointestinal problems within 6 to 12 hours. Scombroid poisoning, which produces nausea and vomiting within an hour, can result if you eat fish that have not been kept chilled. Tetrodotoxin, the most serious fish poisoning, results from eating exotic fish such as a puffer, also called a blowfish (figure 7.3 shows an example of a puffer). Tetrodotoxin poisoning can cause death within minutes.

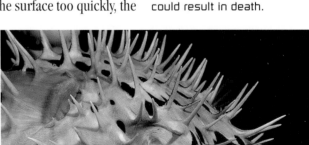

Avoid eating large and unusual-looking fish. Check with people who fish in the local area to determine which fish are safe for consumption.

Many large swimming mammals—sea lions, seals, dolphins, whales, and manatees—inhabit the water world. They are graceful, beautiful, and sometimes awesome in appearance. Some are curious and will approach you. Aquatic mammals usually will not harm you in the water if you leave them alone. But sea lions and seals are defensive on land and might bite if you get too close.

Bottom Dwellers

Bottom dwellers include animals that are stationary, such as sea fans and some hydroids, as well as animals that move about, such as crabs and lobsters. Generally speaking, living stationary bottom dwellers are not included in fish and game regulations, and you should not take them. Don't take coral, sea fans, and animals that appear stationary, such as starfish. If you hunt crabs and lobsters for food, know how to determine the sex of the animals, how to catch them without harming them, and how to measure them for minimum size. Do not take females, particularly those bearing eggs. Some divers take only one claw from a crab to conserve the species. A crab can feed and defend itself with one claw and can regenerate a new claw to replace the one taken.

Hydroids

If you dive in salt water, you should know about hydroids, a category of animals that includes bottom dwellers, such as coral, and swimmers, such as jellyfish (see figure 7.4). Some hydroids, like the beautiful sea anemone, have a round, columnlike body with a mouth surrounded by tentacles. This is a polyp form of hydroid. Another type, called the colonial form, can assume many different shapes. Colonies of hydroids can encrust a surface, and groups of colonies form jellyfish.

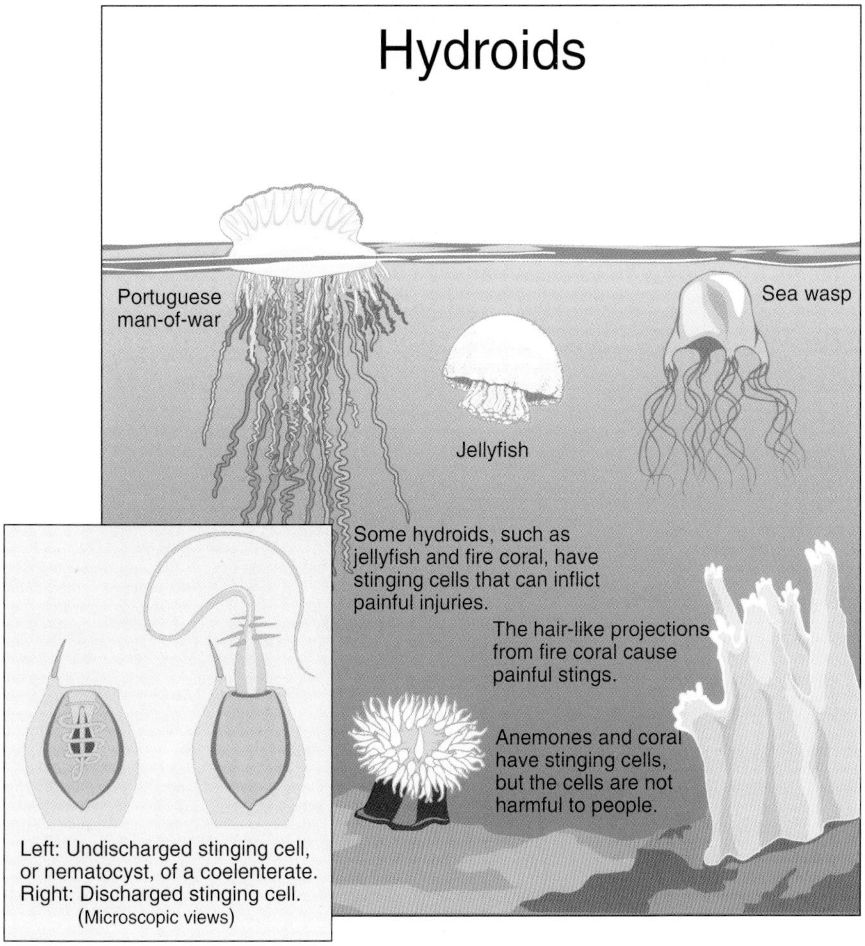

▶ Figure 7.4 There are several types of hydroids, which have stinging cells.

Hydroids

Portuguese man-of-war

Jellyfish

Sea wasp

Some hydroids, such as jellyfish and fire coral, have stinging cells that can inflict painful injuries.

The hair-like projections from fire coral cause painful stings.

Anemones and coral have stinging cells, but the cells are not harmful to people.

Left: Undischarged stinging cell, or nematocyst, of a coelenterate. Right: Discharged stinging cell. (Microscopic views)

POTENTIALLY DANGEROUS AQUATIC ANIMALS

Aquatic animals use a variety of mechanisms to obtain food and to defend themselves from attack. You can minimize your chances of injury by being familiar with the ways in which animals inflict injury. Aquatic animals rarely are aggressive toward humans; they flee, hide, or stand still as you approach. If you do not touch, threaten, or provoke an animal, it is unlikely to injure you intentionally. But remember, aquatic animals are wild animals. If you feed them, and they bite you in the process, you should not blame the animals. Figure 7.5 lists types of injuries you could sustain from aquatic animals and recommended first aid.

Animals That Cause Abrasions or Cuts

Many animals, such as some types of coral and barnacles, are sharp, hard structures that easily cut flesh. Such cuts can be painful and slow to heal and can get infected. Avoid contact with reefs and rocks covered with sharp animals. Also, some fish have knifelike protrusions on their gill plates or at the base of their tails. They defend themselves by flailing rapidly back and forth and slashing anything near them.

Animals That Puncture

Sea urchins are the porcupines of the seas. Cold-water urchins have short, thick spines, while warm-water urchins have spines that are long and thin. The spines of all urchins can penetrate an exposure suit if you bump into them. The spines break off in your flesh and produce a painful, red, swollen wound. The spines can be difficult to remove, so if you are unable to avoid a sea urchin injury, see a physician to have the spines removed.

Some fish have a row of long sharp spines along their back. The scorpion fish has hollow dorsal spines, at the base of which are sacs filled with venom. If you are punctured by the spines and compress the venom sacs, you inject yourself with a toxin. The toxin of some species, such as the stonefish, can cause serious symptoms. The lionfish (also called a turkey fish and a zebra fish), has spines in other fins, and its toxin produces serious symptoms in humans. Freshwater catfish also have venomous spines.

A tropical marine worm, called a bristle worm, has tufted, silky bristles along the sides of its body. The bristles, which are fine and brittle, penetrate the skin easily, are difficult to remove, and cause a burning sensation. Do not touch or handle these worms.

Retreat from snakes if you encounter them. Do not handle them. Sea snakes in tropical waters are extremely venomous; a sea snake puncture bite can produce a life-threatening emergency. Some fresh water snakes, such as the cottonmouth, also are venomous.

Some seashells, called cone shells, have a venom apparatus they use to kill animals for food. The venom is highly toxic, and the animals can inject their venom into a human. Do not handle conical shells in tropical waters.

Animals That Bite

Use discretion to avoid being bitten by aquatic animals. A large freshwater fish that can bite is the gar. Turtles can inflict serious wounds, muskrats may attack in defense, and moray eels in the ocean can deliver a serious bite. Alligators also have the potential to inflict an injury and have been known to bite divers. Sharks can bite, but attacks on scuba divers are nearly nonexistent. Hollywood has exaggerated the danger of sharks; only a few species of sharks are aggressive, and it is rare to encounter these types in the waters visited by divers. Most divers would be delighted to see a shark because the animals usually retreat from an area frequented by scuba divers.

Animals That Cause Lacerations

Rays are round, flat bottom dwellers. Some rays have a sharp, serrated barb at the base of the tail. The rays blend into the sea bottom. When someone disturbs a ray, it defends itself

Coral

Moray eel

▶ Fig. 7.5 Potential injuries and recommended first aid.

Potentially Dangerous Aquatic Animals

Injury	First Aid
Abrasions or cuts	
Barnacle	Scrub and disinfect the wound.
Coral	
Bites	
Barracuda	Stop the bleeding, clean and
Moray eel	disinfect the wound. For a sea
Sea snake	snake bite, apply pressure,
Shark	immobilize the area, and get
Turtle/muskrat/alligator	prompt medical attention.
Stings	
Bristle worm	Soak the injured area in
Cone shell	vinegar. For a cone shell sting,
Fire coral	apply pressure and immobilize
Jellyfish	the injured area.
Puncture	
Sea urchin	Soak the injured area in hot water.
Venomous fish	
Laceration	
Stingray	Soak the injured area in hot water.

Place a constricting band between the heart and the wound for any toxic injuries caused by venomous fish, cone shells, or sea snakes.

Get medical attention as needed for all injuries.

Fire coral

Sea urchin

Stingray

by arching its back and thrusting its barb into the attacker. A sheath, which often remains in the laceration wound, covers the barb and contains a toxin. Stingray wounds in the ankles of divers, waders, and swimmers are common in some areas. Avoid stingray wounds by shuffling your feet along the bottom instead of walking. The torpedo ray, an animal found on the West Coast of the United States, can generate electricity. This ray can stun a diver, so be able to recognize it, and avoid contact if you encounter one.

Animals That Sting

Many animals sting. Learn to identify and avoid contact with jellyfish, featherlike or whip-like hydroids, and even some sponges. Hydroids have tiny stinging cells, called nemato-cysts, that they use to kill food. The sting of some animals, such as encrusting fire coral, is merely annoying; but the sting of others, such as the Portuguese man-of-war or the box jellyfish, can cause a medical emergency. Your should wear an exposure suit at all times while diving in the ocean. The suit provides protection from stings, but be careful when you remove it. The stinging cells of marine animals remain active even if they are not on the animal. Parts of jellyfish and other animals that are on your equipment may come into contact with your skin when you remove the equipment. Some jellyfish come to the surface at night in tropical waters. Dangerous stinging animals are seasonal in some regions. Check with local divers to find out what to avoid and when to be on the alert.

Avoiding Danger

Many aquatic animals are potentially hazardous. Tropical waters have the most dangerous animals. But serious injuries to divers are not common because divers avoid animals that can hurt them. Respect animals but do not be overly concerned about them. Do not panic or flee when you see a potentially dangerous animal; just avoid contact with it. Learn to recognize the dangerous animals in an area, know where to look for them, be alert for them, and keep clear of them. Move slowly and look carefully. Shuffle your feet when wading. Don't touch anything unless you know it is safe. Neutral buoyancy—the ability to hover—is an excellent defense against aquatic injuries.

The biology of the underwater world is so interesting that many divers study it as a hobby. They enjoy learning about animals and plants and then observing them in their natural habitats. Some divers, fascinated with aquatic life, pursue biology as a career.

CONSERVING AND PRESERVING LIFE

Life in the waters is beautiful and precious, but pollution from people jeopardizes life in the lakes and seas. Even divers physically ruin beautiful reefs. Unless we take action immediately, there is a real danger that many areas of the underwater world will become barren and lifeless. We must preserve and conserve the resources of our waters.

Because the waters are so vast, people often take them for granted. Lakes and seas seem too big to be harmed, but that is not the case. The underwater environment is fragile; the balance of nature can be upset more easily than many people realize. We think of the seas as being great and powerful because we see big waves and pounding surf. People who do not see beneath the surface may not realize the delicate nature of the animals that inhabit the waters. Some living things in the seas grow slowly—only a fraction of an inch (a few centimeters) per year.

As a diver, you can help reduce damage to the underwater world. Every diver should take two actions: (1) do everything possible personally to preserve the diving environment, and (2) do everything possible to educate others and help them learn to preserve the aquatic environment. You will get closer to the aquatic environment than most of your friends, and you will see firsthand the effects of pollution, litter, and exploitation. You also will see the beauty and abundance that are possible when the environment is clean and unmolested. Your influence in society can make a difference. If you do not become part of the solution to problems in the aquatic environment, you are part of the problem.

Pollution

Stemming pollution is one of the greatest challenges facing the world. Humans are incredible polluters of the environment; we have polluted the air, the land, and the waters.

People dump billions of gallons and billions of pounds of waste into water every day. People seem to think that when something is out of sight, it no longer is a problem. This is not true of pollutants. Sewage, industrial waste, garbage, and sediment have killed many underwater environments and are continuing to kill. If we stopped all pollution today, the aquatic environment would continue to suffer for decades from the waste materials that are already in the water.

Runoff from land that enters rivers and streams and flows into the ocean also causes pollution. Chemicals used in agriculture, on lawns, and in gardens cause death and destruction in the aquatic environment. Sediment from construction and drilling finds its way into water and blocks out life-giving sunlight and smothers bottom-dwelling creatures.

Lakes and oceans have been viewed as bottomless toilets for waste disposal. There are two problems with this narrow view: (1) animals and plants live in the water and are killed by the pollution, and (2) the water cannot be replaced because large bodies of water cannot be flushed.

Diver Impact

As a diver, you can harm the environment in several ways. You can remove living things from the environment, you can smash and kill life while moving about underwater, and you can stir up clouds of silt on the bottom. The silt can choke and kill some organisms. Good intentions also can cause problems; handling and feeding animals can kill them.

You can be an effective predator underwater. There are many animals you can hunt and take. A few callous individuals kill things for "sport," but most people take only that which they will eat. Although the impact of divers is of little significance compared with commercial fishing, you do have an effect. If you spearfish on a reef, it will not be long before the fish in the area will be unapproachable by divers. If you want to be a predator, do so in a responsible manner. (Conservation and preservation of aquatic resources are discussed later in this section.)

It is difficult to resist touching animals underwater, but you should refrain until you know what animals may be touched and how to touch them without harming them. Many animals are delicate; rough handling will kill them. Predators will eat animals removed from a protected area for viewing. Some animals, including fish, have a protective coating of mucus. If you remove the coating by handling a creature, the animal can develop an infection and die. The stress of being handled by a gigantic, bubble-blowing monster may be more than some aquatic animals can take. Sea turtles may abort their eggs after being harassed by a playful diver. Do not be guilty of killing things for your amusement. After you learn how, you will be able to get extremely close to animals underwater. You can interact with them and enjoy them without handling them.

Feeding animals underwater was a popular activity until environmentalists showed that this is harmful (not to mention dangerous). There are several potential problems. Unnatural food can interfere with the digestive process. The animals may become dependent on the food fed to them by divers and may not be able to forage if the food supply is discontinued. And food can make animals overcome their natural fear of divers. When an animal that would normally take cover at the sight of a diver becomes accustomed to divers providing food, the animal will readily approach a diver who is a hunter.

A diver underwater can be like a bull in a china shop. Overweighted divers plow along the bottom with their fins pointed downward, stirring up great clouds of silt. Buoyancy difficulties cause divers to hold on to and crash into reefs and living things. Divers who rest on the bottom crush life without realizing it. Divers who swim too close to a reef often kick animals to death.

Minimizing Diver Impact

One of the most important reasons for good buoyancy control skills is to prevent damage to the underwater environment. An environmentally responsible diver is properly weighted and in control of buoyancy at all times. Make your diving "no-contact" diving. You should be able to hover above a reef, move your mask within inches of an animal, and view the animal without touching anything but water and without stirring up silt. Learn to use your hands to scull into position while your fins remain still. Sculling is positioning achieved with short movements of the hands (not the arms). Buoyancy control and sculling are excellent skills for reducing diver impact. Figure 7.6 shows a diver sculling.

Another way to protect the environment is to keep your equipment secured close to you so it does not dangle and drag. Equipment that drags along the bottom for an entire dive can do a lot of damage. Streamline your equipment. Moving slowly underwater conserves energy and air and makes you less likely to make contact with things. This helps you avoid injury to both yourself and animals.

▶ Figure 7.6　Sculling helps reduce diver impact.

If you must hold on to something underwater or push yourself away from something, look before you touch, and avoid touching anything that is living. If you must settle on the bottom for some reason, select an area where there is no visible life. If you are weightless, keep in mind that one finger may be all you need to provide the leverage to move. Leave no evidence that you ever visited an underwater area.

Conservation

Many animals that once were plentiful are nearly extinct because of a lack of conservation. Buffalo and passenger pigeons are good examples of land creatures. In some areas, this is happening to aquatic animals. Bait fish, which once swarmed in enormous schools in some areas, no longer exist. With no food to eat, larger predatory fish no longer frequent the areas.

Fish and game regulations are designed to conserve natural resources. Rules regarding sizes, seasons, limits, and the means by which game may be taken have been established to help ensure an ongoing supply of a resource. Obey fish and game regulations, and encourage others to abide by them as well. The rules can benefit everyone in the long run.

If you take life from the water, do it in a responsible manner. Avoid taking animals from areas that are popular dive sites. Limit hunting and collecting to remote areas where the impact of divers is much less. Take only what you need, not what you can get or what you are allowed. The two types of hunters most harmful to the environment are the quantity hunter and the trophy hunter. The quantity hunter seeks to take as much and as many of everything as possible to build an image as the mighty hunter. The trophy hunter seeks the largest animals, which destroys the fittest of the breeding stock. If you kill an animal, you have a duty to know how large one must be to breed and what the maximum size of the animal is. You should take animals that have had the opportunity to reproduce, but do not take the largest ones. It is difficult at times to be selective, but you should attempt to conserve life.

Nature, left undisturbed, maintains a balance of life. Animals are both predator and prey. An animal eats other animals and is, in turn, eaten by others. If there are too many predators, their population will diminish because of an inadequate food supply. If there is a temporary overpopulation of prey, the number of predators will increase. People upset nature's balance. We are the most efficient predators of all. We disturb the food cycle with pollution, hunting, fishing, boating, and every way in which we affect the aquatic environment. It takes nature longer to recover from our impact than from any natural disaster. It is important today to lessen the effect of people on the environment so that nature will have less interference with the management of the life within the waters.

Preservation

Preservation is everyone's business, but it is more of your business now than it was before you became a diver. You know more than your friends and neighbors about the aquatic environment. Be an ambassador for preservation, and educate and motivate people to help preserve the diving environment.

What people do above water affects life beneath the surface. What people put down their drains and toilets winds up in the aquatic environment. So do the chemicals they use on their lawns and gardens. Litter in and around the water kills animals, birds, and fish. Think twice about the products you buy, how you use them, and how you dispose of your wastes. Where will the toxic chemicals and waste end up? Be environmentally conscientious; then teach others to be so. A simple act, such as the use of detergents without phosphates, can make a difference. Phosphates are powerful nutrients that upset the balance of nature in the aquatic environment. Figure 7.7 shows the effects of environmental pollution.

Be involved in your community. Be concerned about issues such as sewage treatment, toxic wastes, and construction. Construction and drilling on shorelines or on waterways can be extremely harmful. So are waste products from manufacturing. Help others understand the seriousness of pollution.

Get more informed and keep informed. Join groups that are working to preserve the environment, such as the Center for Marine Conservation, Project Reefkeeper, and the Oceanic Society. These groups provide up-to-date information and specifics on how you can help. Various organizations sponsor underwater cleanups from time to time; these are enjoyable and worthwhile. (For a list of environmental organizations you can join, see the appendix.)

There are actions you can and should take when diving. Dispose of trash properly, and encourage others to do the same. If you have a boat for diving, anchor it away from reefs to avoid reef damage caused by the anchor and chain. Retrieve trash you find in the environment, especially plastic. Collect plastic, monofilament, lead, and stainless steel leaders. Not all trash is bad. Bottles and cans provide homes for animals. Report unlawful dumping and lost or discarded fishing nets and traps, which continue to catch and kill after abandonment.

▶ Figure 7.7 Litter is ugly, and it kills sea life.

INTRODUCTION TO AQUATIC CONDITIONS

The particular state of the environment or the physical situations in which divers find themselves are conditions. The conditions of concern to divers include the temperature, visibility, and degree of movement of the water. You need to be familiar with aquatic conditions in general and local aquatic conditions specifically.

The Big Picture

Many factors affect the seas. The sun bears down on the earth at the equator more directly than on other parts of the earth. The climate and waters near the equator are warm; the greater the distance from the equator, the colder the water. The difference in water temperatures in different parts of the world causes the movement of air and water by convection currents. Winds move from areas of high pressure to areas of low pressure, and winds and the turning of the earth move water. On a global scale, water currents move in a clockwise direction in the Northern Hemisphere and in a counterclockwise direction in the Southern Hemisphere. Weather moves from west to east. The gravitational attraction between the earth and other planetary bodies produces changes in the water level called tides. Storms at sea produce energy in the form of waves that travel thousands of miles before giving up their energy in the form of surf.

Temperature changes, winds, and storms affect inland bodies of water. Water from snow and rain in the mountains and hills flows into streams, rivers, and lakes. Water seeping into the ground resurfaces in quarries and springs.

Weather, seasons, geography, and other factors affect two categories of diving conditions: surface and underwater. The water may be rough at the surface and calm at depth. There may be a current at the surface but none on the bottom. The visibility may be good at the surface but poor on the bottom. The temperature usually is warmer at the surface than it is at depth. You should become familiar with both surface and underwater conditions and their effect on your diving.

Perhaps the most important fact to remember about diving conditions is that they vary from place to place. Thus, an environmental orientation is important when you dive in a new region. The diving conditions usually dictate the way you dive. What works well in one area may be totally ineffective for another. An understanding of the effects of diving conditions in an area is important. You should know the conditions to expect, how the conditions affect your approach to diving, and how to manage the effects of the conditions.

General Freshwater Diving Conditions

Fresh water is 2.5 percent less dense than salt water, so you are less buoyant in fresh water than in salt water. The density of water varies with temperature. Fresh water is most dense at a temperature of 39.2° F (3.99° C)—the usual temperature and density of the water at depths greater than 60 ft (18 m) in fresh water lakes and quarries. The water becomes lighter when it is either warmer or cooler than this.

Fresh water often forms layers—a layer of warmer, lighter water on top of a layer of colder, denser water. The change from the warm water to the colder water, called a thermocline, is abrupt. When the water is calm, the thermocline appears to have wisps of smoke on top of it when viewed from above. The refraction of light is different when the density of the water is different, so there is a slight visual blurring at the interface of a thermocline. When you dive in fresh water, you must insulate yourself for the water temperature below the thermocline. Although the surface of the lake may be warm, the water at the bottom may be close to freezing.

The best season for diving in a freshwater lake or quarry varies depending on the body of water. Spring and fall are often good times because the water temperature is the same from surface to bottom, there is oxygen for fish at all depths, populations of plankton are low, and visibility usually is good.

In later spring, the sun warms the surface water, and the lack of wind keeps it from mixing with the colder water at depth. The water stratifies, and a thermocline forms that remains until fall. The layer of water below the thermocline stagnates in most lakes during the summer. Decaying matter depletes oxygen and creates toxins. Fish seek refuge

Scuba Wise

There are similarities between the environments above and below the water. Temperature, weather, plants, and animals change when you travel from region to region on land. We enjoy the variety of mountain, plain, forest, and desert regions. The world beneath the water changes similarly when we travel from region to region. The enjoyment that the varying underwater environment provides is a major reason why dive travel is so popular.

When you go to places on land that are rugged, remote, and hazardous, you need special training and equipment. Careful planning and preparation are essential. A guide makes exploration safer and more enjoyable. When you go diving in places that are rugged, remote, and hazardous, the same requirements apply. Enjoy the wonderful differences beneath the waters—coral reefs, vertical walls, wrecks, and so forth—but always be properly prepared and equipped and always obtain orientations to new areas.

above the thermocline. Sunlight and warm water often lead to plankton blooms, which are aggravated by pollution.

In the fall, surface waters in lakes and quarries cool until they equal the temperature of the water at depth. Colder water and reduced sunlight stifle plankton growth and visibility improves. Winds cause water circulation. The movement of water from the top to a depth of about 60 ft (18 m) is called an **overturn**, which carries oxygenated water to the bottom and leads to the spring conditions. Visibility tends to be poor during an overturn.

In the winter, the surface water in a lake or quarry is colder than the water at the bottom. A **reverse thermocline** exists and remains until the surface water temperature warms to that of the water at the bottom. This allows the spring overturn to begin. Water becomes 10 percent lighter

Freshwater conditions

when it freezes. If ice sank when it froze, bodies of water could become solid ice from top to bottom. Ice that forms over water insulates the water beneath it. Figure 7.8 shows the annual cycle of freshwater lakes and the concept of thermoclines.

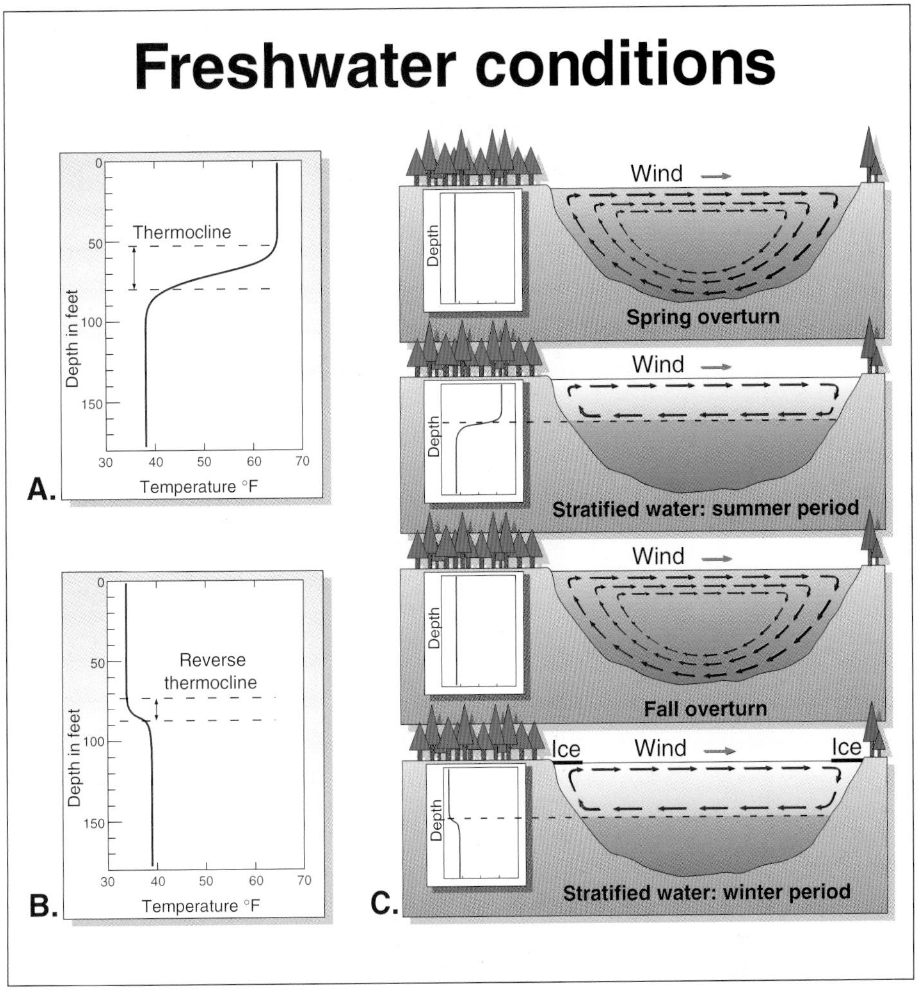

▶ Figure 7.8 Thermocline (a), reverse thermocline (b), and a depiction of the annual cycle of overturn in lakes (c).

When a strong wind blows along a shore for a sustained period over a body of water, the wind pushes the surface water away from shore. This water is replaced by colder water flowing up from the depths. This is called an **upwelling**, which also can occur in the ocean. If the wind conditions persist, the water temperature can become constant throughout the water column, even in the summer. An upwelling carries nutrients from the depths into shallow water and brings animals into the area. Following an upwelling, a bloom may occur because of the increase in nutrients in warm, shallow water.

Specific Freshwater Diving Conditions

There are good diving experiences in many kinds of freshwater environments. Springs, low-altitude lakes, and quarries are good sites for divers who do not live near a coast. Other freshwater environments, such as rivers, caverns and caves, high-altitude and frozen lakes, and areas with submerged wreckage, can be dangerous (see figure 7.9). Complete specialty courses before diving in any hazardous area.

You may encounter strong currents in rivers. The currents are strongest at the surface and on the outside of bends. Countercurrents and swirling currents, called **eddies**, are

upwelling—The replacement of warm water at the surface with colder water flowing up from the depths as a result of a strong wind blowing along a shore for a sustained time

169

▶ Figure 7.9 Diving in rivers provides unique experiences but shouldn't be attempted without specific training.

common, and entanglements are likely in many rivers. Currents can undercut the bank of a river, so direct access to the surface may be impossible at times. Rivers are especially prone to seasonal changes and are often unpredictable.

Freshwater springs can provide beautiful diving environments. The flow of clean, calm water, which usually is at a moderate temperature (65° to 78° F or 18° to 25.6° C), provides excellent visibility. The water often flows through underground limestone cave systems that extend for thousands of feet. Diving in open-water basins in a spring is appropriate for certified divers, but entering any overhead area that lacks a direct, vertical ascent to the surface is not appropriate. A large roomlike opening where light from the surface can be seen is called a **cavern**. Areas that extend farther than a cavern where no surface light can be seen are called **caves** (see figure 7.10). Divers must complete specialty courses and must meet several requirements to dive in caverns and caves. Entering such an environment—even a short distance—without the required training and equipment can lead to your death. It is easy to become disoriented, to stir up thick clouds of silt that instantly reduce visibility to nothing, and to panic and drown. You may dive in spring basins, but stay out of caverns and caves unless you meet the requirements to dive in them. The appendix contains contact information for organizations that offer cavern and cave diving training.

Sometimes the earth collapses into an underground cave system and forms a **sink**. The water flowing into the sink forms a basin. An opening called a **syphon** channels water from a sink back into the system. Diving in syphons can be dangerous. The amount of water moving through a system depends on the amount of rainfall in the area. Under extreme conditions, the normal flow of water can reverse.

People dig pits to excavate sand, gravel, and stone. At some depth they encounter the water table, and the pit floods, forming a quarry or sand pit. At some of these sites, you may view submerged construction equipment, which was abandoned when the pit flooded. Sand pits and quarries tend to have fair to good visibility, although the disturbance of silt

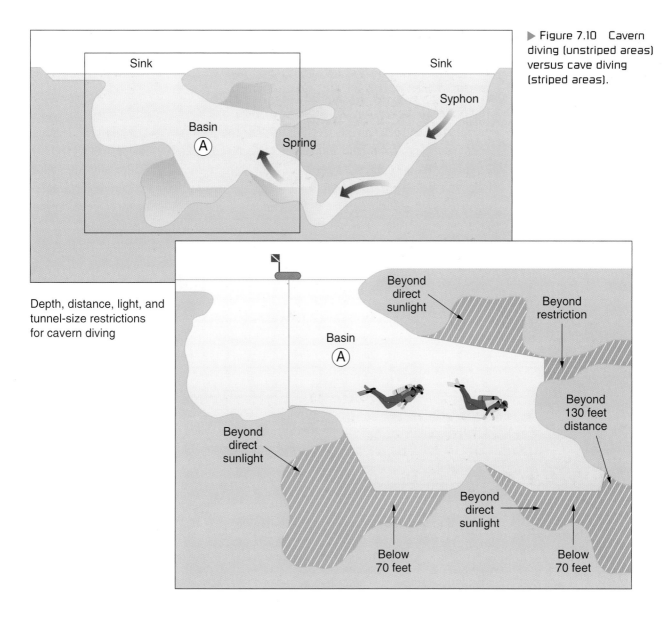

▶ Figure 7.10 Cavern diving (unstriped areas) versus cave diving (striped areas).

Sink   Sink

Syphon

Basin
(A)   Spring

Depth, distance, light, and tunnel-size restrictions for cavern diving

Beyond direct sunlight

Beyond restriction

Basin
(A)

Beyond 130 feet distance

Beyond direct sunlight

Beyond direct sunlight

Below 70 feet

Below 70 feet

that has settled to the bottom can ruin the visibility quickly. Gravel quarries usually are siltier than other types of quarries, so the water may be turbid.

Lakes can be excellent dive sites. There are freshwater lakes at altitudes above 10,000 ft (3,048 m). Diving at altitudes above 1,000 ft (305 m), a specialty called altitude diving, presents many hazards because the rate of change of pressure is greater when you descend into water from atmospheric pressure that is less than the pressure at sea level. You must follow special procedures to avoid decompression sickness. Problems also can result from the thinner air, which provides less oxygen with each breath taken above water.

When ice forms over water in the winter, diving becomes hazardous. Perils include hypothermia, the freezing of regulator and buoyancy control valves, and getting lost beneath the ice. Ice diving can be beautiful and adventurous, but it is dangerous to attempt it without the proper training, equipment, and procedures.

Hazards of freshwater include body heat loss; submerged trees; wire; fishing line, hooks, and lures; logjams; debris; currents; rapids; whirlpools; poor visibility; silt; and overhead restrictions. You can minimize these hazards with training, experience, equipment, correct diving techniques, area orientations, and good judgment.

General Saltwater Diving Conditions

There are five oceans on the earth; seas, gulfs, and bays are smaller sections of the oceans. The land beneath the oceans is not flat. The continental shelf is an underwater area that extends from land and slopes gradually to a depth of about 600 ft (183 m). Beyond the continental shelf are great underwater canyons and mountains as well as hills, valleys, and great plains. In some areas, the tips of some mountains and volcanoes extend above the surface of the ocean from great depths. In other areas, deep canyons sever the continental slope, creating deep-water conditions close to shore.

The saltwater environment varies greatly from one part of the earth to another. The clear waters of the Caribbean, with temperatures that can exceed 85° F (29.4° C), feature coral reefs covered with beautiful, lush animals that look like plants. Schools of colorful tropical fish abound. Temperate waters, with temperatures ranging from 55° F to 70° F (13° C to 21° C), may have great forests of kelp, which contain more life per cubic foot than a tropical rain forest. Cold ocean waters in northern latitudes are nutrient-rich and team with life. There are beautiful sights and wonders to behold in all the oceans. Figure 7.11 shows one example.

Oceans always are in motion. Tides, winds, and currents cause water movement. An underwater earthquake can move water by creating gigantic seismic waves known as tsunami. Although these giant waves are sometimes called tidal waves, the tide has nothing to do with them. Tsunamis can cause great destruction, but they are rare and can be forecasted.

The energy source for the movement of the water may be local or may originate thousands of miles away. You need to understand what causes water to move, how it moves, and how to dive in ocean water that is in motion.

▶ Figure 7.11 Sights like this are common in the temperate waters of the Caribbean.

Tides

The gravitational attraction between the moon and the earth pulls water toward the moon. The resulting increase in water depth is called high tide. Water pulled away from the sides of the earth in the process produces a decrease in water depth called low tide. A high tide forms on the side of the earth opposite the moon because the attraction of the moon is least at that point and because of centrifugal force created by the rotation of the earth. At any given time, two areas on the earth are experiencing high tides and two areas are experiencing low tides. There is a brief period of time, called a stand, when the tide neither rises nor falls; there can be four tidal stands per day, two high and two low. Geographical formations interfere with or enhance the rising and falling of the water in some areas.

The sun also affects the tides, but only about half as much as the moon because the moon is much closer to the earth. When the moon and the sun are aligned with the earth, which occurs twice monthly (during the new and full moons), tides are highest and are called spring tides (see figure 7.12). When the moon and sun are at right angles to each other in relation to the earth, tides are lowest and are called neap tides

The moon rotates around the earth in the same direction that the earth spins, and the duration of a lunar day is nearly 25 hours. This causes tides to occur at different times each day and explains why the heights of subsequent tides vary.

To change the height of the water during a tidal change, water must flow from one area to another. The water movements caused by the tides are called tidal currents, and they vary in velocity between tides. The flow of water into an area because of high tide is called a flood. The flow of water away from an area because of low tide is called an ebb. There is a period of time between flood and ebb when the water has minimal movement. The term for this period is slack water. Because of geographical features of the earth, water cannot move instantly in many areas. There usually is a delay between the predicted time of a tide and the time when the water is slack.

Tidal changes affect diving activities and operations. Large differences in the water level between tides affect visibility and other conditions. Water height also affects entries and exits, shoal areas when boating, the mooring of boats, and the loading and unloading of vessels. It is a good idea to know how high the tide will be. Tidal changes are small (less than 2 ft or 0.6 m) in some areas or on some days and large (more than 6 ft or 1.8 m) in other areas or on other days. The greater the difference between high and low tide, the greater the effect of the tides.

Because the earth, moon, and sun follow set courses, the tides are predictable. Tides vary because the distance between the bodies in the solar system and their positions relative to one another change constantly. Despite all the variables, scientists predict with accuracy when the tides will occur and the heights of the tides. The government publishes tide tables, and national weather channels broadcast tidal information

spring tide—The twice-monthly period of highest tides; occurs when the moon and sun are aligned with the earth

neap tide—The twice-monthly period of lowest tides; occurs when the moon and sun are at right angles to each other in relation to the earth

▶ Figure 7.12   The effect of the sun and moon on tidal patterns.

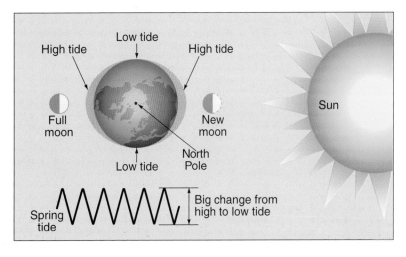

November 1986							
Low tide				High tide			
a.m.	ht.	p.m.	ht.	a.m.	ht.	p.m.	ht.
Sunrise 6:19		-PST-		Sunset 5:08			
1 Sa 1:35	1.0	2:35	0.5	7:49	6.4	8:46	4.7
2 Su 2:06	1.3	3:17	0.9	8:21	6.7	9:36	4.4
3 M 2:38	1.7	4:06	1.0	8:56	8.8	10:35	4.0
4 Tu 3:14	2.1	5:02	0.9	9:33	6.7	11:44	3.7
5 W 3:50	2.6	6:03	0.7	10:19	6.5	—	—
Sunrise 6:24		-PST-		Sunset 5:03			
6 Th 4:42	3.0	7:17	0.4	1:14	3.5	(11:15	6.0)
7 F 6:00	3.3	8:36	0.2	2:57	3.8	12:28	5.4
8 Sa 8:23	3.3	9:43	0.1	4:15	4.0	2:03	
9 Su 10:12	2.8	10:42	0.1	5:01	4.4	3:39	
10 M 11:22	2.1	11:27	0.3	5:37	4.9	4:55	
Sunrise 6:28		-PST-		Sunset 5:00			
11 Tu —	—	12:14	1.4	6:09	5.3	5:?	
12 W 12:06	0.6	12:59	0.8	6:34	5.6	6:?	
13 Th 12:38	0.9	1:38	0.3	6:59	5.9		
14 F 1:07	1.3	2:13	0.1	7:24	8.1		
15 Sa 1:31	1.6	2:45	0.3	7:47	6.2		
Sunrise 6:33		-PST-		Sunset			
16 Su 1:56	2.0	3:21	0.4	8:1?			
17 M 2:21	2.2	3:53	0.3				
18 Tu 2:40	2.5	4:33	0.?				
19 W 3:03	2.7	5:1?					
20 Th 3:21	3.0						

▶ Figure 7.13 An example of a tide table.

wave height—The distance from a wave crest to the trough

wavelength—The distance between waves

wave period—The time it takes two waves to pass a given point

continually. Local correction tables and current tables can provide more precise information. Tide tables refer to the height of the tide in relation to an average of the low tides in an area (see figure 7.13). Wind and barometric pressure affect the height of tides, aiding or opposing the movement of tidal waters.

Generally it is best to dive at high tide, but you may need to coincide your diving with slack water in areas with strong tidal currents. The timing may not be important in areas where tidal changes are small. Consider local knowledge about the effects of tides when planning dives.

Waves and Surf

Ripples form when wind blows across water. You can see this in a puddle on a windy day. When ripples form on a large body of water and the wind continues to blow, the sides of the ripples form a surface against which the wind can push to set the water in motion. The longer and harder the wind blows in a constant direction, the larger the waves that form. As waves move away from the area in which they were created—an area called the fetch—the tops of the waves become rounded and become undulating waveforms called swells. The water within swells moves in a circular motion but has little forward motion. The effect is similar to the transmission of a waveform along a rope that is tossed up and down at one end. Waves of energy travel along the rope, but the rope itself does not move forward.

Swells are energy forms that can travel thousands of miles through water and still contain a great deal of energy. The top of a wave is called its crest. The bottom is called the trough. The distance from the crest to the trough is the wave height. The distance between waves is a wavelength. The time it takes two waves to pass a given point is a wave period. A long series of waves is a wave train. The greater the height of a wave and the greater the wavelength of a wave train, the greater the energy contained in the waves. Two trains of waves can have phases during which the waves of each train reinforce one another and produce larger waves, called wave sets. The formation of larger and smaller waves may occur in phases. By timing the "beat" of the surf, you can make entries and exits easier by moving through the surf zone when the wave sets are small. Figure 7.14 illustrates fundamental concepts of waves and surf.

The water within a passing wave moves in a circular motion. The diameter of the motion equals the height of the wave at the surface and diminishes with depth. Motion from a passing wave can be felt to a depth equal to half of the wavelength for a series of waves. If it is 100 ft (30 m) between waves, you can feel the effect of a passing wave to a depth of 50 ft (15 m).

When waves enter shallow water, contact with the bottom interrupts the circular motion of the water within the waves. The circular movements flatten and eventually become a back-and-forth subsurface motion called surge. Wave contact with the bottom causes waves to slow and to become steeper. The wave height increases as the water depth decreases. When the water depth is about the same as the wave height, the wave becomes unstable and tumbles forward. At this point the water within the wave moves forward and gives up its energy in breaking waves known as surf. In areas with offshore reefs, sandbars, and underwater obstructions, waves can break in shallow water, pass over the obstruction, reform, and break again in shallow water near the shore. Waves that break offshore indicate the presence of shallow water in the area where the waves are breaking.

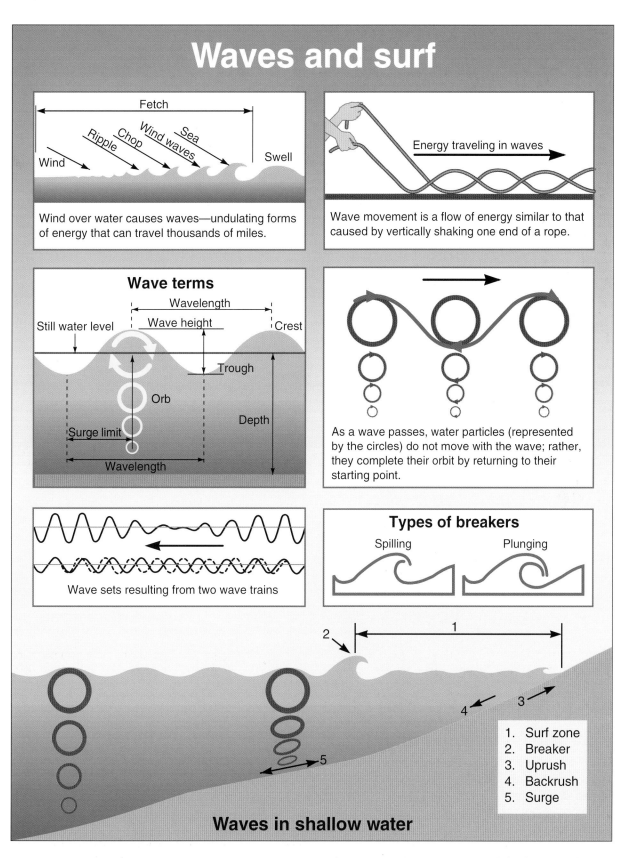

Waves and surf

Fetch

Ripple · Chop · Wind waves · Sea · Swell

Wind

Wind over water causes waves—undulating forms of energy that can travel thousands of miles.

Energy traveling in waves

Wave movement is a flow of energy similar to that caused by vertically shaking one end of a rope.

Wave terms

Wavelength

Wave height

Still water level · Crest

Trough

Orb

Depth

Surge limit

Wavelength

As a wave passes, water particles (represented by the circles) do not move with the wave; rather, they complete their orbit by returning to their starting point.

Wave sets resulting from two wave trains

Types of breakers

Spilling · Plunging

1. Surf zone
2. Breaker
3. Uprush
4. Backrush
5. Surge

Waves in shallow water

▶ Figure 7.14   Wind speed, the absence or presence of obstacles, and the shape and depth of the ocean floor influence the formation of waves and surf.

Waves can break and release their energy all at once, or they can spill forward and expend their energy over a wide area. Waves that build quickly and break suddenly form plunging breakers. Waves that spill forward over some distance to shore are spilling breakers. Plunging breakers build quickly and break suddenly; they occur on steeply sloping shores. Spilling breakers spill forward over some distance to shore and occur on bottoms that slope shallowly. Spilling breakers tend to reduce visibility more than plunging breakers.

The crashing water of surf contains air. The white water and foam in the surf area, called the surf zone, does not provide as much buoyancy as water that does not contain air. It can be difficult to remain above water in the foam of surf, but you should not attempt to rise above the breakers because you can be picked up and tossed forward by the moving water. It is best to remain low in the wave and breathe from your scuba regulator.

Surf rushes up the face of a beach, then flows back again to the still water level. The return flow of water is called the backrush. This countercurrent, mistakenly called an undertow by some, does not extend beyond a depth of 3 ft (1 m). Although backrush can be strong when surf is large on a steep beach, there is no undertow that will carry a swimmer out to sea.

The surf's crashing onto the shore moves sand. Gentle summer waves carry sand onto the beach; and large, rough, winter waves carry the sand offshore, where it forms sandbars. That's why some beaches are rocky in the winter and smooth in the summer.

Currents

Currents are in water what wind is in air—fluid in motion. Because water is 800 times more dense than air, water poses much more resistance to movement than air. You need to know how and why water moves and how to move with it. The force of water in motion is too great to resist. You must learn to use the flow of water to your advantage.

Wind, gravity, tides, and convection cause currents; the most common currents are wind-generated surface currents. Because of the rotation of the earth, currents flow at an angle to the wind that generates them. When the wind pushes water away from an area, another current, a compensating current, replaces the water displaced. Overall, the effect on the earth is to produce large circulating currents, called gyres, that move clockwise in the Northern Hemisphere and counterclockwise in the Southern Hemisphere.

When wind blows along a coast, a vertical compensating current—an upwelling— occurs. The opposite of an upwelling is a downwelling. A strong downwelling current is rare, but it can occur under the right conditions where there is a steep drop-off near shore. It is frightening to be pulled downward in water. Learn if and where a downwelling occurs in an area, and avoid that location. If you should get caught in a downwelling, swim horizontally until you are clear of the current. Trying to swim up may lead to exhaustion and panic.

Water flows in layers. The water at the surface moves quickly with the wind, whereas the water a few feet beneath the surface moves slower. The deeper the depth, the less the effect of a surface current. After 12 hours of a sustained wind in a given direction, the speed of a surface current is approximately 2 percent of the speed of the wind that drives it. Because water flows in layers, it is possible for a surface current to flow in one direction and for a subsurface current to flow in the opposite direction only a few feet (about 1 m) beneath the surface (see figure 7.15).

downwelling—A compensating current that occurs when wind blows along a coast where there is a steep drop-off near shore and which pulls the water downward

Surface water at the equator expands as it is warmed and flows slowly toward the poles of the earth. At the same time, water cooled near the poles increases in density and sinks. Slow-moving convection currents result. These currents do not affect diving procedures, but they greatly affect the oceans by the movement of nutrients and pollution.

Water can move swiftly, and water movement intensifies whenever an amount of water passes through a restriction. When water encounters irregular formations during its movement, turbulence produces dangerous eddies and whirlpools. Swift-water diving is a specialty considered hazardous even with experience and training.

Incoming waves can pass over an underwater obstruction, such as a sandbar, and pile up water on a shore. If the backrush of water flows back to sea through a narrow opening in the obstruction, a **rip current** exists. The current will be narrow, strong, and away from shore. The current will dissipate shortly after passing through the restricted area. You can identify rips by a fan-shaped area of water on the shore; by muddy, foamy water in the rip area; and by a section of waves that breaks before the remainder of the waves. Rip currents may be stationary or moving. Recognize and avoid rip currents. If you are unable to swim toward shore, you probably are in a rip current. Swim parallel to the shore for about 60 ft (18 m) to get clear of the rip; then turn and proceed toward shore (see figure 7.16).

Waves breaking upon a shore at a slight angle move water along the shore. The current, called a longshore current, affects diving. On steep beaches, the current can cut a

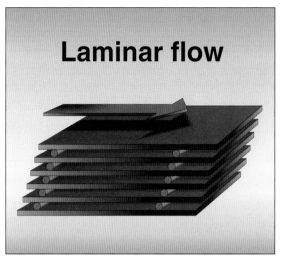

Laminar flow

▶ Figure 7.15   The flow of water is similar to a tipped stack of boards with rollers between them. When the stack is tipped, the top board moves much farther than the bottom board. Surface water moves more than water at depth.

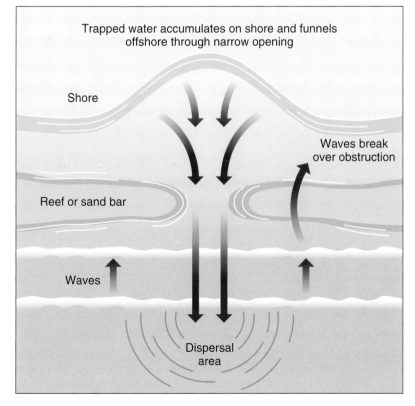

Trapped water accumulates on shore and funnels offshore through narrow opening

Shore

Waves break over obstruction

Reef or sand bar

Waves

Dispersal area

rip current—The narrow, strong current that moves away from shore as a result of water flowing back to sea through a narrow opening in an underwater obstruction

▶ Figure 7.16   A classic rip current.

shallow trough in the bottom close to shore. The trough, called a longshore trench, is a sudden drop-off for a wading diver and can cause an unsuspecting diver to fall. Items dropped into the surf zone move along the shoreline in the direction of the longshore current. The movement of sand on beaches occurs because of wave action combined with longshore currents.

Two types of currents result from the combined forces of nature: standing currents, which are constant, and transitory currents, which occur briefly. The Gulf Stream that flows around Florida and up the eastern coast of the United States and the Antilles Current that flows through the Caribbean are examples of standing currents. A longshore current is a transitory current. A rip current may be either type. Be familiar with the currents you will encounter or may encounter in an area. (This is one more reason for encouraging area orientations for diving.)

Currents can flow at a rate of hundreds of feet (meters) per minute. The speed of a current is its drift, and the direction assumed by a current is its set. A fully equipped diver can swim at a rate of 60 to 100 ft (18 to 30 m) per minute. Attempting to fight even a mild current is futile and a waste of energy. Strong water movement can dislodge equipment, cause regulators to free-flow, and cause rapid heat loss. You must learn to recognize and estimate currents. If the currents are strong, avoid them. Even if they are mild, avoid struggling against them. The primary rule for diving in currents—when you begin and end your dive at the same point—is to dive in a direction opposite the flow at the surface; then use the surface current to aid you when you return at the end of the dive. (See chapter 6 for suggestions on estimating currents.)

There are other general rules for diving in currents. Water movement is minimal at the bottom. Whenever possible, descend along a line from the surface to the bottom. If the current is still strong when you reach the bottom, ascend on the line and abort the dive. When unsure of your location during a dive, it may help to surface, determine the direction to the exit point, redescend, and move along the bottom toward your destination.

When there is a surface current, minimize the time spent at the surface. Whenever possible, hold on to a fixed object at the surface to keep from drifting downcurrent at a dive site. When a surface current is mild, swim against it to maintain your position at the surface. Develop the habit of noting your surface position in relation to a fixed reference. If you are caught in a sudden, strong current, swim across it to escape from it.

For diving operations conducted from a boat, the crew usually extends a long floating line, called a trail line, from the stern (back) of the vessel. This line, which has a float attached to the end, can be used by divers to pull themselves to the boat if they surface downcurrent from the vessel (see figure 7.17). Because an anchored vessel points into the current, you should plan to end your dives in front of the boat so the surface current will aid your return. If you end a dive downcurrent from a boat, are unable to return to the bottom to move upcurrent, and are unable to swim against the current, get buoyant, signal the vessel, and wait to be picked up. This is embarrassing but better than exhausting yourself to no avail.

A dive made with the flow of current is a drift dive. Simple drift dives along a coast are acceptable when planned. You enter the water at one point, move along the shore with the current, and exit at another point downstream. Another type of drift diving, which is a specialty activity, involves diving in currents from a boat. This type of diving is hazardous because the boat must be operated while divers are in the water. Do not at-

drift dive—A dive made with the flow of current

▶ Figure 7.17 Divers may use a trail line to pull themselves to the boat if they surface downcurrent.

tempt drift diving from boats unless you have completed specialty training and have a trained, experienced captain for the vessel.

Potential saltwater diving hazards include body heat loss, currents, surf, marine life, poor visibility, and fishing nets and equipment. You can minimize the hazards of ocean diving by following the recommendations described in this section.

SUMMARY

The aquatic environment is a vast, great, wonderful area. We depend on it for our existence. We need to learn about it, care for it, and respect it. We must protect the environment and encourage everyone we know to assist in that effort. Because the environment varies greatly from place to place, divers need area orientations. There are hazards in the underwater world just as there are hazards on land, but you can minimize aquatic hazards with training, experience, planning, proper procedures, and common sense.

Diving
Opportunities

8

As a qualified scuba diver, you can do many things. You can learn more, dive in different areas, be recognized for expertise, help others, or earn money, to name just a few. Opportunities abound.

By the end of this chapter, you will be able to

- list ten special-interest areas for novice divers and six special-interest areas for advanced divers,
- list at least five ways to continue your scuba diving education,
- list at least three ways to get involved with the local diving community, and
- list several actions to take when preparing for a dive travel trip.

CONTINUING EDUCATION

A good diver never stops learning. You cannot learn everything you need to know about diving during a single course of instruction. After you complete your entry-level course, you can enroll in an intermediate or advanced scuba course. These courses allow you to gain additional experience under supervision, help you develop important skills (such as navigation), and introduce you to special-interest areas of diving (see figure 8.1). When you have identified the diving specialty you would like to pursue, complete a specialty course for that topic. A specialty course helps you begin enjoying the special-interest area from the outset and helps you avoid mistakes and injury. Specialty areas that are of interest to new divers include the following:

- Underwater photography
- Underwater hunting and collecting
- Underwater environment
- Diving rescue techniques
- Night diving

- Boat diving
- Dry suit diving
- Drift diving
- Cavern diving
- Altitude diving

▶ Figure 8.1 Underwater photography is an enjoyable diving activity.

The following specialty courses are of interest to experienced scuba divers with advanced training:

- Wreck diving
- Ice diving
- Cave diving
- Deep diving
- River diving
- Search and recovery

Courses are only one way to learn about diving. Many diving seminars, workshops, and conferences are also available. Check the calendar section of diving publications to learn of events scheduled for your area. Diving changes constantly, so you need to keep updating your knowledge of diving medicine, diving equipment, and diving procedures. Continuing education programs give you the opportunity to learn from professionals who are continually involved in diving.

You can learn more about scuba diving by reading books, magazines, and newspapers. Subscribe to a scuba periodical and read all you can about diving. The appendix contains a listing of scuba periodicals.

If you have a computer and a modem, you can use computer bulletin boards that have sections for scuba divers. The scuba bulletin boards feature libraries, conferences, and topic discussions; they are "living" publications in which you may participate.

Another good way to continue your diving education is to join a dive club. Dive clubs offer many benefits to divers, including education. A talk on an interesting subject by a good speaker usually is part of a local club's monthly meeting.

Continuing your diving education is important for your safety and enjoyment. When you have increased your knowledge about diving, you may become interested in helping others to learn.

LOCAL OPPORTUNITIES

You do not need to live in a coastal area to dive regularly or to get involved in diving. You can dive nearly anywhere you can find water, and there are dive stores, dive clubs, and diving events in noncoastal areas.

Get involved in diving in your area right away. Find all the diving-related businesses and groups in your area—dive clubs, dive stores, dive boats, diving events, and diving publications. Join a dive club, attend the meetings, and participate in club dives. Use the scuba bulletin board of a computer network to make contact with other divers in the area. Complete continuing education courses. Attend local diving seminars, workshops, conferences, and shows, and talk to other divers when you attend diving events. Seize every opportunity to learn and every opportunity to dive with those who are more experienced than you.

DIVE TRAVEL

Many divers enjoy taking dive trips to exotic destinations, and there are thousands of beautiful and exciting diving locations to choose from around the world (see figure 8.2). If you are a diver, you will probably travel somewhere to dive. You need to know how to arrange dive travel, how to prepare to travel, and how to enjoy your trip.

Scuba Wise

Scuba equipment is a means to an end—a mechanism that enables you to go to areas that are otherwise unreachable by the average person. I think of scuba as a means of transporting myself to a destination where I can explore or participate in a special activity. Scuba diving without an objective loses its thrill after only a few dives. You need to develop an interest area, which can be anything from bottle collecting to wreck diving. When you have an objective for your dives, diving can be extremely rewarding. Over the years, I have participated in many *different diving activities. My favorite underwater pursuit is underwater photography. I can collect priceless memories without removing anything from the environment. In my opinion, underwater photography is the most challenging and the most satisfying dive activity. Select a diving activity that appeals to you, complete training for the activity, and then pursue it. You may choose several different activities. No matter what you choose to do while diving, I hope that your experiences will be as wonderful as mine have been.*

Travel agencies that specialize in dive trips provide valuable information, so it is a good idea to book your trip through one of them. You might want to consider a dive package that includes accommodations and diving. Dive resorts advertise these packages in diving publications and often offer packages for bargain prices at dive shows. There are many toll-free numbers you can call to obtain information about dive packages. To ensure the best value for your money, compare several packages before you book a trip. If a brochure from a dive resort is out-of-date, check with the resort for current offers.

When planning a dive travel trip, you need to decide where you would like to dive and whether you want to dive from a live-aboard dive boat or from a shore-based dive resort. A live-aboard trip allows you to dive in a variety of locations. The vessel moves from place

▶ Figure 8.2 Scuba diving can take you to some exotic destinations.

▶ Figure 8.3 Vacationing on a live-aboard boat immerses you in scuba diving.

to place in the mornings, evenings, and at night. You dive in remote areas that only a few divers visit. A live-aboard dive trip can be a wonderful experience if diving is the only objective of your trip and you are not affected by motion sickness (see figure 8.3).

Consider a shore-based dive trip if you do not care for confinement and if you want to participate in activities other than diving. Many beautiful islands and resorts offer a great deal to do in addition to diving (see figure 8.4). Nondiving members of your group or family usually can find many sources of enjoyment at a land-based diving destination.

Many diving magazine articles and diving location publications are available to help you decide where to dive, although choosing from all the destinations available can be difficult. Recommendations from other divers, trips sponsored by your dive club or dive store, and travel presentations can help you decide.

When you have decided on the region for your dive trip, get as much information as possible about diving in the area. Obtain and review brochures, books, articles, videotapes,

▶ Figure 8.4 Dive resorts accommodate any need a vacationing diver may have.

and any other materials you can get on the region. Find out who has been to the location you plan to go to, and talk to them. The more you know in advance, the more enjoyable you can make your experience.

After you select your diving destination, you should make your reservations well in advance, confirm all financial arrangements in writing, and get clarification regarding cancellations, refunds, and so forth.

Research and plan your dive trip by learning about the water temperature for the time of year when you will be diving, and obtain appropriate exposure protection. Remember that too much insulation is better than too little. Also make sure that all your equipment is in good working order.

Plan to avoid sunburn. Sunlight in tropical areas is more intense than in other climates. Use a sunscreen, and unless you are well tanned, keep yourself covered at all times—even while in the water. Use lip balm with a sunscreen ingredient. You cannot develop a tan in a few days, so it is silly to try if you do not have one. Sunburn can ruin an expensive vacation, and it is painful to don an exposure suit when you are burned. It takes only a few minutes for an untanned person to get burned in the tropics, so be careful!

Obtain all required documentation well in advance. Obtaining passports and visas can take months. Be sure to find out whether the country you will be traveling to requires immunizations.

Learn what to expect when you arrive at your destination. Know the frequency and voltage of the electricity; take converters if you are taking electrical appliances that operate on a different voltage. Know the monetary exchange rate. Consider taking a small pocket calculator to help compute the conversion of money.

If you have an expensive camera, video equipment, or jewelry, take your property to a customs office before you leave the country and have it documented to avoid being charged duty on the items when you return home.

Do not procrastinate in making your preparations. Procrastination can cause a cancellation of your trip, a forfeiture of your deposit, and a great deal of frustration.

Limit what you take when you pack for your trip. You do not need much clothing for a dive trip unless you plan to attend formal events. A few sets of shorts and T-shirts, some swimsuits, and a couple of sets of nice clothes for dinner should suffice. Experienced dive travelers travel light when it comes to clothing and personal effects.

Diving destinations provide tanks and weights, so you do not need to take those items with you (see figure 8.5). When you pack, keep in mind that there may be weight limitations for your baggage. Excess baggage costs can be very high. To guard against theft, avoid advertising expensive diving, photography, and video equipment. Use inconspicuous containers to ship your equipment, and it will be less likely to disappear. Insure luggage that contains expensive equipment.

▶ Figure 8.5 It's not necessary to transport tanks because most diving destinations provide them.

SCUBA DIVING

Be prepared for travel illnesses. It is easier to obtain medications for nausea, diarrhea, and colds before a trip than it is if you become ill in a foreign country.

Flying is the most common method of transportation for dive travel. Air travel usually produces jet lag and dehydration. A viral illness a couple of days after reaching your destination is common because many virus germs are concentrated inside the cabins of airliners. Following are some tips and suggestions concerning air travel.

First, schedule your flight to arrive the day before you start diving. It is unwise to plan to dive the same day you arrive. Drink a full glass of water or apple juice every hour during your flight to help prevent dehydration. Avoid alcohol, milk, and drinks containing sugar. The humidity in an aircraft is about 8 percent, so you will become dehydrated unless you drink plenty of fluids. Avoid eating heavy meals and salty foods when flying. Light foods cause less dehydration than fatty foods. Consider ordering a special meal of salad and fruit.

Wash your hands frequently when traveling. If you rub your eyes or your nose, germs from your hands that get into your eyes and nose can lead to viral infections.

Baggage compartments on airliners are unpressurized, and the reduced atmospheric pressure can damage your gauges. Either take your gauges inside the airplane in your carry-on luggage or store them in airtight containers.

As soon as possible after reaching your destination, get some exercise and drink plenty of liquids. Limit the consumption of alcohol, which causes dehydration. Getting intoxicated at the outset of a diving vacation is one of the worst things you can do because you increase your chances of getting DCS.

Confirm your return air reservations as soon as you arrive at your destination, especially if you travel to another country. If you fail to do this, you are likely to lose the reservations. It is frustrating to arrive at the airport to go home and discover that your tickets are not valid.

Your first dive at your destination should be an orientation dive. In addition to learning about diving in the area, use the dive to check your buoyancy and make any needed adjustments. Work out any equipment problems during a dive in shallow, still, calm water. Avoid deep dives or moving water until you have become acclimated to the area.

After three days of repetitive diving, refrain from diving for one day so your system can outgas. Go shopping or take a land tour for a refreshing change of pace. Allow one day between your final scuba dive and your scheduled flight home. The nondiving day before flying helps prevent DCS caused by altitude and gives you the opportunity to rinse, dry, and pack your diving equipment. Snorkeling is a good last-minute activity, and your mask, snorkel, and fins dry quickly for last-minute packing.

Dive travel can be fun, exciting, and memorable when you plan it well. Avoid unpleasant, frustrating, and disappointing experiences by researching your destination and preparing properly. Good diving to you.

CAREER OPPORTUNITIES

Some people love diving so much that they want it to be their vocation. Career opportunities do exist for those who are willing to put forth the effort to achieve their desires. Jobs within the recreational dive industry include resort dive guide, instructor, journalist, dive travel coordinator, retail sales person, and sales representative for equipment manufacturers. There are also nonrecreational scuba jobs such as scientific research, archaeology, engineering studies, hull cleaning, salvage, and underwater repairs. Two of the same rules that apply to recreational pleasure diving also apply to underwater work: (1) complete training for an activity before you attempt it, and (2) use complete, proper equipment for the activity. Career training opportunities abound. If you are interested in scuba diving as a vocation, you can find information about training in dive periodicals.

SUMMARY

Always remember that a good diver never stops learning. Complete additional training, be trained for any special activity before you attempt the specialty, read as much as possible, join a dive club, attend educational events, and take advantage of every opportunity to learn more about diving.

Increase your diving abilities and experience together. Apply what you learn. Participate in dive trips and charters. Research and plan your excursions thoroughly to maximize your enjoyment and minimize your disappointment. Be sure to plan a nondiving day before flying home. There are many opportunities for diving adventures throughout the world.

There is another opportunity for you as a diver. It is the opportunity to make a positive contribution to the diving community. You can do this by conducting yourself in a responsible manner at all times and encouraging other divers to act responsibly. Help establish a good image of diving, get involved in issues that pertain to the diving environment, and help educate people who do not dive. Whether your contribution is small and personal or vast and international, you can and should make a difference. Decide now that your involvement in the wonderful activity of scuba diving will be a positive one.

Lists and Checklists

DIVER-TRAINING ORGANIZATIONS

International Diving Educators
Association (IDEA)
Box 17374
Jacksonville, FL 32245

Multinational Diving Educators
Association (MDEA)
Box 52433
Marathon Shores, FL 33052

National Association for Cave
Diving
Box 14492
Gainesville, FL 32604

National Association of Scuba
Diving Schools (NASDS)
Box 17067
Long Beach, CA 90807

National Association of
Underwater Instructors (NAUI)
Box 14650
Montclair, CA 91763

National Speleological Society
Cave Diving Section
Box 950
Branford, FL 32008-0950

National YMCA Scuba Program
Oakbrook Square
6083-A Oakbrook Parkway
Norcross, GA 30092

Professional Association of
Diving Instructors (PADI)
Box 15550
Santa Ana, CA 92705

Professional Diving Instructors
Corporation (PDIC)
1015 River Street
Scranton, PA 18505

Scuba Schools International (SSI)
2619 Canton Court
Fort Collins, CO 80525

ENVIRONMENTAL ORGANIZATIONS

Center for Marine Conservation
1725 DeSales Street Northwest
Washington, DC 20036

Cousteau Society
930 West 21 Street
Norfolk, VA 23320

CEDAM
Fox Road
Croton-on-Hudson, NY 10520

Greenpeace
Box 3720
Washington, DC 20007

NOAA Sanctuary and Reserves Ocean
and Coastal Resource Management
Universal Building Room 714
1825 Connecticut Avenue Northwest
Washington, DC 20235

Oceanic Society
1536 16th Street Northwest
Washington, DC 20036

Project Reefkeeper
16345 West Dixie Highway
Suite 1121
Miami, FL 33160

Sea Shepard
Box 7000-S
Redondo Beach, CA 90277

Wildlife Conservation
International
Bronx Zoo
New York, NY 10460

SCUBA PERIODICALS

DAN Alert Diver
Box 3832
Duke University Medical Center
Durham, NC 27710

Discover Diving Magazine
Box 83727
San Diego, CA 92138

Dive Training Magazine
405 Main Street
Parkville, MO 64152

Rodale's Scuba Diving Magazine
6600 Abercorn Street #208
Savannah, GA 31405

Scuba Times
Box 6268
Pensacola, FL 32503

Skin Diver Magazine
6420 Wilshire Blvd
Los Angeles, CA 90048-5515

Sources
NAUI
9942 Currie Davis Dr #11
Tampa, FL 33619-2667

DIVING EQUIPMENT CHECKLIST

- [ ] Mask, snorkel, and snorkel keeper
- [ ] Fins and boots
- [ ] Scuba tank (filled)
- [ ] Buoyancy compensator
- [ ] Exposure suit, hood, and gloves
- [ ] Weight system
- [ ] Regulator with pressure gauge
- [ ] Alternate air source
- [ ] Instruments to monitor depth, time, and direction
- [ ] Signaling devices (whistle, mirror, safety tube)
- [ ] Dive knife
- [ ] Float, dive flag, and anchor
- [ ] Dive tables
- [ ] Dive light
- [ ] Slate and pencil
- [ ] Marker buoy
- [ ] Collecting bag
- [ ] Gear bag

- [ ] Spare equipment
  - [ ] Scuba tank(s)
  - [ ] Weights
  - [ ] Straps
  - [ ] O-rings
  - [ ] Snorkel keeper
- [ ] Secondary equipment
  - [ ] First aid kit
  - [ ] Emergency phone numbers and radio frequencies
  - [ ] Logbook
  - [ ] Swimsuit
  - [ ] Towel
  - [ ] Jacket
  - [ ] Hat or visor
  - [ ] Sunglasses
  - [ ] Dive kit
  - [ ] Save-a-dive kit
  - [ ] Drinking water

Glossary of Scuba Diving Terms

AAS—See alternate air source.

absolute pressure—The combined force of atmospheric pressure and gauge pressure.

actual dive time—The total time spent underwater from the beginning of descent until surfacing at the end of a dive; does not include precautionary decompression time.

adjusted maximum dive time—The maximum dive time for a specific depth minus the residual nitrogen time for a specific letter group for that depth.

ADT—See actual dive time.

AGE—See arterial gas embolism.

alternate air source—An additional second-stage regulator for emergency use by a buddy diver (also called an octopus) or a completely independent scuba unit for emergency use.

AMDT—See adjusted maximum dive time.

ambient pressure—The surrounding pressure.

arterial gas embolism—The blockage of blood flow to the brain caused by air bubbles escaping into the blood from the lungs.

atmospheric pressure—The pressure exerted by the atmosphere.

backpack—An item of dive equipment that holds a scuba tank on a diver's back.

barotrauma—A pressure-related injury.

BC—See buoyancy compensator.

bezel—A movable reference ring on a dive instrument.

bloom—A plankton overpopulation that can color the water, destroy underwater visibility, and form toxins in animals that feed by filtering water.

blowout plug—A rubber plug on the back of a submersible pressure gauge to prevent the face of the gauge from exploding if the high-pressure tube inside ruptures.

Bourdon tube—A curved or spiral tube that tries to straighten under pressure; the movement is mechanically coupled to a needle to indicate pressure.

Boyle's law—The inverse relationship between pressure and volume.

buddy breathing—Two divers sharing a single air source.

buddy system—A standard practice for people to dive in teams of two.

buddy line—A short line extended between two divers to help the divers maintain contact in limited visibility.

buoyancy—An upward force on an object placed in water; equal to the weight of the water displaced.

buoyancy compensator—An item of dive equipment that a diver can inflate to increase buoyancy and deflate to decrease buoyancy.

burst disk—A thin, metal disk in a scuba valve; designed to rupture and relieve pressure when the tank pressure exceeds a safe limit.

capillary gauge—A gauge made with a hollow tube that is open on one end and closed on the other. The gauge indicates pressure on a dial when Boyle's law compresses the air inside the tube.

cave—A naturally occurring room or passage in bedrock or coral, large enough for a human to enter. Extends farther than a cavern and beyond the point where surface light can be seen.

cavern—A large roomlike natural formation where light from the surface can be seen.

C-card—A card that documents successful completion of scuba diving training.

ceiling—A minimum depth to which a diver may ascend with minimal risk of DCS.

ciguatera—A type of fish poisoning that results from eating fish that consume a certain species of algae.

compartment—A decompression mathematical model that represents a body tissue half-time.

compass course—A direction determined by a compass bearing.

compass heading—A direction relative to magnetic north.

console—Devices that hold instruments near the SPG.

contact descent—A descent controlled by maintaining contact with something such as a line or a slope.

continental shelf—A region of relatively shallow water surrounding each continent.

contingency plan—A backup plan for unexpected developments.

controlling compartment—The area of the body that determines how long a diver can remain at a given depth. The determination is made by how quickly a gas diffuses from that compartment.

crest—The highest part of a wave.

Dalton's law—The partial pressure of a given quantity of gas is the pressure it would exert if it alone occupied the same volume. Also the total pressure of a mixture of gases is the sum of the partial pressures of the components of the mixture.

DCS—See decompression sickness.

decompression illness—Neurological injury caused by barotrauma.

decompression sickness—Identifiable signs and symptoms caused by the formation of inert gas bubbles within a diver's body.

decompression stops—Delays in ascent at specified depths to allow the elimination of excess nitrogen before surfacing.

defogging—Applying a substance to a mask lens to prevent condensation.

dehydration—A lack of adequate body fluids.

density—Mass per unit volume; for example, pounds per cubic foot.

DIN-valve—A new type of outlet for a scuba tank valve that is threaded and has a recessed O-ring seal. It was designed for pressures greater than 3,000 psi.

dive profile—A graphic representation of a diver's times at various depths.

diver's push-ups—The use of buoyancy to raise and lower the body by breath control.

dolphin kick—An undulating kick that uses the entire body for propulsion.

downwelling—A compensating current that occurs when wind blows along a coast where there is a steep drop-off near shore and which pulls the water downward.

drag—Resistance to movement through a fluid.

drift—The speed of water current.

drift dive—A dive in which divers use water current as the primary propulsion means.

eardrum—The membrane separating the middle and outer ears.

ebb—An outgoing tide.

eddies—Circulating currents caused by turbulent flow.

EDT—See equivalent dive time.

emergency decompression—A required delay in ascent to eliminate excess and help avoid DCS; must be taken if ADT or EDT exceeds the MDT for a dive.

equalization—Techniques used to prevent squeezes.

equivalent dive time—The sum of ADT and RNT.

eustachian tubes—The tubes that connect the middle ears to the throat; allow divers to equalize pressure in the middle ears.

Farmer Johns—An over-the-shoulders wet suit design.

fetch—The distance over which wind blows to create waves.

flaring—A technique of maximizing a diver's cross-sectional area to slow the speed of an ascent.

flood—An incoming tide.

flutter kick—A means of propulsion in which each leg moves upward and downward in opposite directions.

fronds—Kelp leaves.

gauge pressure—Absolute pressure minus atmospheric pressure; the pressure indicated by a gauge that reads zero at sea level.

Guy-Lussac's law—For any gas at a constant volume, the pressure of the gas will vary directly with the absolute temperature.

gyre—Large circulating currents.

half-time—The rate of absorption and/or elimination of gas in tissues at an exponential rate.

heat exhaustion—An illness caused by overheating and characterized by fatigue, weakness, and collapse.

heatstroke—A life-threatening illness caused by overheating and characterized by hot, dry, flushed skin.

Henry's law—At a constant temperature, the amount of gas that dissolves in a liquid with which it is in contact is proportional to the partial pressure of that gas.

hyperthermia—Higher than normal body core temperature.

hyperventilation—Rapid, deep breathing in excess of the body's needs.

hypothermia—Excessive loss of heat from the core of the human body.

hypoventilation—Shallow breathing that doesn't allow carbon dioxide to be flushed out of the lungs.

ingassing—The absorption of gas by tissues.

J-valve—A spring-loaded scuba cylinder reserve valve; also known as a constant reserve valve.

jumpsuit—A one-piece wet suit that covers nearly all of the body.

kelp—A collective term for large, brown seaweed.

K-valve—A nonreserve scuba cylinder valve; a simple on-off valve.

letter group designation—A letter of the alphabet used to designate the amount of residual nitrogen that remains in a diver's body after diving.

limiting line—The point at which a decompression stop changes from precautionary to required.

lubber line—A reference line on a compass.

maximum dive time—The maximum time that a diver may spend underwater for the deepest depth attained during a dive.

MDT—See maximum dive time.

mediastinal emphysema—A lung injury caused by overexpansion and characterized by air in the middle of the chest.

middle ear—The air-filled space between the outer ear and the inner ear.

modified frog kick—A kick with the ankles rotated so the tips of the fins are pointed outward, the feet are moved apart, and then the bottoms of the fins are pulled together quickly in an arcing motion.

multilevel dive profile—A dive to multiple depth levels, from the deepest depth to shallower depths.

neap tide—Tides with the minimum range between high water and low water.

nitrogen narcosis—A dangerous state of stupor caused by the narcotic effect of nitrogen in the body under pressure.

noncontact descent—A descent controlled by buoyancy and swimming motions and without maintaining contact with something such as a line or a slope.

octopus—A common term for an alternate air source.

open-valve ascent—A method for maintaining neutral buoyancy during an ascent by keeping the BC inflator-deflator valve open while holding the valve in a special way.

O-ring—A circular sealing ring for underwater equipment.

outgassing—The elimination of gas from tissues; occurs when gas dissolved in a liquid comes out of solution.

overturn—The process of surface water in lakes moving to deep water (up to 60 ft or 18 m) as a result of temperature differences and wind movement.

partial pressure—The pressure exerted by individual gases in a mixture of gases.

perfusion—The delivery of oxygen and other nutrients to body cells and the elimination of waste products; results from the constant, adequate circulation of blood through body capillaries.

plankton—Minute aquatic animals and plants, and their eggs, spores, larvae, and so forth that drift in the water. Generally occur near the surface in the sea.

pneumothorax—A lung injury caused by overexpansion and characterized by air in the pleural cavity.

pony tank—A small, redundant scuba system attached to the primary scuba system.

port—A threaded opening in the first stage of a scuba regulator. Also the left-hand side of a vessel when facing the bow with your back to the stern.

precautionary decompression stop—A 2- to 5-minute delay in ascent at 15 ft (4.6 m) made at the end of every dive to minimize the risk of DCS.

pressure—Force per unit area.

pulmonary barotrauma—A pressure-related injury to the lungs.

reciprocal compass course—A course in which a diver moves in a given heading for a given distance and returns to the origination point by reversing the direction of travel.

red tide—An extremely heavy bloom of plankton or algae.

repetitive dive—Any dive made within 6 to 24 hours (depending on dive table used) of a previous dive.

residual nitrogen—Nitrogen remaining within a diver following a dive.

residual nitrogen time—The time in minutes, converted from a letter group designation, that is equivalent to the nitrogen remaining in the body from a previous dive.

reverse block—A situation in which some form of blockage prevents compressed air from escaping along the route by which it entered a body air space.

reverse thermocline—A horizontal, abrupt transition from a colder layer of water to a warmer layer of water where the colder layer is shallower than the warmer layer.

rip current—A strong, narrow current that moves away from shore and forms when water in a surf zone accumulates on shore and funnels out through a narrow gap.

RNT—See residual nitrogen time.

sawtooth dive profile—A dive that progresses repeatedly from deep to shallow during a given time.

scissors kick—A resting fin kick done by extending one leg backward and the other forward while lying on the side, then pulling the legs together quickly.

scombroid—A type of fish poisoning, which can result from eating fish that has not been kept chilled.

scrolling—A dive-planning function of a dive computer to display the time limits for various depths sequentially.

set—The direction of a current; also a group of larger-than-average waves.

shorty—A one-piece wet suit with short legs and sleeves.

sink—An area where the ground collapses into an underground cave system.

SIT—See surface interval time.

skip breathing—A dangerous attempt by a scuba diver to extend an air supply by holding each breath for several seconds.

slack water—The time during high tide when water movement is minimal.

Spare Air unit—A small backup scuba unit designed for use during an emergency ascent.

SPG—See submersible pressure gauge.

spike dive—A dive in which a diver descends to a depth and ascends again quickly.

spring tide—Tides with the greatest range between high water and low water.

square compass course—A series of headings that allow the diver to travel in a square pattern so that the dive ends where it began.

squeeze—An injury that results when the pressure inside a body air space or an air space that is attached to the body is less than the surrounding pressure.

stage—A pressure-reduction step in a regulator or compressor.

stand—Time during which the tide neither rises nor falls.

step dive—A dive that progresses from deep to shallow during a given time.

stipes—Strands of kelp.

subcutaneous emphysema—A lung injury caused by overexpansion and characterized by air around the base of the neck.

submersible pressure gauge—An instrument used to measure the pressure in a scuba cylinder while submerged.

surface interval time—The time spent at the surface between repetitive dives.

surf—Breaking waves releasing their energy in shallow water.

surge—The back-and-forth subsurface movement of water produced by passing waves in shallow water.

swells—Rounded, undulating waves moving through deep water.

syphon—An area where water in an underground cave system is channeled from a sink back into the system.

tetrodotoxin—The most serious type of fish poisoning; results from eating exotic fish such as puffer.

thermocline—A horizontal, abrupt transition from a warmer layer of water to a colder layer of water.

Toynbee maneuver—A method of opening the eustachian tubes by blocking the nostrils, closing the mouth, and swallowing.

trail line—A line with a float extended behind a boat to assist divers in returning to the vessel if they surface downcurrent.

trapdoor effect—The situation that exists when a diver cannot equalize pressure in the middle ear because ambient pressure holds the opening of the eustachian tube closed.

trough—The lowest part of a wave.

tsunami—Giant waves caused by underwater geological disturbances; erroneously called tidal waves.

upwelling—The vertical, upward movement of water in a body of water and the subsequent replacement of that water from beneath.

Valsalva's maneuver—A method of opening the eustachian tubes by blocking the nostrils, closing the mouth, and gently trying to exhale.

valve seat—The portion of the valve that closes and stops the flow of air.

vasoconstriction—Narrowing of the blood vessels.

vertigo—A feeling of dizziness or disorientation.

wave height—The vertical distance between the crest and trough of a wave.

wave period—The time required for two consecutive waves to pass a given point.

wave train—A long series of waves.

wavelength—The horizontal distance between waves.

Bibliography

Auerbach, P. (1987). *A medical guide to hazardous marine life.* Jacksonville, FL: Progressive Printing.

Barnhart, R., & Steinmetz, S. (1986). *Dictionary of science.* Maplewood, NJ: Hammond.

Bascom, W. (1964). *Waves and beaches.* Garden City, NY: Anchor Books.

Bove, A., & Davis, J. (1990). *Diving medicine.* Philadelphia: W.B. Saunders.

Divers Alert Network. (1989). *Medical requirements for scuba divers.* Durham, NC: Author.

Edmonds, C., Lowry, C., & Pennefather, J. (1981). *Diving and subaquatic medicine.* Mosman, NSW, Australia: Diving Medical Centre.

Foley, B. (1989). *Physics made simple.* New York: Doubleday.

Groves, D., & Hunt, L. (1980). *Ocean world encyclopedia.* McGraw.

Lee, P., Lidov, M., & Tyberg, T. (1986). *The sourcebook of medical science.* New York: Torstar.

Lehrman, R. (1990). *Physics the easy way.* Hauppauge, NY: Barron's Educational Series.

Lippmann, J. (1992). *The essentials of deeper sport diving.* Locust Valley, NY: Aqua Quest.

Maloney, E. (1983). *Chapman piloting seamanship and small boat handling.* New York: Hearst Marine Books.

Miller, J. (Ed.) (1979). *NOAA diving manual* (2nd Ed.). Washington, DC: U.S. Government Printing Office, U.S. Department of Commerce.

National Association of Underwater Instructors (NAUI). (1991). *Advanced diving technology and techniques.* Montclair, CA: Author.

Professional Association of Diving Instructors (PADI). (1998). *The encyclopedia of recreational diving.* Santa Ana, CA: Author.

Sebel, P., Stoddart, D., Waldhorn, R., Waldmann, C., & Whitfield, P. (1985). *Respiration: The breath of life.* New York: Torstar.

Skin Diver. Various equipment articles from 1991 and 1992 issues. Los Angeles: Peterson.

Taylor, E. (Ed.) (1985). *Dorland's illustrated medical dictionary.* Philadelphia: W.B. Saunders.

Whitfield, P., & Stoddart, D. (1984). *Hearing, taste, and smell: Pathways of perception.* New York: Torstar.

Index

Locators followed by *f* indicate figures; locators followed by *t* indicate tables.

About the Author

With over a quarter-century of experience as a scuba instructor and instructor trainer, Dennis Graver has authored 27 books and manuals on the subject of scuba diving. In his position as director of training for the Professional Association of Diving Instructors (PADI), he designed the PADI modular scuba course and wrote the PADI Dive Manual, which revolutionized scuba instruction. During his tenure as director of education for the National Association of Underwater Instructors (NAUI), Graver wrote the NAUI Openwater I Scuba Diver Course Instructor Guide. He has also contributed hundreds of published articles on diving in such magazines as *Skin Diver*, *Sources*, and *Undercurrents*, as well as several NAUI technical publications.

From the Red Sea off the coast of Egypt to the barrier reefs of Australia, Dennis Graver has spent the past 30 years photographing all of the wonders under the water. He has won numerous awards from the Underwater Photographic Society, and his photos have graced the covers of many magazines and illustrated several diving texts and audiovisual education programs.

Graver has also influenced scuba diving with his development of a dive table multilevel diving technique for recreational diving and a breathing mask technique for diving rescue. In addition, he designed the NAUI Dive Time Calculator and the first PADI dive tables.

Graver is currently a member of NAUI, the Handicapped Scuba Association, the Undersea Hyperbaric and Medical Society, the Diver's Alert Network, the Underwater Photographic Society, and the Underwater Society of America. Dennis and his wife, Barbara, reside in Camano Island, Washington.

www.humankinetics.com

Dive into the Human Kinetics web site

Our site gives you a personalized online experience—you go right to the subject area you're interested in (tennis, hiking, strength training, etc.) and navigate from there.

Get the latest scuba news

Then browse through news, events, associations, job opportunities, books, and videos. You'll also be able to scan through the aquatics forum for bulletin board style conversation on the best diving spots, the newest scuba equipment, or just helpful diving tips.

Make your Human Kinetics purchase

Place your order with real-time shopping, and we'll send your new books, videos, or software right away. We've also scheduled chat events, so you may get a chance to interact with one of your favorite coaches or experts from the sports and fitness fields.

The next time you're online, bookmark our address—**www.humankinetics.com.** And be sure to visit frequently—we're always updating the site with fresh content!

HUMAN KINETICS
The Premier Publisher for Sports & Fitness